Advanced Techniques in dBASE II

Advanced Techniques in dBASE II™

ALAN SIMPSON

Berkeley • Paris • Düsseldorf • London

Cover art by Nicolae Razumieff
Book design by Lisa Amon

CP/M is a trademark of Digital Research Incorporated.
dBASE II is a trademark of Ashton-Tate.
IBM Personal Computer is a registered trademark of International Business Machines Corporation.
WordStar and MailMerge are trademarks of MicroPro International.

SYBEX is not affiliated with any manufacturer.

Every effort has been made to supply complete and accurate information. However, SYBEX assumes no responsibility for its use, nor for any infringements of patents or other rights of third parties which would result.

Copyright©1985 SYBEX Inc., 2344 Sixth Street, Berkeley, CA 94710. World rights reserved. No part of this publication may be stored in a retrieval system, transmitted, or reproduced in any way, including but not limited to photocopy, photograph, magnetic or other record, without the prior agreement and written permission of the publisher.

ISBN 0-89588-228-0
Printed by Haddon Craftsmen
Manufactured in the United States of America
10 9 8 7 6 5 4 3 2 1

ACKNOWLEDGMENTS

Thanks to Carole Alden, my editor/mentor from SYBEX, for her countless contributions to the development of this book. Also, thanks to Valerie Robbins, word processing; Jeremy Elliott, technical review; Lisa Amon, book design; Donna Scanlon, typesetting; and Dawn Amsberry, Brenda Walker, and Sarah Seaver, proofreading.

TABLE OF CONTENTS

INTRODUCTION   xiii

    Why Program in dBASE II?   xiv
    The Structure of this Book   xvi
    What Version Should You Use?   xvi

TYPOGRAPHICAL CONVENTIONS   xvii

CHAPTER 1:   CREATING COMMAND FILES   1

    Creating Command Files with MODIFY COMMAND   1
    Creating Command Files with SED   3
    Creating Command Files with WordStar   5
    Structured Programming   7
    Summary   10

CHAPTER 2:   MAXIMIZING PERFORMANCE   13

    Trimming Minutes Down to Seconds with FIND and WHILE   13
    Faster Math   15
    Faster Reports   16
    Faster Copying   17

Faster Edits   17
Faster Sorts   18
Estimating Performance   19
Managing Multiple Index Files   20
Performance Trade-offs   21
Programming for Performance   23
Summary   24

CHAPTER 3:   PROGRAM DESIGN AND DEVELOPMENT   27

Software Design and Development   28
Defining the Goals of the Project   28
Designing the Database Structure   30
Designing the Software Structure   32
Designing and Developing Each Command File in the System   33
Summary   38

CHAPTER 4:   CUSTOM DATA-ENTRY SCREENS   41

Creating Formatted Screen Displays   41
Using ZIP   43
Using SED   45
Using Format Files   47
Adding Templates   49
Command File for Custom Data-Entry Screen   50
Summary   52

CHAPTER 5:   MENU-DRIVEN SORTS AND SEARCHES   55

The REPORTS Command File   55
Menu-Driven Sorting   60
Menu-Driven Searching   61
Summary   67

CHAPTER 6: <u>CUSTOM REPORTS</u> 69

Screen and Printer Formatting   69
Multicopy Labels with Alignment Check   77
Creating a MailMerge File   84
Summary   87

CHAPTER 7: <u>CUSTOM COMMAND FILES FOR
EDITING AND DELETING</u>   91

Automating the Editing Process   92
Deleting Records from the Database   98
Summary   105

CHAPTER 8: <u>ADDITIONAL OPTIONS</u>   107

Quick Lookup of a Single Record   107
Quick Check for Duplicates   114
Summary   120

CHAPTER 9: <u>A CUSTOM INVENTORY SYSTEM</u>   123

Inventory System Goals   125
Inventory System Database Design   126
Inventory System Software Design   128
Inventory System Main Menu   129
Summary   132

CHAPTER 10: <u>THE MASTER INVENTORY FILE</u>   135

Master File Software Design   136
Master File Menu   136

Adding Unique Part Numbers   137
Master File Reports   143
Current Stock Report   144
Reorder Report   145
   Items on Order Report   146
   Placing Orders   147
   Presenting Report Options   148
Editing the Master File   156
Summary   161

CHAPTER 11: INVENTORY SALES SYSTEM   163

Sales System Software Structure   164
Sales System Menu   164
Point-of-Sale Data Entry   165
Sales System Reports   173
A Note on Dates   181
Summary   185

CHAPTER 12: INVENTORY NEW STOCK SYSTEM   187

New Stock System Software Structure   188
New Stock System Menu   188
New Stock Data-Entry Program   189
NEWSTOCK System Reports   193
Summary   200

CHAPTER 13: INVENTORY SYSTEM UPDATING   203

Updating the Master File   204
Editing the Sales Files   208
Editing the New Stock File   215
Summary   224

CHAPTER 14: <ins>A BOOKKEEPING SYSTEM</ins>   227

Bookkeeping System Goals   228
Bookkeeping System Database Design   228
Bookkeeping System Software Structure   232
Summary   233

CHAPTER 15: <ins>BOOKKEEPING SYSTEM INSTALLATION   235
AND MENU PROGRAMS</ins>

Bookkeeping System Installation Program   236
Bookkeeping System Main Menu   244
Summary   246

CHAPTER 16: <ins>ADDING AND UPDATING TRANSACTIONS</ins>   249

Recording Bookkeeping Transactions   249
Updating the Chart of Accounts   256
Summary   266

CHAPTER 17: <ins>MANAGING THE CHECK REGISTER</ins>   269

Recording Deposits, Calculating Balances   271
Printing the Check Register   275
Summary   280

CHAPTER 18: <ins>THE BOOKKEEPING SYSTEM REPORTS</ins>   283

Bookkeeping System Reports Menu   284
Income Statement   285
Chart of Accounts Report   292
Writing Checks   300
Summary   311

CHAPTER 19: EDITING THE BOOKKEEPING DATA   317

Bookkeeping Edit Screens   318
Add, Change, or Delete Bookkeeping Data   322
Adjustment Transactions   328
Expanding the Bookkeeping System   332
Summary   334

CHAPTER 20: A LIBRARY CROSS-REFERENCING SYSTEM   337

Library System Goals   338
Library System Database Structure   338
Library System Software Design   330
Library System Main Menu   340
Adding References   342
Editing References   342
Deleting References   348
Summary   351

CHAPTER 21: LIBRARY SYSTEM REPORTS   353

Searching For References   354
Underlining   378
Library Subjects Report   381
Summary   389

INDEX   392

INTRODUCTION

If you have a great idea for a programming project in mind, and you want to turn it into a dBASE II software reality, then this book is written for you. In these pages you will learn how to turn great ideas into dBASE II programs that accomplish exactly what you specify with speed and efficiency.

It is not necessary that you understand every dBASE II command prior to reading this book. Some of the complex commands will be discussed in detail, particularly those not fully explained in the dBASE II User's Manual. If you do come across an unfamiliar command in one of these programs look it up in the manual to get more information.

The dBASE command is always the first word in a program line. For example, if you see the line:

UPDATE ON CODE FROM TRANS ADD AMOUNT REPLACE DATE

you can look up the UPDATE command in the dBASE II manual for more information. The first word in a dBASE sentence is the main dBASE command of the entire sentence.

dBASE II *functions* usually precede a field or memory variable name surrounded by parentheses. For example, in the line:

STORE STR(X,5) TO Y

STORE is the command, and STR is a function which changes the variable X to a character string (in this example, a character string that is five digits long). If this or any other function is unfamiliar, take the time to look it up in the dBASE manual; you'll save yourself a great deal of time in the long run.

Also, keep in mind that this book is a tutorial text, and is designed to be read as such. It starts with relatively easy programs and builds upon acquired skills to more complex programs. Therefore, if you skip chapters one through nine, you're likely to run into quite a few surprises in Chapter 10. You should take the time to read this book from cover to cover.

To write a custom dBASE II software system, you must have several skills. First, you need to know the dBASE language. My introductory book, *Understanding dBASE II*, was designed to teach you the basic commands of dBASE II. Second, you need to know how to program. The goal of this book is to teach you how to program in dBASE II. We'll approach this goal by drawing upon three primary techniques:

1. *Software design techniques.* Designing a software system involves many steps: writing down the basic goals of the project, deciding what you need to store on the database, or on several databases, and breaking the big job down into small discrete steps, each of which is relatively easy to program. Then your programming task begins: you will write a series of small, simple *routines* which, when combined into a single *system*, work together to accomplish your goal. In this book, we'll follow these steps for creating command files.

2. *Techniques for maximum performance.* A program that accomplishes a given task in an hour may be a good program, but a program that accomplishes the same task in five minutes is preferable. Maximizing the performance of a software system is a key issue in this book. Chapter 2 discusses many techniques for maximizing the speed of dBASE programs.

3. *Fundamental algorithms.* Another programming technique is creating *algorithms*, separate routines that solve common problems, and can later be used in a variety of programming situations. For example, in Chapter 18, you will find a program that writes checks for a bookkeeping system. If you were to develop a payroll system, or accounts payable system, you could use the same check-writing program, rather than build a new one from scratch. The basic logic, or *algorithm*, for check writing is the same for all types of systems.

Why Program in dBASE II?

dBASE II is so rich in commands that you can accomplish many tasks without any programming effort whatsoever. But there are at least three very good reasons why you should consider writing programs in the dBASE II language:

1. *Expand the capabilities of dBASE II.* Although dBASE has a variety of commands that you can type on the screen to perform a given task, these commands are far from being exhaustive. For example, if you wish to print mailing labels from your database, you will find no command to do so. You must write a dBASE command file to accomplish this task. Therefore, to get the maximum mileage from dBASE II, you will need to write some command files.

2. *Develop user-friendly systems.* By now, you've probably learned how to create and manage data on a database. Undoubtedly, you've had to invest some time and effort to do so. However, chances are that once you set up the database system, you'll want someone else to manage it so you can move on to other dBASE projects. That person may not be quite so willing to invest the time necessary to learn the dBASE II language. Therefore, you can write a series of command files that allow a novice to manage your data through a series of menus from which he or she can select options. This frees you to move on to other dBASE projects.

3. *Increase programmer performance.* If you are a professional programmer, you are probably aware of how much time it takes to develop a custom software system. However, most custom software systems must perform the same basic tasks: the user should be able to add data to a database, sort, search, and edit it, and print formatted reports from it, and perhaps add numbers to it. In lower-level languages, such as C or Pascal or COBOL or FORTRAN, the time required to write programs to perform these tasks is usually pretty hefty. dBASE can perform most of these tasks with a single command, which can cut programming time considerably.

Since dBASE II already has the routines to add new data, sort, search, edit, and print formatted reports, you can write a program that performs these tasks in a relatively short period of time. Furthermore, dBASE II offers the programmer debugging utilities that speed up the programming process even more.

There is another good reason for learning to program in dBASE II. The excellent design of the product, coupled with Ashton-Tate's outstanding marketing effort, has made the program an industry standard. Whether you are an established pro, or an aspiring one who wishes to keep up with the times, you will find lots of advantages in mastering dBASE II.

The Structure of this Book

Chapter 1 discusses general techniques for creating dBASE II command files. This includes using the MODIFY COMMAND, as well as using the WordStar and Screen Editor (SED) programs. Chapter 2 discusses general techniques for maximizing the performance of your dBASE II software.

Chapters 3 through 8 discuss a mailing list system, and cover basic programming techniques such as menus, custom screens, and custom reports. Chapters 9–13 discuss an inventory system and general programming techniques used in managing multiple data files. Chapters 14–19 discuss a bookkeeping system, with more advanced techniques for managing multiple data files. Finally, Chapters 20–21 present a library cross-referencing system, with advanced techniques for presenting menu-driven searches, keyword cross-referencing, and word wrapping.

What Version Should You Use?

To make life simple, all the software systems in this book were written in dBASE II version 2.4. If you are still using an earlier version, you should upgrade to version 2.4 because many of the bugs in earlier versions have been fixed. More capabilities have also been added to version 2.4 to simplify the programming process.

TYPOGRAPHICAL CONVENTIONS

Alt-H   Hold down Alt and H at the same time.

^D   Hold down CTRL and D at the same time.

CHAPTER 1
CREATING COMMAND FILES

In this chapter, we'll cover techniques for creating command files with MODIFY COMMAND, as well as with the alternative Screen Editor (SED) and WordStar packages. We'll also discuss structured programming.

Creating Command Files with MODIFY COMMAND

A *command file* is simply a series of commands that dBASE II can read and process as a group. dBASE II provides a *text editor* to create command files. When the dBASE *dot prompt* (.) is showing, use MODIFY COMMAND (or the abbreviated MODI COMM) to call up the text editor and create a command file.

Let's create a command file named TEST on the disk in drive B. Type in:

MODI COMM B:TEST

Note: If you've already used SET DEFAULT TO B, you can omit B:. dBASE will briefly display the message NEW FILE and then give you a blank screen on which to write the command file.

You can write your command file by typing in each line followed by pressing RETURN. Try typing this simple two-line program:

    ERASE
    ? "Hi, I'm a test program"

To save this short command file, type ^W (hold down the control key and type W). dBASE will save this command file on the specified drive under the name TEST, and add the extension .CMD (or .PRG on computers with the MS-DOS or PC-DOS operating systems). dBASE will then redisplay the dot prompt.

To run the command file, type in DO, followed by the name (and, if necessary, the drive location) of the command file. In this example, type in:

    DO B:TEST

and press RETURN. dBASE will perform both lines in the command file: it will clear the screen, then print the message in the second line. The screen should now look like this:

    Hi, I'm a test program

Now you will modify the TEST command file. Type in:

    MODI COMM B:TEST

and press RETURN. The screen will clear, then the command file will be displayed with the cursor beneath the first character in the first line, like so:

    ERASE
    ? "Hi, I'm a test program"

At this point, you can add, change, and delete lines and characters by using the following control-key commands:

    ^E   Move cursor up one line.
    ^X   Move cursor down one line.
    ^D   Move cursor right one character.
    ^S   Move cursor left one character.
    ^G   Delete character over cursor.

Creating Command Files 3

    ^T   Delete entire line over cursor.
    ^N   Insert a new, blank line at cursor position.
    ^V   Turn Insert mode on/off.

   On some keyboards, such as the IBM, the arrow keys that normally control the cursor will also work. In addition, the Del key can be used to delete a character and the Ins key can be used to turn the Insert mode on and off.

   For example, typing ^D (or pressing the down-arrow key) will cause the cursor to move down one line in the TEST command file, as below:

    ERASE
    ? "Hi. I'm a test program."

Typing ^N will cause a new blank line to be inserted into the command file, like this:

    ERASE

    ? "Hi. I'm a test program."

Now you can type in a new line, as shown below:

    ERASE
    ? "This is a new line"_
    ? "Hi. I'm a test program."

When you are done editing the command file, use ^W to save your changes. If you accidentally make a mess while editing the command file, you can abandon it with the command ^Q. This will leave the TEST command file on the disk in its unedited form.

   After you edit any command file and save it with ^W, dBASE automatically creates a backup file with the extension .BAK. Just remember that the .BAK file is always one edited version behind the current command file.

Creating Command Files with SED

   MODI COMM is a somewhat primitive text editor. As an alternative to MODI COMM for IBM users, Ashton-Tate has created the Screen-Editor program (SED). SED offers many features, including a User's

Manual on disk. If you need to look up information, even in the middle of creating a command file, just hold down Alt-H. A brief description of SED commands will appear on the screen. You can also view the table of contents of the SED manual. From there, just type in the page number you wish to view, and that page appears on the screen (and printer, if you like). When you are done, press RETURN to get back to the command file you were working on.

To create a command file with SED, you put the SED disk in drive A, and the disk you wish to use for storing the command file in drive B. Then, type in SED and press RETURN. The SED main menu of options appear on the screen. To create a command file, select N (edit a new file), and SED will ask you to type in:

Name of new file:

You should include the drive specification and extension; so type in the filename as B:TEST.PRG, and press RETURN. SED provides a blank screen to work with. As with MODI COMM, you just type in the command file. To move the cursor around on the screen, use the IBM keyboard arrow keys. To view all of the commands for using SED, just type Alt-H. Keystrokes for moving the the cursor are summarized below:

up-arrow	Move cursor up one line.
down-arrow	Move cursor down one line.
left-arrow	Move cursor left one character.
right-arrow	Move cursor right one character.
Del	Delete character over cursor.
^D	Delete entire line.
^M	Insert a new blank line at cursor position.
Ins	Turn Insert mode on/off.

When you've finished your command file, type Esc-X to save it and return to the dot prompt. To run the command file, load up dBASE and DO B:TEST. You can edit the command file further by using MODI COMM, or you can quit dBASE to return to the A> prompt. From the A> prompt, load up SED again, and select the E option to edit an existing file. Once again, SED asks for the name of the file, like so:

Name of file:

Type in the name B:TEST.PRG. The command file will appear on the screen for editing once again.

SED also provides commands for marking blocks of text. These blocks can be copied, moved, or deleted. Again, all of the commands to do so are presented on the screen when you type Alt-H. When you are done editing, save the command file and exit SED. Then just use the dBASE DO command to run the edited command file.

Creating Command Files with WordStar

You can also use most standard word processing packages to create command files. One example, Micropro's WordStar program, offers many useful features to programmers. To use WordStar, place the WordStar disk in the currently logged drive (e.g., A> designates drive A as the currently logged drive). Then call up WordStar by typing WS, and pressing RETURN.

The WordStar No-file menu will then appear on the screen, and wait for a command. Press N to specify that you want to edit a nondocument file. WordStar asks:

NAME OF FILE TO EDIT? :

Type in the drive specification, the filename, and the extension. If you wish to create a command file on the disk in drive B, type in the filename B:TEST.CMD (for a CP/M-based computer), or the filename B:TEST.PRG, (for a PC-DOS or MS-DOS-based system).

WordStar then presents a blank screen on which you can compose your command file. (The top of the screen, however, contains brief instructions for controlling the cursor.) Here are the basic commands for moving the cursor:

^E	Move cursor up one line.
^X	Move cursor down one line.
^D	Move cursor right one character.
^S	Move cursor left one character.
^G	Delete character over cursor.
^Y	Delete entire line over cursor.
^N	Insert a new, blank line at cursor position.
^V	Turn Insert mode on/off.

To save the command file and return to the A> prompt, type ^KX. From the A> prompt, just call up dBASE in the usual fashion, and type DO B:TEST. You can use MODI COMM to make additional changes to the command file, or quit dBASE and use the WordStar Nondocument mode again.

If you have both dBASE II and WordStar stored on the same disk, you can create your command file with WordStar's Nondocument mode, and save it with the ^KD. WordStar will save the command file and return to the No-file menu. From there, you can select the R command to run a program. WordStar will ask:

    COMMAND? :

You type in:

    DBASE B:TEST

and dBASE will run the command file.

To edit the command file with WordStar again, just quit dBASE in the usual fashion. The message:

    Hit any key to return to WordStar

will appear on the screen, and you'll be right back at WordStar's No-file menu, ready to edit your command file, using the Nondocument mode again. This procedure is as convenient as having the entire WordStar program embedded in dBASE.

The most valuable WordStar capability for dBASE programmers is the ability to mark blocks of text and move, copy, delete, and write those blocks to disk files. You can also read one disk file into any portion of the command file you are currently editing. This is essential to the seasoned programmer, because it allows him to use portions of various command files to build new command files. This simple capability greatly reduces the time required to develop and debug a command file, because you can use tried-and-true routines in your command file without having to retype and debug them again.

Here are the WordStar commands to mark and move blocks of text:

^KB	Mark the beginning of a block.
^KK	Mark the end of a block.
^KC	Copy marked block to current cursor position.
^KV	Move marked block to current cursor position.
^KY	Delete entire marked block.
^KW	Write marked block to a disk file.
^KR	Read a file from disk into this file at the current cursor position.

Although you can use many other word processing systems to create command files, WordStar is one of the best. It will certainly be worth your while to learn to use a good word processing program to enhance your dBASE programming.

Structured Programming

In the mid-1970's, the concept of *structured programming* evolved as an answer to the problem of modifying and maintaining large software systems on large computers. The same techniques can be used with dBASE II to simplify the processes of debugging and modifying command files. The basic rules-of-thumb for structured programming are:

1. Embed highly-visible programmer comments in the program so that you can easily locate portions of the program that perform a specific task.
2. Indent program lines within loops and decision-making routines, so you can see the beginning and endpoints of these routines while working with the program.
3. Try to use commands that are self-descriptive, rather than mysterious.

Let's compare two programs; one which does not use these structured programming techniques, and one which does. Both programs perform *exactly* the same job; they present a main menu for a hypothetical library management system, ask the user for his choice from the menu, and then perform the task that the user requested.

Figure 1.1 presents an *unstructured* MAIN MENU program.

Notice first that while there are some programmer comments in the program (lines preceded by an asterisk), they are not highly visible. For example, you must skim through many lines of dBASE code to find the comment that reads * EXIT.

Second, the indentations do not necessarily make the program easier to read. The indents are awkward and confusing, particularly near the bottom of the program where there are a series of seemingly disconnected ENDIF statements that must be traced upward. If for some reason this program bombed, it would not be easy to find out why.

Third, some of the commands are not self-descriptive. For example, the third line from the top reads DO WHILE T. In dBASE, T is always true. Therefore, this line suggests that the loop will run forever. However, if you examine the lines below, you'll find that the loop will not

8 Advanced Techniques in dBASE II

```
* MAIN MENU
USE B:LIBRARY
DO WHILE T
ERASE
@ 1,20 SAY "Library Management System"
@ 3,25 SAY "1. Add New Records"
@ 4,25 SAY "2. Print Reports"
@ 5,25 SAY "3. Edit Data"
@ 6,25 SAY "4. Exit"
STORE " " TO CHOICE
@ 8,20 SAY "Enter choice (1-4) " GET CHOICE
READ
* BRANCH ACCORDINGLY
IF CHOICE="1"
   APPEND
   ELSE
      IF CHOICE="2"
      REPORT FORM LIBRARY
      ELSE
         IF CHOICE="3"
         EDIT
         ELSE
            * EXIT
            IF CHOICE="4"
            RETURN
         ENDIF
      ENDIF
   ENDIF
ENDIF
ENDDO
```

Figure 1.1: *An unstructured MAIN MENU program.*

actually run forever. When the user selects option 4, dBASE performs a RETURN command which, in a sense, jumps out of the loop back to the dot prompt. Also note that at the bottom of the command file is the ENDDO command, which has no comments associated with it. If this were a larger program with many DO WHILE commands, it would be difficult to determine which DO WHILE this ENDDO belonged to. The same is true for the many ENDIF commands.

Compare this program to the one in Figure 1.2, which is written using the rules-of-thumb for structured programming.

Notice how much easier this command file is to read than the first. To begin with, all of the programmer's comments are visible at a glance. That's because there are many asterisks in front of them which make them stand out. Furthermore, they're written in plain English syntax (upper- and lowercase), so you don't need to look for them. Also, at the top of the program, you will see the name of the program and a brief description of what the program does.

```
****************************************** LIBRARY.PRG.
*************************** Library system Main Menu.
USE B:LIBRARY
STORE " " TO CHOICE

DO WHILE CHOICE # "4"
   ERASE
   @ 1,20 SAY "Library Management System"
   @ 3,25 SAY "1. Add New Records"
   @ 4,25 SAY "2. Print Reports"
   @ 5,25 SAY "3. Edit Data"
   @ 6,25 SAY "4. Exit"
   @ 8,20 SAY "Enter choice (1-4) " GET CHOICE
   READ

   ****************** Perform according to user's request.
   DO CASE

      CASE CHOICE =  1"
           APPEND

      CASE CHOICE="2"
           REPORT FORM B:LIBRARY

      CASE CHOICE = "3"
           EDIT

   ENDCASE

ENDDO (while choice # 4)

********************************* When choice = 4, exit.
RETURN
```

Figure 1.2: *A structured MAIN MENU program.*

Notice that all the lines with the DO WHILE . . . ENDDO loop are indented at least three spaces. You can easily find the beginning and endpoints of the DO WHILE loop simply by running your finger down the margin from the DO WHILE command to the ENDDO in the same column.

The program also uses the DO CASE . . . ENDCASE commands to decide which task to perform based upon the user's request. This eliminates confusing ENDIFs in the first program, which makes the program easier to read. The commands within the DO CASE . . . ENDCASE lines are also evenly indented, which makes the entire DO CASE . . . ENDCASE clause stand out.

Finally, compare the commands in the two sample programs. The commands in the structured program are more descriptive than the commands in the unstructured program. The command **DO WHILE CHOICE # 4** immediately informs us that this loop is not going to repeat itself forever. It is going to stop when the memory variable CHOICE equals 4. We need not find the mysterious end to a seemingly infinite loop. In addition, the ENDDO command at the bottom of the program is followed by (while choice # 4). This simple comment pinpoints the DO WHILE command that is associated with this ENDDO, and makes the program easier to work with at a later date. In dBASE, *anything* that you type in to the right of an ENDDO or ENDIF command is a programmer comment: it does not affect how the program runs. Therefore you can do yourself a big favor by putting in reminders as to which particular DO WHILE or IF each ENDDO or ENDIF command belongs.

Summary

The procedure for creating and saving a dBASE II command file is to use either MODIFY COMMAND, or a word processor such as SED or WordStar to type in the command file. To run the command file, call up the dBASE dot prompt, and use the DO command along with the name of the command file (e.g. DO B:TEST). Follow the rules-of-thumb for structured programming while writing your command files; this will make your command files easier to read, and therefore easier to debug and modify in the future.

In the next chapter we'll discuss techniques for maximizing the performance of the custom dBASE II systems.

CHAPTER 2
MAXIMIZING PERFORMANCE

We all want to maximize the performance of our computers. We are happy that our computers can trim down to minutes what might take a human hours to perform. But not all of us realize that these minutes can be trimmed down to mere seconds. In this chapter, we'll discuss and compare general techniques for maximizing the performance of dBASE II.

Trimming Minutes Down to Seconds with FIND and WHILE

Let's compare a few different techniques for performing basic tasks with dBASE II. We'll use a simple mailing list database for our examples. Its name is MAIL.DBF, and it has this structure:

FLD	NAME	TYPE	WIDTH	DEC
001	LNAME	C	020	000
002	FNAME	C	020	000
003	ADDRESS	C	020	000
004	CITY	C	020	000
005	STATE	C	010	000
006	ZIP	C	010	000
007	AMOUNT	N	009	002

Let's assume that the MAIL.DBF database already has 1,000 records on it. Ten individuals on this database have the last name (LNAME field) Miller. How long would it take to LIST, COUNT, or COPY all the Millers to another database? How long would it take to print a formatted report with only Millers, or to sum the amounts for the Millers? Of course, the length of time depends on the technique you use.

To compare techniques, we'll assume that the database has already been indexed on the LNAME field, using the commands:

```
USE MAIL
INDEX ON LNAME TO NAMES
```

If you had typed in these commands, an index file named NAMES.NDX would exist on the disk, so you could use the command USE MAIL INDEX NAMES to specify the MAIL database, as well as the NAMES index file for dBASE to use.

Let's compare processing times using three different command files and approaches. The first method will use the standard LIST FOR approach to find all the Millers. The command file would look like this:

```
* * * * * * * * * * * * * * * * * * * * * Method 1: LIST FOR approach.
ERASE
USE MAIL INDEX NAMES
ACCEPT " List all people with what last name? " TO SEARCH
LIST FOR LNAME = SEARCH
```

If you do this command file, it will clear the screen and display the prompt:

List all people with what last name?

Suppose you type in the name Miller, and press RETURN. The program will then display the records for all 10 Millers on the screen. The time required for the command file to display the Millers and return to the dot prompt is about 148 seconds (two and a half minutes) on a floppy disk system.

A second approach to solve the same problem is to use the FIND command to look up the first Miller in the NAMES index, and a DO . . . WHILE loop to display the remaining 9 Millers. The command file for the second approach looks like this:

```
* * * * * * * * * * * Method 2: FIND and DO . . . WHILE approach.
ERASE
USE MAIL INDEX NAMES
ACCEPT " List all people with what last name? " TO SEARCH
FIND &SEARCH
```

```
DO WHILE LNAME = SEARCH
    DISPLAY
    SKIP
ENDDO (while lname = search)
```

When you do the method 2 command file, it also asks which people you wish to list, then lists those people. The time required for this command file to display all 10 Millers and redisplay the dot prompt is about 29 seconds (less than half a minute) which is roughly one-third the time of the first method.

An even faster and simpler approach is to use the FIND command to find the first Miller on the database, then use the LIST WHILE command to display the remaining Millers. The third approach is displayed in the command file below:

```
*********** Method 3: FIND and LIST WHILE approach.
ERASE
ACCEPT " List all people with what last name? " TO SEARCH
FIND &SEARCH
LIST WHILE LNAME = SEARCH
```

It takes less than 9 seconds of processing time to display all 10 Millers, then redisplay the dot prompt on the screen. Obviously, this third method is preferable. (Unfortunately, it isn't applicable to *all* situations, as we'll see in coming chapters.)

You can see the difference in these three methods in Table 2.1. Although each of the three methods performs exactly the same task, the processing times vary dramatically.

Faster Math

The FIND and WHILE approach with an indexed database can offer significant time savings with dBASE commands other than LIST. For example, if you want dBASE to count how many Millers are on the

Method No.	Commands Used	Time Required
1	LIST FOR	148.75 seconds
2	FIND and DO WHILE	29.91 seconds
3	FIND and LIST WHILE	8.94 seconds

Table 2.1: *Comparison of Processing Times Using Three Methods*

database, you can use the commands:

    USE MAIL
    COUNT FOR LNAME = "Miller"

This approach requires about 55.5 seconds to display the fact that there are 10 Millers on the database then redisplay the dot prompt. You can cut this time down significantly using these commands:

    USE MAIL INDEX NAMES
    FIND Miller
    COUNT WHILE LNAME = "Miller"

This approach performs the same task in about 3.20 seconds, which offers significant time savings.

Suppose you wish to sum the amount field for just the Millers? You could use these commands:

    USE MAIL
    SUM AMOUNT FOR LNAME = "Miller"

Processing time using this method is about 58 seconds. Here is an alternative approach:

    USE MAIL INDEX NAMES
    FIND Miller
    SUM AMOUNT WHILE LNAME = "Miller"

This approach takes 5.28 seconds, about one-tenth the time.

Faster Reports

You can use the WHILE command with the REPORT command also. For example, suppose you've already created a formatted report called MAILIST using the REPORT command. To display all the Millers on the formatted report, you could use the commands:

    USE MAIL
    REPORT FORM MAILIST FOR LNAME = "Miller"

This approach requires about 135.3 seconds to display all the Millers on the report, then redisplay the dot prompt. We can use the faster approach with these commands:

    USE MAIL INDEX NAMES
    FIND Miller
    REPORT FORM MAILIST WHILE LNAME = "Miller"

These commands perform the same job in a slim 14.03 seconds.

Faster Copying

For copying portions of the MAIL database to a database called TEMP, the commands:

    USE MAIL INDEX NAMES
    COPY TO TEMP FOR LNAME = "Miller"

require a hefty 200.6 seconds, more than three minutes. You can perform the same job using these commands:

    USE MAIL INDEX NAMES
    FIND Miller
    COPY TO TEMP WHILE LNAME = "Miller"

These commands trim the copying time down to a comfortable 18.7 seconds.

Faster Edits

Indexing files can also speed up the editing process. For example, suppose you want to browse through the database to edit data for one of the Millers. You could type in the commands:

    USE MAIL
    BROWSE

which will set up the dBASE BROWSE screen with the names and addresses in their original order, as displayed in Figure 2.1. You will need to use lots of ^C commands to scroll through the database to find the Miller you're looking for. It might take a long time to find the

LNAME	FNAME	ADDRESS
Bond	James	007 Spy St.
Kenney	Dave	123 Clark St.
Newell	Jeff	341 Lou Drive
Mohr	Richard	350 W. Leadora St.
Rosiello	Rick	999 Buddy Way
Wallace	Doug	345 Killer St.
Miller	Mike	601 Lemon Dr.

Figure 2.1: An unindexed BROWSE screen.

particular Miller you wish to edit, because the Millers will be placed randomly throughout the database.

On the other hand, you can use these commands to browse:

```
USE MAIL INDEX NAMES
FIND Miller
BROWSE
```

The BROWSE screen will display the first Miller on the database, and all the remaining Millers immediately beneath, as displayed in Figure 2.2. There is no need to go scrolling through pages and pages of BROWSE screens to find the Miller you wish to edit, because all 10 Millers are displayed immediately and simultaneously on one BROWSE screen.

Similarly, if you wish to use the EDIT command to change the data for a particular Miller, you can use the commands:

```
USE MAIL INDEX NAMES
FIND Miller
EDIT WHILE LNAME = "Miller"
```

The first Miller will quickly be displayed in the database on the EDIT screen. Each subsequent ^C command will immediately position you to the next Miller on the database. Once again, you can save a great deal of time because you don't have to search for the each Miller.

Faster Sorts

In some cases, a database should be sorted physically rather than indexed. For example, the UPDATE command works best if the file

LNAME	FNAME	ADDRESS
Miller	Mollie	601 Mission Blvd.
Miller	Sheila	1234 Genessee
Miller	Ms. Stephanie S.	734 Rainbow Dr.
Miller	Patti	626 Mazda Way
Miller	George	P.O. Box 2802
Miller	Julie	999 Love St.
Miller	Caron	123 Princess Way
Miller	Ms. Chrissie	321 Hynde St.
Miller	Mrs. Sally S.	355 Seco Ct.
Miller	Dr. James T.	701 Newport Dr.

Figure 2.2: A BROWSE screen with an indexed database.

you are updating from is physically presorted. You use the SORT command to create a sorted database called TEMP from the MAIL database using the commands:

    USE MAIL
    SORT ON LNAME TO TEMP

This approach takes about 940 seconds (about 15 minutes) of processing time. If the NAMES index file already exists, you can achieve the same result using the commands:

    USE MAIL INDEX NAMES
    COPY TO TEMP

Copying the contents of the indexed file only requires about 326 seconds of processing time (about one-third the time). When you copy an indexed file to another database, the records on the database you copied to will be physically sorted.

Estimating Performance

Quick performance is an important attribute of a custom dBASE II software system. Generally, processing times tend to increase linearly with the size of a database. Therefore, on a database with 5,000 records on it, displaying all the Millers could take as long as 740 seconds (a little over 12 minutes), with the LIST FOR approach. Using an indexed file with the FIND and LIST WHILE approach will perform the same task in about 45 seconds (less than a minute), a whopping 24 minutes (almost half an hour) for a database with 10,000 records in it with the LIST FOR approach, and only 88 seconds (under a minute and a half) with the FIND and LIST WHILE approach.

But what about the time it takes to INDEX ON LNAME TO NAMES in these comparisons? After all, it takes a healthy 529.06 seconds to index a database with 1,000 records on it. However, you can virtually eliminate the indexing time by performing the INDEX command immediately after creating the database.

If you create the MAIL.DBF database, then immediately INDEX ON LNAME TO NAMES, the indexing time is virtually nill. The average time required to index an empty database is only a couple of seconds. If you then USE MAIL INDEX NAMES before you append or edit (or in any other way modify the contents of the database), the index file will be updated automatically rather quickly. Therefore, there is no need to go through the INDEX ON LNAME TO NAMES procedure after adding or changing data on the database. Indexing time is thus reduced to a few seconds or less.

Managing Multiple Index Files

In the previous examples, we compared processing times using an index file called NAMES. This index file is ordered only by the LNAME field. Realistically, a mailing list will probably require two separate sort orders:

1. A sort by last and first name for printing a directory listing.
2. A sort by zip code for bulk mailings.

When two sort orders are used regularly, you can create two index files to manage the two different sort orders. One index file, which we'll call NAMES, will keep the mailing list data in last name and first name order. A second index file, which we'll call ZIPS, will maintain a zip code order for handling bulk mailings. To create both of these index files, first you'll need to create the MAIL.DBF database with the CREATE command, then create the two index files using these commands:

```
USE MAIL
INDEX ON LNAME + FNAME TO NAMES
INDEX ON ZIP TO ZIPS
```

The MAIL.DBF database now has two index files associated with it; NAMES.NDX and ZIPS.NDX. You can keep both index files up-to-date using the command:

```
USE MAIL INDEX NAMES,ZIPS
```

By specifying two index files in this fashion, all future modifications to the database with the APPEND, EDIT, BROWSE, READ, or REPLACE commands will automatically update both index files.

If you list or display all the records in the database, they will be displayed in last name order, since NAMES is the first-listed index file in the INDEX portion of the command line. Furthermore, you can only use the FIND command with the first listed index, NAMES. Therefore, to display all the records in the database in zip code order, you need not go through the INDEX ON ZIP TO ZIPS procedure again.

Instead, you can simply type in the command:

    SET INDEX TO ZIPS

Because this procedure eliminates the time required to index the file again, your dBASE software systems will speed up dramatically.

Performance Trade-offs

You will have to make some trade-offs when you use multiple index files. Generally, the more index files you have active at any given moment, the longer it takes to perform an APPEND, EDIT, or REPLACE procedure. For example, if you want to add records to the MAIL database without any active index files, you can use the commands:

    USE MAIL
    APPEND

As you type in the data for each new individual, the screen will immediately accept each new record and redisplay the next APPEND screen. However, if you create four index files, and keep them all active like so:

    USE MAIL INDEX NAMES, ZIPS, CITIES, STATES

you will notice a delay before the appearance of each new blank APPEND screen. On a large data file with over 1000 records on it, this delay could be as much as 20 seconds, depending on how many fields are in each index file.

In general, however, one or two active index files are sufficient for most databases, as we'll see throughout the examples in the book. The delays caused by one or two active index files are relatively insignificant, and are more than compensated for by the time that the FIND and WHILE commands save, as well as by the time you save by avoiding reindexing.

Another disadvantage to indexed files occurs during global replaces. For example, if for some reason you wish to set all the AMOUNT fields back to zero in our hypothetical MAIL database, you could use the commands:

    USE MAIL INDEX NAMES,ZIPS
    REPLACE ALL AMOUNT WITH 0

On a database with 1000 records on it, this process could take 45 minutes. However, these commands waste processing time because they update the index files unnecessarily.

Recall that the NAMES index contains the LNAME and FNAME fields, and the ZIPS index contains the ZIP field. The AMOUNT field has no direct effect on either index. When that is the case, you can use the NOUPDATE option (supplied in dBASE II versions 2.4 and higher) to perform the replace. These commands perform the update in about six minutes:

```
USE MAIL INDEX NAMES,ZIPS
REPLACE NOUPDATE ALL AMOUNT WITH 0
```

The NOUPDATE option informs dBASE that, even though there are two active index files, there is no need to update them while performing this REPLACE command.

There are some important points to keep in mind about the INDEX and FIND commands. First, the FIND command *only* works on an indexed field. If a database is in use with multiple index files, the FIND command only works with the first listed index file. For example, if you open the MAIL database with the two index files as below:

```
USE MAIL INDEX ZIPS, NAMES
```

the FIND command can only be used to locate a zip code.

Second, if the data you wish to look up in a database is stored in a variable, then the variable name must be "macro-ized" in order to be used with the FIND command, as below:

```
ACCEPT "Look up whom? " TO SEARCH
FIND &SEARCH
```

Also, FIND does not support functions or operators. That is, you cannot use the commands FIND Miller .OR. Smith, or FIND LNAME > &SEARCH.

If you create two index files, but later add, edit, or delete data with only one or neither of the index files active, the index files will be corrupted, and you will most likely get a RECORD OUT OF RANGE error later. In this case, you must recreate both index files by typing in these commands:

```
USE MAIL
INDEX ON LNAME + FNAME TO NAMES
INDEX ON ZIP TO ZIPS
```

Again, you can avoid the reindexing if you always keep both index files active with the command USE MAIL INDEX NAMES, ZIPS when working with the database.

Programming for Performance

The manner in which you structure your command files can also influence the performance of your overall software system. For example, you can use the following simple program to print mailing labels in zip code order:

```
*********************************** LABELS.CMD.
*********** Print mailing labels from MAIL.DBF.
USE MAIL INDEX ZIPS
DO WHILE .NOT. EOF
   DO MFORMAT
   SKIP
ENDDO
```

Notice that this command file, called LABELS, continually branches to another command file called MFORMAT to print each mailing label. The MFORMAT command file looks like this:

```
******************** MFORMAT.CMD
? TRIM(FNAME),LNAME
? ADDRESS
? TRIM(CITY)+", "+STATE,ZIP
?
?
?
RETURN
```

The LABELS program above will take about 20 minutes to print 1000 mailing labels in zip code order if you have created the ZIPS index. You can cut this processing time in half if you do not force dBASE to DO MFORMAT every time it needs to print a label. Use the following single command file instead:

```
*********************************** LABELS.CMD.
********************** Print mailing labels from MAIL.DBF.
USE MAIL INDEX ZIPS
DO WHILE .NOT. EOF
   ? TRIM(FNAME),LNAME
   ? ADDRESS
   ? TRIM(CITY)+", "+STATE,ZIP
   ?
```

```
    ?
    ?
    SKIP
ENDDO
```

This command file will print 1000 labels in zip code order in about ten minutes. Since dBASE does not need to find out the MFORMAT command file's instructions at every pass through the DO WHILE loop, it can process the same amount of data in half the time.

In general, you can speed up your programs if you do not call external command files from within a DO WHILE . . . ENDDO loop. All of the programming examples throughout this book follow this important rule.

When you develop larger software systems, you can't always use the fastest method for every task in the program. Since most databases contain many fields, it is not practical to keep indexes of every field in the database. But a little planning can speed up many tasks considerably, as we'll see throughout the sample systems in the following chapters.

Summary

In this chapter we've seen several techniques for maximizing the speed of custom dBASE II software systems. The use of index files can greatly enhance the performance of a dBASE II software system because first they eliminate the need to re-sort the database after records have been added, deleted, or changed, and second, the FIND command allows for rapid searching for data in the index field. In addition, the WHILE option, rather than the FOR option, can be used to define the scope of the records accessed (e.g. WHILE LNAME = "Miller" as opposed to FOR LNAME = "Miller").

Multiple index files allow a custom dBASE system to maintain several sort orders at a time. Once an index file has been created with the INDEX ON command, it can be made active by inclusion in the USE command. For example, to keep two index files, named NAMES and ZIPS, active with a database named MAIL, use the command:

```
USE MAIL INDEX NAMES,ZIPS
```

That way, whenever records are added, edited, or deleted, both index files will be updated automatically.

When multiple index files are active with a database, the first listed file (NAMES in the example above), is *primary*. When the records are displayed with LIST, DISPLAY, REPORT, COPY, BROWSE, or any other command, they will be displayed in the order specified by the primary index file. Also, the FIND command only works with the primary index file. A single database can have up to seven active index files associated with it.

Programs can also be made to run a little faster by avoiding DO commands within DO WHILE loops. Calling the same program over and over again from within a command file can take up a lot of disk-accessing time, and double the time required to perform a given task.

CHAPTER 3
PROGRAM DESIGN AND DEVELOPMENT

Writing a custom software system is much like writing a school term paper. The first question is "Where do I start?" Like the term paper, a software system can become an unorganized mass of information if you do not have a definite goal in mind, and a plan of attack for attaining your goal. In this chapter, we'll discuss techniques for defining and obtaining the goal of a software project. Along the way, we'll examine a variety of programming techniques that will be useful for many applications. These techniques include:

1. Creating custom screen displays for adding and editing data.
2. Using ZIP and SED to create custom screens.
3. Creating menu-driven sorts and searches.
4. Managing multiple index files.
5. Creating custom reports with screen pauses and page breaks.
6. Checking for duplicate records in a database.

Software Design and Development

The steps involved in designing and developing a software project can be summarized as follows:

1. Define the goal of the project.
2. Design the database structure.
3. Design the software structure.
4. Design and develop each command file in the system, following the steps below:

   - Design the input screens and reports,
   - design the program with pseudocode, and
   - write, test, and debug each program in the system independently.

The best way to examine each of these steps is by performing them, so let's begin by designing and developing a custom dBASE II software system. We will begin at step one: defining the goals of the project.

Defining the Goals of the Project

For our first programming example, we'll design and develop a sophisticated mailing list system that is user-friendly, fast, and flexible. A mailing system is a good example to start with because it is a relatively easy-to-learn application.

Defining the goals of the project can be as simple as thinking about all the jobs you want the software to perform and writing them down on paper. Here is a simple explanation of our program.

The mailing system will allow the user to store names, addresses, and keywords, on a database. When the user enters the system, he'll first see the main menu which presents the primary options. These options will be shown in the main menu as follows:

Mailing System Main Menu
1. Add new names and addresses
2. Print reports
3. Do a quick look-up

4. Edit names and addresses
5. Delete names and addresses
6. Check for duplicates
7. Exit

Option 1 allows the user to add new names and addresses using a custom-designed screen that provides instructions for controlling the cursor.

Option 2 allows the user to print mailing labels, print a directory, or create a MailMerge file for writing form letters with WordStar's MailMerge option. Prior to printing a report, the user can select a sort order (name, zip code, city, or state) from a simple menu of options. The user may also specify a search criterion from a simple menu, such as requesting to include only people with the last name Smith, or only people with the keyword EXPIRES 10/31/84. Optionally, the user may request that all names and addresses be printed or sent to the MailMerge file.

When printing labels, the user may request that multiple copies of each label be printed. Also, the mailing label program will allow the user to check the alignment of the labels in the printer and make adjustments prior to printing the labels.

Option 3 allows the user to look up an address or phone number quickly. When the user needs to change data for an individual on the database, he selects option 4 and simply types in the last name of the person whose data he wishes to edit. Then a custom edit screen, complete with instructions for managing the cursor, appears and allows him to make changes. Similarly, option 5 allows the user to delete people from the list by specifying the names of the individuals he wishes to delete. The delete option double-checks with the user prior to deleting the names permanently.

Option 6 gives the user a listing of all potential duplicates on the database.

Option 7 allows the user to exit the mailing system and return to the A> prompt.

The description above provides a set of goals to work toward. We've provided many options, and have ensured that the system will be easy for a novice to use. For example, dBASE usually requires that the user know the number of the record he wishes to edit or delete, but we'll make life easier by allowing the user to type in the name instead. The user can define sort and search options from a menu without knowing the dBASE II commands and syntax normally required to perform these tasks.

The next step is to design a database that will hold the appropriate information.

Designing the Database Structure

Contrary to popular belief, the term *database* actually refers to *all* the database and index files used by a given system, rather than a single dBASE II .DBF data file. In this system, we only need a single data file with names and addresses, but a couple of index files will also come in handy here.

The names and addresses will be stored on the disk in drive B on a data file called MAIL.DBF. It will have the structure displayed in Figure 3.1.

The KEYWORD field allows the user additional flexibility in defining search criteria. For example, this structure could be used for a membership mailing list for a club. The user could store expiration dates here to simplify the task of creating form letters and mailing labels for individuals whose memberships expire on a particular date. If the user included occupations in this field, he or she could send letters to a specified professional group, like attorneys or teachers.

This structure also includes phone numbers, because the quick lookup option we are going to provide allows the user to search for a phone number.

STRUCTURE FOR FILE: B:MAIL .DBF

FLD	NAME	TYPE	WIDTH	DEC
001	LNAME	C	020	
002	FNAME	C	020	
003	COMPANY	C	020	
004	ADDRESS	C	025	
005	CITY	C	020	
006	STATE	C	005	
007	ZIP	C	010	
008	PHONE	C	013	
009	KEYWORD	C	020	
** TOTAL **			00154	

Figure 3.1: *Data file structure for the mailing system.*

Next, we need to think about what kind of index files the user will need. Since the user will probably want to print mailing labels in zip code order for bulk mailing, we should create an index of zip codes.

We've also stated that the user will be able to edit, delete, and do quick lookups based on name. Therefore, we will create an index of names so that the program can use the FIND command to look up names. (This index will also be useful for printing the directory, which will probably be in alphabetical order by name.) Of course there may be 10 Smiths and 15 Millers on the database, so the index will assure that all people with common last names are alphabetized by first name.

We can also have the system handle any problems a user might encounter with upper- and lowercase when searching through a database. We'll simply create the index of names in all uppercase. Every time the user types in a name to look up, the command file will change that name to uppercase prior to performing the search. Therefore, we take the responsibility of worrying about upper- and lowercase off of the user, and give it to the command file.

When you decide what you want to store on the database and what index files you'll need, you are ready to write them into the program. In this example, load up dBASE, then SET DEFAULT TO B (or the drive you'll use). Then CREATE MAIL with the structure previously displayed in Figure 3.1.

Then, while the MAIL data file is still empty, you can create the zip code index by typing in the commands:

```
USE MAIL
INDEX ON ZIP TO ZIPS
```

To create the names index in all uppercase, type in the commands:

```
USE MAIL
INDEX ON !(LNAME) + !(FNAME) TO NAMES
```

Now the entire database consists of three files:

```
MAIL.DBF
ZIPS.NDX
NAMES.NDX
```

They are all empty and ready for input. Once you have the database structure defined, the next step is to develop a plan of attack for developing the command files.

Designing the Software Structure

The goals we defined earlier in this chapter will require a fair amount of software. It would be very difficult to write one gigantic command file to perform all these tasks. Instead, let's break the job down into smaller tasks, each representing a single command file that we can design, write, and test independently. This will make our programming task much simpler in the long run. As any professional programmer will tell you, the key to developing large software systems is to break down the large, seemingly insurmountable, job into small tasks which are easy to work with. Figure 3.2 shows the software structure for our mailing system.

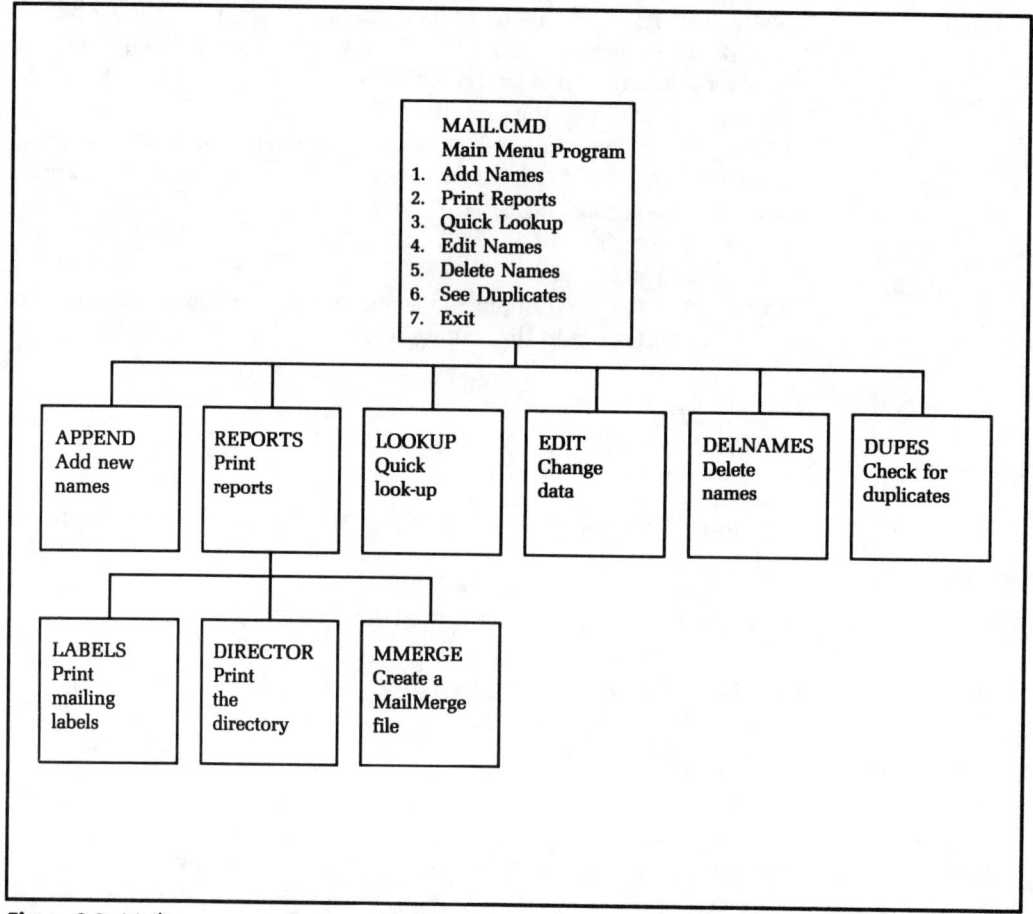

Figure 3.2: Mailing system software structure.

Notice the hierarchical structure of the command files. The MAIN MENU program is at the top of the hierarchy, because its primary job is to determine which task the user wishes to perform. Once the user selects the task, the program branches to the appropriate command file. The REPORTS command file, while subordinate to the main menu, also has many tasks to perform. It needs to find out:

1. the type of report to print (labels, directory, or MailMerge file),
2. the sort order required, and
3. the searching conditions.

Once the REPORTS command file has all of that information, it branches to the appropriate subordinate command file (either LABELS, DIRECTOR, or MMERGE). When the subordinate command file finishes its task, it returns control to the program that called it (immediately above in the hierarchy).

A hierarchical software design such as this allows us to break the overall large system down into small digestible command files which are relatively easy to create and test.

Designing and Developing Each Command File in the System

The first step in designing each individual command file is to decide what input and/or output will appear on the screen or printer. For our first programming example we'll develop the main menu for the mailing system. The output for the user to read from this command file is the main menu, as displayed in Figure 3.3.

The next job is to design the *logical flow* of the command file. This is best achieved by writing *pseudocode*, a plain English description of the various steps that the command file will follow. Figure 3.4 shows our pseudocode for the mailing system main menu.

Once the logical flow of the program is defined in pseudocode, we can translate it to dBASE II code. We'll begin by giving the program a title, setting the talk parameter off, and setting the default drive to B, as below:

```
******************************** MAIL.CMD.
********************** Mailing system main menu.
SET TALK OFF
SET DEFA TO B
```

```
              Mailing System Main Menu
           1. Add new names and addresses
           2. Print reports
           3. Quick look-up
           4. Edit names and addresses
           5. Delete names and addresses
           6. Check for duplicates
           7. Exit
              Enter choice (1–7) from above :   :
```

Figure 3.3: *Mailing system main menu.*

Next, we'll define MAIL.DBF as the data file to use, along with the NAMES and ZIPS index files, as below.

```
*************** Set up data file and index files.
USE MAIL INDEX NAMES,ZIPS
```

We've listed the NAMES index before the ZIPS index, to make NAMES the primary index file in use. With NAMES as the primary index file, the command file can use the FIND command to look up names in the data file quickly. We've tagged on the ZIPS index so that any additions or changes to the database will also automatically update the ZIPS index also. That way, we don't have to reindex the file every time the user wants to print data in zip code order.

Next we'll set up a loop for displaying the main menu:

```
*************** Set up loop for presenting menu.
STORE 0 TO CHOICE
DO WHILE CHOICE # 7
   ERASE
   TEXT
         Mailing System Main Menu
      1. Add new names and addresses
      2. Print reports
      3. Quick look-up
      4. Edit names and addresses
      5. Delete names and addresses
      6. Check for duplicates
      7. Exit
ENDTEXT
```

```
*********************** Ask for user's choice.
@ 12,12 SAY "Enter choice (1–7) from above "';
GET CHOICE PICTURE "9"
READ
```

MAIL.CMD MAIN MENU program for the mailing system

Set dBASE "talk" off
Make drive B the default drive

Use MAIL.DBF with the NAMES and ZIPS index files

Set up loop for the main menu
As long as the user does not ask to exit
    Clear the screen
    Display the main menu of choices

        1. Add new names and addresses
        2. Print reports
        3. Quick look up
        4. Edit names and addresses
        5. Delete names and addresses
        6. Check for duplicates
        7. Exit

Wait for a response from the user

If user chooses option 1
    Branch to the APPEND program

If user chooses option 2
    Branch to the REPORTS program

If user chooses option 3
    Branch to the LOOKUP program

If user chooses option 4
    Branch to the EDIT program

If user chooses option 5
    Branch to the DELNAMES program

If user chooses option 6
    Branch to the DUPES program
If user does not request exit, redisplay the main menu
Otherwise, QUIT

Figure 3.4: *Pseudocode for the mailing system main menu.*

We created a memory variable called CHOICE, and gave it a value of zero. Next, the command DO WHILE CHOICE # 7 assures that the menu will be redisplayed as long as the user does not pick option 7 to exit the mailing system. Within the loop, the command file first clears the screen (ERASE), then presents the main menu using the TEXT and ENDTEXT commands.

To find out what the user wants to do next, we set up the prompt "Enter choice (1–7) from above" beneath the menu on line 12 at column 12. The GET and READ commands wait for the the user to type in a single number. The PICTURE statement will only accept a number, since this is what the command file expects.

Once the user types in an answer, the command file branches to the appropriate subordinate command file to perform the requested task. The next few lines of code perform that task.

```
********** Branch to appropriate command file.
DO CASE
    CASE CHOICE = 1
        DO APPEND
    CASE CHOICE = 2
        DO REPORTS
    CASE CHOICE = 3
        DO LOOKUP
    CASE CHOICE = 4
        DO EDIT
    CASE CHOICE = 5
        DO DELNAMES
    CASE CHOICE = 6
        DO DUPES
ENDCASE
```

Next, we need to close the DO WHILE loop, and allow the user to exit dBASE. These next few lines take care of that job:

```
ENDDO (while choice # 7)
************ When choice = 7, end loop and quit.
QUIT
```

Figure 3.5 shows the MAIL.CMD command file in its entirety. If you are following along on-line, be sure to create the MAIL.DBF data file, and the two INDEX files described earlier. Then key in the MAIL.CMD program (or MAIL.PRG, if you are using MS-DOS) using MODIFY COMMAND or a word processor.

```
**************************************** MAIL.CMD.
*********************** Mailing system main menu.
SET TALK OFF
SET DEFA TO B

*************** Set up data file and index files.
USE MAIL INDEX NAMES,ZIPS


*************** Set up loop for presenting menu.
STORE 0 TO CHOICE
DO WHILE CHOICE # 7
   ERASE
   TEXT
                Mailing System Main Menu

                1. Add new names and addresses
                2. Print reports
                3. Quick look-up
                4. Edit names and addresses
                5. Delete names and addresses
                6. Check for duplicates

                7. Exit
   ENDTEXT

   *********************** Ask for user's choice.
   @ 12,12 SAY "Enter choice (1-7) from above ";
      GET CHOICE PICTURE "9"
   READ

   ********** Branch to appropriate command file.
   DO CASE

      CASE CHOICE = 1
           DO APPEND

      CASE CHOICE = 2
           DO REPORTS

      CASE CHOICE = 3
           DO LOOKUP

      CASE CHOICE = 4
           DO EDIT

      CASE CHOICE = 5
           DO DELNAMES

      CASE CHOICE = 6
           DO DUPES

      ENDCASE

ENDDO (while choice # 7)
************* When choice = 7, end loop and quit.
QUIT
```

Figure 3.5: *The mailing system main menu (MAIL.PRG).*

Summary

In this chapter we've explored techniques for moving a software project from the idea stage to a manageable specification. The steps used in designing and defining the project are:

1. Define the goals of the project.
2. Define the database structure.
3. Design the software structure.
4. Design and develop each program in the system.

Along the way, we've designed a mailing system, defined the database and software structure, and written the MAIN MENU command file for the system.

We will develop the rest of the command files for our sophisticated mailing system in chapters that follow, beginning with a discussion of custom screen displays for adding new names and addresses and editing existing ones.

CHAPTER 4
CUSTOM DATA-ENTRY SCREENS

For simple programming applications, the EDIT and APPEND commands allow the user to edit and add records to a database. When you type in APPEND, the screen displays the field names, and spaces for typing in data, as in Figure 4.1.

This screen is not easy for a novice user to understand. By creating your own data-entry screens, you can include clearer prompts, such as Last Name instead of LNAME. You can also provide instructions on the screen, such as commands for managing the cursor. Let's examine how to use the @, SAY, GET, READ, and PICTURE commands to design the screen to your exact specifications.

Creating Formatted Screen Displays

For the novice or occasional user, a custom screen for adding new data or editing data should provide some brief instructions for managing the cursor on the screen. Figure 4.2 shows the custom screen that

```
LNAME      :_              :
FNAME      :               :
COMPANY    :               :
ADDRESS    :               :
CITY       :               :
STATE      :    :
ZIP        :         :
PHONE      :       :
KEYWORD    :          :
```

Figure 4.1: A typical APPEND screen.

will be used for adding new data and editing data in our sample mailing system.

There are three basic methods for creating custom screen displays. The first method is to use MODI COMM to create a file, then type in the @ sign and the coordinates (row and column number) of each prompt, followed by the prompt, the GET command, and the name of the field. *Note:* If you want to use MODI COMM to create the screen, you *must* remember to give the file the extension FMT. For example, to create a custom screen display called MSCREEN1, you would type in MODI COMM B:MSCREEN1.FMT, then type in the contents (shown in Figure 4.3), and save the file with ^W.

As an alternative to typing in all of those @, SAY, and GET commands, Ashton-Tate provides the ZIP (for CP/M) and SED (for PC-DOS) programs. ZIP and SED allow you to draw your custom screen as you wish it to appear during an APPEND or EDIT. Then, the ZIP or

```
Cursor Movement: (The ^ symbol means 'hold down the CTRL key ...')
^E up : ^X down : ^D right : ^S left : ^G delete : ^V insert

Last Name    :              : First Name :              :
Company      :              :
Address      :              :
City         :              : State :         : Zip :        :
Phone number : ( ) - :
Keyword      :              :
```

Figure 4.2: Custom data-entry screen.

Custom Data-Entry Screens

```
@  1, 0 SAY "Cursor Movement: (The ^ symbol means "
@  1,37 SAY "^hold down the CTRL key...^)"
@  3, 0 SAY "^E up : ^X down : ^D right : ^S left "
@  3,37 SAY ": ^G delete : ^V Insert"
@  4, 0 SAY "-------------------------------------"
@  4,37 SAY "-------------------------------------"
@  6, 0 SAY "Last Name"
@  6,10 GET LNAME
@  6,32 SAY "First Name"
@  6,43 GET FNAME
@  8, 0 SAY "Company"
@  8,10 GET COMPANY
@ 10, 0 SAY "Address"
@ 10,10 GET ADDRESS
@ 12, 0 SAY "City"
@ 12,10 GET CITY
@ 12,32 SAY "State"
@ 12,38 GET STATE
@ 12,46 SAY "Zip"
@ 12,50 GET ZIP
@ 14, 0 SAY "Phone number"
@ 14,13 GET PHONE
@ 16, 0 SAY "Keyword"
@ 16, 8 GET KEYWORD
```

Figure 4.3: *Format file for displaying custom data-entry screen.*

SED program takes care of writing all the @, SAY, and GET commands.

Using ZIP

To create a custom screen using ZIP, put your zip disk in drive A, and the command file disk in drive B. With the CP/M A> prompt showing, type in the command ZIP. This will bring up a menu of options as displayed in Figure 4.4.

To draw a custom screen, simply press RETURN. ZIP asks:

<NEW> or <OLD> file (Q to Quit)? _

Since this is a new file, type N (new). The ZIP program asks:

FILE NAME (drive opt): _

Type in a filename with the disk drive specification. To create a command file called MSCREEN1 on the disk in drive B, type in the filename B:MSCREEN1, and press RETURN. ZIP will display a blank screen for you to work with, and display a reminder at the bottom of

```
ZIP<tm>              <C> 1982 Hal Pawluk
 @: DISPLAY value           #: INPUT value
 []: EMBED commands
 /<Tab>: Edge              /C: Center text
 /K: Kill Row/Col           /A: Add Row/Col
 /H: Horizontal line        /V: Vertical line
 /T: Top /B: Bottom         /M: Middle
 /D: Delete    /I: Insert   /P: Prior Scrn
 /F: First     /L: Last     /N: Next Scrn
 /S: SAVE      /E: Erase    /Q: Quit no save
 T>abs:     5   V>ert: .        H>oriz:
                M>argin:    0
 Enter L>etter to change or <RETURN> _
```

Figure 4.4: The ZIP main menu.

the screen to inform you of the cursor's current position, like so:

   Row 0, Col 0

Type in the custom screen exactly as you wish it to appear to the user. At the location you want dBASE to get a field or memory value, type in the # symbol, followed by the name of the field or memory variable to get. To create a format file similar to the one displayed in Figure 4.3, fill out the blank ZIP screen as shown in Figure 4.5. (*Note:* Type /H to draw a quick horizontal line.)

If you ever feel lost while drawing a screen in ZIP, type two slashes (//) to call the ZIP main menu to the screen. Then press RETURN to go back to your custom ZIP screen.

```
Cursor Movement: (The ^ symbol means 'hold down the CTRL key . . .')

^E up : ^X down : ^D right : ^S left : ^G delete : ^V insert
─────────────────────────────────────────────────────────────
Last Name      #LNAME         First Name #FNAME
Company        #COMPANY
Address        #ADDRESS
City           #CITY          State #STATE Zip #ZIP
Phone number   #PHONE
Keyword        #KEYWORD
```

Figure 4.5: A ZIP screen.

Once you've drawn your screen, type in /S to save it. ZIP will ask:

> SAVE B:MSCREEN1: (Cmd, Fmt, Stop)? _

You must specify whether this is a .CMD or a .FMT file (or Stop to cancel). For a custom format screen, type F for a format file. Then ZIP will ask:

> B:MSCREEN1: Change name (Y or N)? _

Answer N (no). Then ZIP will ask:

> B:MSCREEN1: Print format (Y/N)? _

We've created this screen for adding new data, not for printing data on the printer, so type N (no). ZIP will then create a command file called MSCREEN1.FMT on the disk in drive B, as well as the files SCREEN1.ZPR and SCREEN1.ZIP that can be used for revising the custom screen at a later date.

After creating and saving the custom screen format, ZIP will return you to the custom ZIP screen. To quit ZIP, type in /Q. ZIP will ask:

> QUIT to system (Yes or No)? _

Answer Y (yes). The operating system A> prompt will reappear.

Now, to view the format file that ZIP created, load up dBASE. When you see the dot prompt, type in SET DEFAULT TO B. Next, type MODI COMM MSCREEN1.FMT. You should see the format file that ZIP created, similar to the one shown in Figure 4.6.

To become proficient with ZIP, just practice. Remember to use the // command to review your options while you are drawing the custom screen. For more information, refer to the ZIP section of your dBASE II manual (if your version of dBASE II includes the ZIP program).

Using SED

If you wish to use the SED program to generate custom screen displays, begin by putting the SED disk in drive A, and the disk with your command files in drive B. Then, type in the command SED, and press RETURN.

To create a custom screen display, select option N to create a new file. SED will ask:

> **Name of new file?** _

```
* MSCREEN1.FMT
@  1, 0 SAY "Cursor Movement: (The ^ symbol means "
@  1,37 SAY "^hold down the CTRL key...^)"
@  3, 0 SAY "^E up : ^X down : ^D right : ^S left "
@  3,37 SAY ": ^G delete : ^V Insert"
@  4, 0 SAY "--------------------------------------"
@  4,37 SAY "--------------------------------------"
@  6, 0 SAY "Last Name"
@  6,10 GET LNAME
@  6,32 SAY "First Name"
@  6,43 GET FNAME
@  8, 0 SAY "Company"
@  8,10 GET COMPANY
@ 10, 0 SAY "Address"
@ 10,10 GET ADDRESS
@ 12, 0 SAY "City"
@ 12,10 GET CITY
@ 12,32 SAY "State"
@ 12,38 GET STATE
@ 12,46 SAY "Zip"
@ 12,50 GET ZIP
@ 14, 0 SAY "Phone number"
@ 14,13 GET PHONE
@ 16, 0 SAY "Keyword"
@ 16, 8 GET KEYWORD
```

Figure 4.6: The MSCREEN1.FMT format file generated by ZIP.

In our example, we'll type in the filename B:MSCREEN1.SCN, and press RETURN. The screen will clear, and SED will present a blank screen on which to draw the custom screen. To create the display presented earlier, just draw the screen as shown in Figure 4.7.

Notice that the screen in Figure 4.7 resembles the previous ZIP screen, except that < rather than # is used to specify GET fields.

```
Cursor Movement: (The ^ symbol means 'hold down the CTRL key ...')
^E up : ^X down : ^D right : ^S left : ^G delete : ^V insert

Last Name     <LNAME           First Name <FNAME
Company       <COMPANY
Address       <ADDRESS
City          <CITY             State <STATE Zip <ZIP
Phone number  <PHONE
Keyword       <KEYWORD
```

Figure 4.7: A SED screen to generate a custom dBASE screen.

Once you have typed in the SED screen, save it by pressing Esc, and pressing D. This will return you to the SED main menu.

From the SED main menu, select option G to generate a dBASE II command file. SED will ask:

   Name of screen file: B:MSCREEN1.SCN

SED is asking for the name of the screen file, while proposing MSCREEN1 as the likely answer, since we just created this screen file a moment ago. Just press RETURN, and SED will state:

   Will generate dBASE command file b:MSCREEN1. (X to cancel) :

There is no need to cancel the command, so press RETURN to allow SED to create the command file for the custom screen. When SED is done, it redisplays its main menu. Select option Q (quit) to redisplay the A> prompt.

Now, put your dBASE II disk in drive A, and call up dBASE. When the dot prompt appears, SET DEFAULT TO B, then call up the format file generated by SED by typing in the command:

   MODI COMM B:MSCREEN1.

The format file will appear on the screen, as presented in Figure 4.8.

There is one problem with the format file generated by SED: it does not have the necessary extension, .FMT. All we have to do is rename the SED-generated file, MSCREEN1 to MSCREEN1.FMT. To do so, you can return to the PC-DOS operating system A> prompt, and type in the command:

   RENAME B:MSCREEN1 b:MSCREEN1.FMT

and press RETURN. From the dBASE dot prompt you can use the command:

   RENAME B:MSCREEN1. TO B:MSCREEN1.FMT

Using Format Files

Once you've created the format (.FMT) file, using it is simple. To add some new records to the MAIL database we've already created, just load up dBASE in the usual manner and set the default drive to B (or the drive you are using). When the dot prompt appears, be sure to type

```
* B:MSCREEN1.
@ 1,1 SAY "Cursor Movement: (The ^ symbol means ´hold down the CTR"
@ 1,56 SAY "L key...´)"
@ 3,1 SAY "^E up : ^X down : ^D right : ^S left : ^G delete : ^V I"
@ 3,56 SAY "nsert"
@ 4,1 SAY "------------------------------------------------------"
@ 4,56 SAY "------------"
@ 6,1 SAY "Last Name"
@ 6,12 GET LNAME
@ 6,33 SAY "First Name"
@ 6,45 GET FNAME
@ 8,1 SAY "Company"
@ 8,12 GET COMPANY
@ 10,1 SAY "Address"
@ 10,12 GET ADDRESS
@ 12,1 SAY "City"
@ 12,12 GET CITY
@ 12,33 SAY "State"
@ 12,40 GET STATE
@ 12,47 SAY "Zip"
@ 12,52 GET ZIP
@ 14,1 SAY "Phone number"
@ 14,15 GET PHONE
@ 16,1 SAY "Keyword"
@ 16,10 GET KEYWORD
```

Figure 4.8: *A custom dBASE screen generated by the SED program.*

in the command:

USE MAIL INDEX NAMES, ZIPS

Again, it is important to specifiy *both* index files here, since we'll be adding new data and we want both index files to be kept current. Now to add a few records, type in the command:

SET FORMAT TO MSCREEN1

and then type in the usual command:

APPEND

The appending procedure will work as usual, except that it will use the custom MSCREEN1 screen shown in Figure 4.9.

In addition, you can SET FORMAT TO MSCREEN1, then type in EDIT or READ to modify existing data using the custom screen.

When you are done using a custom format screen, you should set dBASE back to its normal screen mode by typing:

SET FORMAT TO SCREEN

Otherwise, dBASE may try to use the custom screen for future

```
Cursor Movement: (The ^ symbol means 'hold down the CTRL key . . .')
^E up : ^X down : ^D right : ^S left : ^G delete : ^V insert

Last Name      :                        : First Name :              :
Company        :                        :
Address        :                              :
City           :                        : State :       : Zip :     :
Phone number   :               :
Keyword        :                        :
```

Figure 4.9: Append mode after setting format to MSCREEN1.

APPEND, EDIT, and READ commands inappropriately. The SET FORMAT TO SCREEN command sets dBASE back to its normal screen.

Adding Templates

We can improve the custom screen display by providing a template for the phone number field. As it stands, the screen displays the prompt

    Phone number :   :

with space for 13 digits in it, assuming that the user is going to type in the phone using a format such as (619)555-1212. We can save the user the time of typing in the parentheses and hyphen by including them in the field. That is, we'll have the custom screen display the prompt for the phone number as:

    Phone number :(   )   -   :

As a safety check, we'll assure that the user only types in numbers, since a phone number doesn't have letters in it. To do so, we'll modify the MSCREEN1.FMT format file. This is not a difficult task. You can use MODI COMM B:MSCREEN1.FMT, or use the WordStar program's nondocument mode to edit the MSCREEN1.FMT command file. Then add the PICTURE command next to the GET PHONE command in the format file, as shown in Figure 4.10.

```
*  MSCREEN1.FMT
@  1, 0 SAY "Cursor Movement: (The ^ symbol means "
@  1,37 SAY "^hold down the CTRL key...^)"
@  3, 0 SAY "^E up : ^X down : ^D right : ^S left "
@  3,37 SAY ": ^G delete : ^V Insert"
@  4, 0 SAY "-------------------------------------"
@  4,37 SAY "-------------------------------------"
@  6, 0 SAY "Last Name"
@  6,10 GET LNAME
@  6,32 SAY "First Name"
@  6,43 GET FNAME
@  8, 0 SAY "Company"
@  8,10 GET COMPANY
@ 10, 0 SAY "Address"
@ 10,10 GET ADDRESS
@ 12, 0 SAY "City"
@ 12,10 GET CITY
@ 12,32 SAY "State"
@ 12,38 GET STATE
@ 12,46 SAY "Zip"
@ 12,50 GET ZIP
@ 14, 0 SAY "Phone number"
@ 14,13 GET PHONE PICTURE "(999)999-9999"
@ 16, 0 SAY "Keyword"
@ 16, 8 GET KEYWORD
```

Figure 4.10: *ZIP command file modified to include a PICTURE.*

The parentheses and hyphens will automatically appear on the screen, and will be placed in the data file without the user having to type them in. Furthermore, the 9's in the PICTURE statement will assure that only numeric characters (0–9) will be accepted into the field, therefore reducing the likelihood of an error.

If you are using the SED program, you can have SED automatically create the PICTURE formats too. Simply use the ! symbol when drawing the screen to stand for PICTURE. For example, if you want SED to include the picture statement in the PHONE field, draw the line on the SED screen as below:

Phone number <PHONE!"(999)999-9999"

Command File for Custom Data-Entry Screen

The design of our mailing system called for a command file named APPEND to allow the user to add new names and addresses via the custom screen. Once you've created the MSCREEN1.FMT format file, the next step is to create the APPEND command file. This is very simple; the entire command file is displayed in Figure 4.11.

You can create the command file (after creating the MSCREEN1.FMT format file) using the command MODI COMM B:APPEND, or by using a word processor. To test the command file, ask dBASE to DO MAIL rather than to DO APPEND. When the MAIL main menu appears, select option 1 to add new records. You should then see the custom screen for adding new names and addresses, as displayed in Figure 4.12.

If you are creating the format and command files as we discuss them, test the program now by adding some names and addresses to the database. When you are done, press RETURN rather than typing in a last name. The SET FORMAT TO SCREEN command in the APPEND program will set dBASE back to its original screen mode, and the RETURN command will return control to the MAIL command file, and redisplay the main menu. From there, just select the EXIT option so we can begin developing the remaining command files.

```
*********************************************************** APPEND.CMD
********* Add new data via custom data entry screen, MSCREEN1.FMT

SET FORMAT TO MSCREEN1
APPEND
SET FORMAT TO SCREEN

RETURN
```

Figure 4.11: APPEND command file for the sample mailing system.

```
Cursor Movement: (The ^ symbol means 'hold down the CTRL key ...')

^E up : ^X down : ^D right : ^S left : ^G delete : ^V insert


Last Name    :                    : First Name :           :
Company      :                    :
Address      :                    :
City         :                    : State :      : Zip :    :
Phone number : (   )   -   :
Keyword      :                    :
```

Figure 4.12: Custom screen to add new names and addresses.

Summary

In this chapter, we've discussed techniques for creating custom screens in dBASE II. The @, SAY, GET, and PICTURE commands can be used to format a screen in any fashion. Custom screens can be developed rapidly with the ZIP (for CP/M) and SED (for PC-DOS) programs. Once the custom screen is created, the SET FORMAT TO command can be used to specify the name of the custom screen, the READ, APPEND, and EDIT commands can be used to display the screen. The SET FORMAT TO SCREEN command releases the custom screen, and returns dBASE to its normal mode.

We've also developed a command file, named APPEND, for adding records to the MAIL database through the mailing system main menu.

CHAPTER 5
MENU-DRIVEN SORTS AND SEARCHES

dBASE provides great capabilities for sorting and searching a database, but these require considerable knowledge of the syntax of the dBASE II language. Since we're assuming that the user of our system is not well versed in the dBASE language, we can simplify the sort and search procedures by making them menu options. In our sample mailing system, the REPORTS program will take care of these jobs and ask which report the user wants (mailing labels, directory, or MailMerge file).

The REPORTS Command File

The REPORTS command file will perform four major tasks:

1. Ask the user what report he/she wants.
2. Ask the user what sort order he/she wants.
3. Ask the user what search criteria he/she wishes.
4. Branch to approriate custom report program and print data according to sort and search criteria.

When the user selects option 2 from the main menu (Print Reports), he'll first see a menu of report options:

Report Options

1. Mailing labels
2. Directory
3. MailMerge file

Enter report type (1–3) : :

Then, he selects a report option by keying in the appropriate menu number. The screen then presents another menu, which allows the user to specify how the data should be sorted:

Sort Options

1. Directory order (by last name)
2. Bulk mailing order (by zip code)
3. City order
4. State order
5. Original order

Which sort order (1–5) : :

If the user selects option 1, the data will be presented in alphabetical order by last, then first name. If he selects option 2, the data will be presented in zip code order, and so forth.

Then, the user is asked to define a search condition from the next menu to appear on the screen:

Searching Options

1. Last Name
2. Zip code
3. Keyword
4. Print all names and addresses

Enter search choice (1–4) : :

If he decides to search by name (option 1), the screen asks:

Look for whom?

At this point, the user can type in a name to look for. For example, if the user types in *Smith*, then only people with the last name Smith will be sent to the report. If the user selects option 3, the screen will ask:

Look for what keyword?

The user can then type in a keyword. For example, if he types in EXPIRES 10/84, only names and addresses for people with the keyword EXPIRES 10/84 will be sent to the report. If the user selects option 4, then all names and addresses on the database will be sent to the report.

This very simple series of menus provides the user with a great deal of flexibility. For example, to send a form letter to all people whose membership expires in 10/84, the user could select the MailMerge file as the report option, the zip code as the sort order (for bulk mailing), and EXPIRES 10/84 as the keyword. The program then produces a MailMerge file of individuals whose membership expires on 10/84 in zip code order. To print matching labels, the user could select labels as the report format, zip code as the sort order, and keyword EXPIRES 10/84 as the search criterion again. The letter and labels will be printed in the same order, making it easy to match the labels with the letters.

The pseudocode for the REPORTS program is shown in Figure 5.1.

Let's begin writing the code now. The first task is to display a menu of report options and wait for an answer. The usual comments containing the program name and tasks are included at the top of the program below:

```
* * * * * * * * * * * * * * * * * * * * * * * * * * REPORTS.CMD
* * * * * * * * * * * * * * * * * * * * * * Ask user for report type,
* * * * * * * * * * * * * * * * * * * * * * sort order and for search
* * * * * * * * * * * * * * * * * * * * * * criteria, then branch
* * * * * * * * * * * * * * * * * * * * * * to appropriate report.
ERASE
STORE " " TO RCHOICE
TEXT

        Report Options

     1. Mailing labels
     2. Directory
     3. MailMerge file

ENDTEXT
8,18 SAY "Enter report type (1-3) " GET RCHOICE
READ
```

This menu display is pretty straightforward.

> Clear the screen
> Display menu of report options
>
>> Report Options
>>
>> 1. Mailing labels
>> 2. Directory
>> 3. MailMerge file
>
> Ask user which report, and store answer in RCHOICE
>
> Next, display menu of sort options
>
>> Sort Options
>>
>> 1. Directory order (by last name)
>> 2. Bulk mailing order (by zip code)
>> 3. City order
>> 4. State order
>> 5. Original order
>
> Ask user which order, and store answer to ORDER
>
> Set up sort order according to user's request
>
>> If user chooses 1
>>> Use mail with names index
>>
>> If user chooses 2
>>> Use mail with zips index
>>
>> If user chooses 3
>>> Create a temporary index of cities
>>
>> If user chooses 4
>>> Create a temporary index of states
>>
>> Otherwise
>>> Use mail with no index
>
> Display menu of search options
>
>> Searching Options
>>
>> 1. Last name
>> 2. Zip code
>> 3. Keyword
>> 4. Print all names and addresses

Figure 5.1: *Pseudocode for the REPORTS program.*

Wait for response and store to SEARCH

Set up search condition according to user's request

    If user chooses 1
        Make LNAME field to search on
        Ask whom to search for
        Make answer the search condition

    If user chooses 2
        Make ZIP the field to search on
        Ask which zip code to look up
        Make answer the search condition

    If user chooses 3
        Make KEYWORD the field to search on
        Ask which keyword to look for
        Make answer the search condition

    If user chooses 4
        Set up an "always true" condition
            so all records are printed

Then, branch to appropriate program based
        upon user's request (RCHOICE)

    If report choice was 1
        Print labels

    If report choice was 2
        Print the directory

    If report choice was 3
        Create a MailMerge file

When done with the report

Check to see if temporary index file was created
    If so, delete it

Make NAMES and ZIPS index files active
before returning to main menu

Release memory variables

Return to main menu

Figure 5.1: Pseudocode for the REPORTS program (continued).

Menu-Driven Sorting

Your next task is to create a routine that will present a menu of sorting options, as below:

```
***************** Ask about sort order.
ERASE
STORE " " TO ORDER
TEXT

    Sort Options
  1. Directory order (by last name)
  2. Bulk Mailing order (by zip code)
  3. City order
  4. State order
  5. Original order

ENDTEXT
@ 10,11 SAY " Which sort order (1-5) " GET ORDER
READ
```

Again, this is a simple menu. The next task is to set up the sort order according to the user's request. The following DO CASE clause takes care of this job:

```
**** Set up sort order according to user's request.
ERASE
DO CASE

    CASE ORDER = "1"
       SET INDEX TO NAMES

    CASE ORDER = "2"
       SET INDEX TO ZIPS

    CASE ORDER = "3"
       ? " Sorting . . . please wait."
       INDEX ON CITY TO TEMP

    CASE ORDER = "4"
       ? " Sorting . . . please wait."
       INDEX ON STATE TO TEMP

    OTHERWISE
       USE MAIL
ENDCASE
```

Since the NAMES and ZIPS index files are always up-to-date in this system, the program will SET INDEX TO NAMES if the user wants an alphabetical order. If the user wants zip code order, the program will SET INDEX TO ZIPS. That way, the user does not have to wait for a re-sort because the sort order is already set up.

We've also allowed the user to select either city or state order. We did not create index files for these orders initially, so they will have to be created as needed. Since it takes time to index a database, the prompt:

   Sorting . . . Please wait

is displayed on the screen. Of course, if the original (keyed-in) order is selected, the program will use the MAIL data with no index file.

Notice the design we've used here. Since this is a mailing system, we can be pretty certain that the user is going to need both alphabetical and zip code orders fairly regularly. Therefore, the system will keep two index files active for these, thereby avoiding the need to re-sort every time the user accesses the database. There is an outside chance that the user may want a city or state order, though. We provide these options, but the program creates the index file only as needed.

Menu-Driven Searching

The next task for the REPORTS program is to determine the search criteria. First, the command file will present a menu of search criteria and wait for the user to make a choice in the lines below:

```
********************* Ask about search options.
ERASE
STORE " " TO SEARCH
TEXT

        Searching Options

    1. Last Name
    2. Zip code
    3. Keyword
    4. Print all names and addresses

ENDTEXT
8,13 SAY "Enter search choice (1–4) " GET SEARCH
READ
```

Once the user chooses a field to search on, the command file needs input for the information to search for. That is, if the user opts to search by keyword, the command file needs a specific keyword to search for. Then it stores the answers to memory variables called

SEARCH and CONDITION. The following DO CASE clause handles this task:

```
******************* Set up search condition.
DO CASE
    CASE SEARCH = "1"
       STORE "!(LNAME)" TO SEARCH
       ACCEPT " Look for whom? " TO CONDITION
       STORE !(CONDITION) TO CONDITION
    CASE SEARCH = "2"
       STORE "ZIP" TO SEARCH
       ACCEPT "Look for what zip code? " TO CONDITION
    CASE SEARCH = "3"
       STORE "!(KEYWORD)" TO SEARCH
       ACCEPT "Look for what keyword? " TO CONDITION
       STORE !(CONDITION) TO CONDITION
    CASE SEARCH = "4"
       STORE "X" TO SEARCH
       STORE 1 TO X,CONDITION
ENDCASE
```

Let's look at an example of this concept. If the user selects option 3 (search by keyword), the statement "!(KEYWORD)" is stored to memory variable SEARCH. Then, the screen asks:

Look for what keyword?

and the user's answer is stored to a variable called CONDITION; then the uppercase equivalent of the user's answer is stored to CONDITION. So, if the user opts to search by keyword, and asks to look up the keyword "expires 10/84," two memory variables are created with these contents:

Memory Variable	Contents
SEARCH	= "!(KEYWORD)"
CONDITION	= "EXPIRES 10/84"

Later, when the command file prints the report, it will decide whether or not to include a record with the statement:

IF &SEARCH = CONDITION

When dBASE substitutes in the SEARCH macro and the CONDITION

Menu-Driven Sorts and Searches   63

variable, the decision criterion becomes:

    IF !(KEYWORD) = EXPIRES 10/84

Therefore, only records in which the uppercase equivalent of the keyword field is EXPIRES 10/84 will be selected by the IF statement.

There is one catch, however. If the user wishes to see all the names and addresses in the file, the IF clause must be nondiscriminating. That is, the IF condition needs to be a situation that is always true. Menu option 4 takes care of the "all names and addresses" option. If the user opts to see all individuals in the file, the command file sets up the following memory variables:

Memory Variable		Contents
SEARCH	=	"X"
CONDITION	=	1
X	=	1

The IF clause that makes the decision is IF &SEARCH = CONDITION. When dBASE makes the macro substitution, the IF statement becomes:

    IF X = 1

Above, we can see that the variable X has 1 stored in it, so the IF statement becomes:

    IF 1 = 1

Since 1 = 1 is always true, the IF statement never leaves out a record. Hence, all records in the database are passed to the report.

We'll see the searching clauses more clearly in the report command files in the next chapter. For now, keep in mind that the REPORTS program has set up the proper sort order for the database, and stored vital information to the memory variables SEARCH and CONDITION. SEARCH contains the name of the field to search on, and CONDITION contains the value to search for.

The final tasks for the REPORTS program involve branching to the appropriate command file to produce the report that the user requested. Recall that the user's choice was stored in a memory variable called RCHOICE. The following DO CASE clause handles the branching:

    ************* Branch to appropriate program based
    ************* upon user's request (RCHOICE).

```
    DO CASE
      CASE RCHOICE = "1"
          ************** Print labels.
        DO LABELS
      CASE RCHOICE = "2"
          ************** Print directory.
        DO DIRECTOR
      CASE RCHOICE = "3"
          ************** Create MailMerge file.
        DO MMERGE
    ENDCASE
```

LABELS prints labels, DIRECTOR prints the directory, and MMERGE creates the MailMerge file. These are all described in the next chapter.

When each of those command files is finished, control is returned to the REPORTS program, which checks to see if a temporary index file was created. If so, it deletes that index file. These lines will delete the temporary index file:

```
    ************ Delete TEMP.NDX file, if it exists.
    USE
    IF FILE("TEMP.NDX")
       DELE FILE TEMP.NDX
    ENDIF (temp.ndx exists)
```

Next, the command file releases the memory variables created in this program, as shown below:

```
    ********************** Release memory variables.
    RELEASE RCHOICE,ORDER,SEARCH,CONDITION
```

Then, the command file makes both the NAMES and ZIPS indexes active again, so that any future additions or changes to the MAIL data file keep both index files up-to-date. These lines handle that job, and return control to the MAIN MENU program:

```
    *********** Make NAMES and ZIPS index files active
    *********** before returning to main menu.
    USE MAIL INDEX NAMES,ZIPS
    RETURN
```

The entire REPORTS command file is presented in Figure 5.2.

```
*************************************** REPORTS.CMD
********************** Ask user for report type,
********************** sort order and for search
********************** criteria, then branch
********************** to appropriate report.
ERASE
STORE " " TO RCHOICE
TEXT
                    Report Options

                 1. Mailing labels
                 2. Directory
                 3. MailMerge file

ENDTEXT
@ 8,18 SAY "Enter report type (1-3) " GET RCHOICE
READ

******************* Then ask about sort order.
ERASE
STORE " " TO ORDER
TEXT
             Sort Options

         1. Directory order (by last name)
         2. Bulk Mailing order (by zip code)
         3. City order
         4. State order
         5. Original order

ENDTEXT

@ 10,11 SAY " Which sort order (1-5) " GET ORDER
READ


**** Set up sort order according to user's request.
ERASE
DO CASE

   CASE ORDER = "1"
        SET INDEX TO NAMES

   CASE ORDER = "2"
        SET INDEX TO ZIPS

   CASE ORDER = "3"
        ? " Sorting... please wait."
        INDEX ON CITY TO TEMP

   CASE ORDER = "4"
        ? " Sorting... please wait."
        INDEX ON STATE TO TEMP
   OTHERWISE
        USE MAIL
```

Figure 5.2: The REPORTS command file.

```
ENDCASE

********************* Ask about search options.
ERASE
STORE " " TO SEARCH
TEXT
              Searching Options

                 1. Last Name
                 2. Zip code
                 3. Keyword
                 4. Print all names and addresses
ENDTEXT
@ 8,13 SAY "Enter search choice (1-4) " GET SEARCH
READ

****************** Set up search condition.
DO CASE

    CASE SEARCH = "1"
        STORE "!(LNAME)" TO SEARCH
        ACCEPT " Look for whom? " TO CONDITION
        STORE !(CONDITION) TO CONDITION

    CASE SEARCH = "2"
        STORE "ZIP" TO SEARCH
        ACCEPT "Look for what zip code? " TO CONDITION

    CASE SEARCH = "3"
        STORE "!(KEYWORD)" TO SEARCH
        ACCEPT "Look for what keyword? " TO CONDITION
        STORE !(CONDITION) TO CONDITION

    CASE SEARCH = "4"
        STORE "X" TO SEARCH
        STORE 1 TO X,CONDITION

ENDCASE

************ Branch to appropriate program based
************ upon user's request (RCHOICE).

DO CASE

    CASE RCHOICE = "1"
         *************** Print labels
         DO LABELS

    CASE RCHOICE = "2"
         *************** Print directory
         DO DIRECTOR

    CASE RCHOICE = "3"
         *************** Create MailMerge file.
         DO MMERGE
```

Figure 5.2: *The REPORTS command file (continued).*

```
ENDCASE
*********** Done with report program.

************* Delete TEMP.NDX file, if it exists.
USE
IF FILE("TEMP.NDX")
   DELE FILE TEMP.NDX
ENDIF (temp.ndx exists)

*********************** Release memory variables.
RELEASE RCHOICE,ORDER,SEARCH,CONDITION

*********** Make NAMES and ZIPS index files active
*********** before returning to main menu.
USE MAIL INDEX NAMES,ZIPS
RETURN
```

Figure 5.2: *The REPORTS command file (continued).*

Summary

In this chapter, we've discussed some techniques for defining searches and sorts from within command files. The goal here is to provide the nonsophisticated user with an easy means of specifying sorting and searching parameters without knowing any dBASE commands. In the next chapter, we'll discuss custom reports, which present data in the order specified by the user and limit displays only to records which meet the specified searching criterion.

CHAPTER 6
CUSTOM REPORTS

The dBASE II REPORT FORM command allows the user to design custom reports. However, in many situations the REPORT FORM command won't do the trick, particularly when a database has multiple or very long fields. In these cases, we must write a special command file to print the report. This command file must handle pagination, page breaks, pauses on the screen, and so forth. All of these topics are covered in this chapter.

Screen and Printer Formatting

The sum total of the field lengths for the MAIL data file is 154 characters. If we use the REPORT FORM command to print a report 80 columns wide, we have to break down many of the fields into two or three parts in order to fit them on the page. As an alternative, we can create a command file that divides the entire record for each individual into two separate lines. The DIRECTOR command file will print the directory in this system using the format displayed in Figure 6.1.

	Directory Listing	Page 1
Adams, Andy	ABC Company	123 A St.
San Diego CA	(123)456-7890	EXPIRES 01/85
Anderson, Ruth	XYZ Company	345 Oak St.
Los Angeles CA	(619)455-7442	EXPIRES 03/31
Bovee, Madeline	Ears and Sowbuck	1124 Madison St.
Arlington VA	(111)123-4567	PROSPECT
Carlson, Carrie	Wonder Co.	5328 Bragg St.
Plainsville GA	(123)456-6789	LIFETIME

Figure 6.1: Sample listing from the DIRECTOR command file.

If the user requests that the report be sent to the printer, then the directory will be displayed on individual pages, with the heading and page number at the top of each page, as shown in Figure 6.1. If the user requests that the report only be displayed on the screen, the directory will be presented one screenful at a time. When the screen fills up, this message will be displayed at the bottom of the screen:

Press any key for next page (R to return to menu)

This provides two conveniences. First, it gives the user time to view a screenful of information before any names scroll off the top of the screen. Second, if the user has found what he is looking for, he can press the letter R to quit viewing the directory. That way, he need not sift through every name in the file (or every record listed by the search criteria).

Remember that the DIRECTOR command file is called by the REPORTS command file. The REPORTS command file assigns the appropriate index file so that the directory will be printed in sorted order. The REPORTS command file also sets up the conditions for the DIRECTORY report, and stores the searching information to the memory variables SEARCH and CONDITION. Therefore, when testing the DIRECTOR command file, you should start from the main menu (DO MAIL) and select option 2 (Print Reports) to be sure that the DIRECTOR command file interfaces properly with the MAIL and REPORTS command files.

The pseudocode for the DIRECTOR command file is displayed in Figure 6.2.

Clear the screen

Set up title, page number, and line counter variables

Ask about hardcopy (store answer to variable LP)

If going to the printer, have user ready the printer,
    then set the printer on

Clear the screen
Print title and page number

Start at top of data file
Loop through each record while not at the
    end of file, and user doesn't request exit

    Check for match to requested condition
        If record matches search criterion
           print name, company, address
           print city, state, zip, phone keyword
           print blank line
           increment line counter by 3

    If report going to printer, and 55 or more
        lines have been printed:
        start on new page
        increment page counter by 1
        print title and page number
        reset line counter to 0

    If directory not going to printer, and
    18 or more lines have been displayed:
        display prompt for next page (or exit)
        wait for response
        If user does not request exit
           increment page counter
           print title and page number
           reset line counter to 0

Skip to next record in the database
Continue loop (if not end of file and exit not requested)

When done with report
Turn off printer
If report not going to printer and user did not
    request exit, pause

Release memory variables
Return to REPORTS program

Figure 6.2: *Pseudocode for the DIRECTOR command file.*

Let's translate the pseudocode to dBASE code a step at a time. First we'll add the usual comments and clear the screen, as below:

```
*************************** DIRECTOR.CMD
*************************** Print names and addresses
*************************** in directory format.
ERASE
```

Next we will set up the memory variables to be used by this program:

```
******************* Set up title and counters.
STORE "              Directory Listing" TO TITLE
STORE 1 TO PAGE
STORE 2 TO LF
STORE " " TO DONE
```

TITLE is the directory title, PAGE keeps track of the page number, and LF (linefeed) counts how many lines have been printed. We need this information to know when to pause the screen or start a new page in the printer. The DONE variable is used to exit if the user requests termination prior to printing all the data.

The next routine asks the user if he wants the directory to go to the printer. His answer is stored in a variable called LP (line printer). If he answers yes, the command file sets the printer on.

```
*************************** Ask about hardcopy.
STORE " " TO LP
2,2 SAY "Send directory to printer (Y/N)" GET LP
READ

IF !(LP) = "Y"
   ?
   ? "Ready printer, and press any key to continue"
   WAIT
   SET PRINT ON
ENDIF (yn = y)
```

Now, let's write the routine to print the report. First, we'll have the command file clear the screen, print the title and page number, and begin at the top of the data file. These lines take care of that job.

```
*************************** Print the report.
ERASE
TITLE + "            Page " + STR(PAGE,2)
?
GO TOP
```

Now we must set up a loop so that the command file keeps searching for, and printing records from, the MAIL database, as long as it hasn't encountered the end of the file (EOF), and the user has not requested to return to the menu (DONE = R). The command line to set up this loop is presented below:

```
DO WHILE .NOT. EOF .AND. !(DONE) # "R"
```

Now the command file should check that the record currently being considered for printing matches the search criterion specified in the REPORTS program. If so, it will print the data on two lines, print one blank line, then increment the line counter (LF) by three. Use these command lines to do so:

```
******* Check for match to requested condition.
IF &SEARCH = CONDITION
    ? TRIM(LNAME) + ", " + FNAME,COMPANY,ADDRESS
    ? " ",TRIM(CITY),STATE,ZIP,PHONE,KEYWORD
    ?
    STORE LF + 3 TO LF
```

When the command file prints the data for a record, it has to create page breaks or perhaps pause the screen. The first routine handles page breaks on the printer:

```
************** If going to printer, start
************** new page every 55 lines.
IF !(LP) = "Y" .AND. LF > = 55
    EJECT
    STORE PAGE + 1 TO PAGE
    ? TITLE + "                    Page " + STR(PAGE,2)
    ?
    STORE 2 TO LF
ENDIF (55 lines sent to printer)
```

Notice the IF conditions above. First, !(LP) = "Y" means that the user answered "yes" to the question "Send directory to the printer?" Second, LF > = 55 means that at least 55 lines have been printed. If both of these situations are true, then the program advances the paper in the printer to the next page (EJECT), and increments the PAGE counter by 1 (STORE PAGE + 1 TO PAGE). Then it prints the title and the page number, changing the page number to a string for better formatting. Then it prints a blank line beneath the title and resets the line counter to 2 (STORE 2 to LF).

If the report is not displayed on the printer, then the command file needs to pause the screen about every 18 lines so that the user has a chance to read or jot down information from the screen. This routine handles the screen breaks:

```
* * * * * * * * * * * * * If not going to printer, do
* * * * * * * * * * * * * screen pause every 18 lines.
IF !(LP)#"Y" .AND. LF> = 18
   ?
   ? "Press any key for next page "
   ?? "(R to return to menu)"
   WAIT TO DONE
   IF !(DONE) # "R"
      STORE PAGE + 1 TO PAGE
      ERASE
      ? TITLE +"                    Page " + STR(PAGE,2)
      ?
      STORE 2 TO LF
   ENDIF (done # R)
ENDIF (18 lines sent to the screen)
```

Here the IF condition is !(LP) # "Y" (user did not request printer), and LF > = 18 (at least 18 lines have been printed). When that occurs, this prompt appears on the screen:

   Press any key for next page (R to return to menu):_

If the user does not press R, the page number is incremented by one, the screen is cleared, the title and page number are printed, and the line counter is set back to two. If the user does press R, none of those steps are performed.

The next lines close the main IF clause (IF &SEARCH = CONDITION), skip to the next record in the database (SKIP), and continue the loop (as long as the end of the file has not been encountered and the user has not typed R during a screen break to return to the menu):

```
   ENDIF (search = condition)
SKIP
ENDDO (while not eof and done # R)
```

When the job of printing the directory is complete, the command file can return to the REPORTS program. However, if the user did not ask that the report be printed, and did not opt to exit during a screen break, you should pause the screen one more time so that the last screen does not get erased too quickly. These lines handle that job:

```
* * * * * * * * * * * * * * * * * * * * * * * * * * If report not going to
* * * * * * * * * * * * * * * * * * * * * * * *    printer, pause before return.
SET PRINT OFF
IF !(LP) # "Y" .AND. !(DONE) # "R"
```

```
    ?
    ?
    ? " Press any key to return to main menu."
    WAIT
ENDIF (yn # y)
```

Then the command file must release the memory variables and return to the REPORTS program. Add these lines to complete this task:

```
RELEASE
TITLE,LP,LF,PAGE,DONE
RETURN
```

The entire command file is displayed in Figure 6.3.

```
*********************************  DIRECTOR.CMD
**************************  Print names and addresses
**************************  in directory format.
ERASE

******************* Set up title and counters.
STORE "              Directory Listing" TO TITLE
STORE 1 TO PAGE
STORE 2 TO LF
STORE " " TO DONE

************************** Ask about hardcopy.
STORE " " TO LP
@ 2,2 SAY "Send directory to printer (Y/N)" GET LP
READ

IF !(LP)="Y"
    ?
    ? "Ready printer, and press any key to continue"
    WAIT
    SET PRINT ON
ENDIF (yn=y)

**************************** Print the report.
ERASE
? TITLE+"              Page "+STR(PAGE,2)
?
GO TOP
DO WHILE .NOT. EOF .AND. !(DONE) # "R"
    ****** Check for match to requested condition.
    IF &SEARCH=CONDITION
        ? TRIM(LNAME)+", "+FNAME,COMPANY,ADDRESS
        ? "      ",TRIM(CITY),STATE,ZIP,PHONE,KEYWORD
        ?
        STORE LF+3 TO LF
        ************** If going to printer, start
        ************** new page every 55 lines.
        IF !(LP)="Y" .AND. LF>=55
```

Figure 6.3: The DIRECTOR.CMD command file.

```
                EJECT
                STORE PAGE + 1 TO PAGE
                ? TITLE+"              Page "+STR(PAGE,2)
                ?
                STORE 2 TO LF
            ENDIF (55 lines sent to printer)
            ************* If not going to printer, do
            ************* screen pause every 18 lines.
            IF !(LP)#"Y" .AND. LF>=18
                ?
                ? "Press any key for next page "
                ?? "(R to return to menu)"
                WAIT TO DONE
                IF !(DONE) # "R"
                STORE PAGE + 1 TO PAGE
                ?
                ? TITLE+"              Page "+STR(PAGE,2)
                ?
                STORE 2 TO LF
            ENDIF (done # R)
         ENDIF (18 lines sent to the screen)
      ENDIF (search = condition)
   SKIP
   ENDDO (while not eof)

   *************************** If report not going to
   *************************** printer, pause before return.
   SET PRINT OFF
   IF !(LP) # "Y" .AND. !(DONE) # "R"
       ?
       ?
       ? " Press any key to return to main menu."
       WAIT
   ENDIF (yn # y)

   RELEASE TITLE,LP,LF,PAGE,DONE
   RETURN
```

Figure 6.3: *The DIRECTOR.CMD command file (continued).*

This is a good general purpose command file that can be used in many programming situations, and is easily adapted to other data files. For example, if you were working with a database of references to literature with the fields AUTHOR, TITLE, PUBLISHER, PAGES, DATE, SUBJECTS, and ABSTRACT, you could save yourself considerable work by making a copy of the DIRECTOR command file and changing a few lines. Specifically you would need to change this line:

    STORE "   Directory Listing" TO TITLE

to a more appropriate title, such as:

    STORE "   Bibliography" TO TITLE

Of course you'd need to print the appropriate fields too. To do this, change these lines:

```
? TRIM(LNAME)+", "+FNAME,COMPANY,ADDRESS
? "           ",TRIM(CITY),STATE,ZIP,PHONE,KEYWORD
?
STORE LF+3 TO LF
```

to a more appropriate format, such as:

```
? AUTHOR,TITLE
? PUBLISHER,PAGES,DATE
? SUBJECTS
? ABSTRACT
?
STORE LF+5 TO LF
```

Notice the line counter (LF) now increments by five, since each record in the database now requires five lines of print.

To eliminate the search element from the command file, just remove these two lines:

```
IF &SEARCH=CONDITION
```

and

```
ENDIF (search = condition)
```

Multicopy Labels with Alignment Check

In my introductory dBASE II book, *Understanding dBASE II* (SYBEX, 1984), I presented a simple mailing-labels program, and a more complex one for handling multi-column labels. In this book, we'll develop a label program with some new features.

One of the inconveniences of any mailing-label program is simply that you have to load the labels into the printer every time you need labels. Some wise companies prefer to make several copies of each label while printing them. That way, the user can load up the labels, and print out, say, ten copies of each and then store the printed labels. The user can just peel off a label from the preprinted stack without having to go through the printing routine again.

Our LABELS command file handles this by simply asking the user:

How many copies of each label? :   :

The user types in a number from 1 to 99, and the command file prints that many copies of each label.

There is another inconvenience in working with mailing labels: sometimes they aren't lined up quite right in the printer. If they begin printing crooked, the user must stop the program, adjust the alignment, and try again. Our LABELS command file handles this by asking the user:

    Check alignment of labels first? :   :

If the user answers yes, the command file will print two fake labels like this:

```
NNNNNNNNNNNNNNNNNNNNNNNNNNNNNN
CCCCCCCCCCCCCCCCCCCCCCCCCCCCCC
AAAAAAAAAAAAAAAAAAAAAAAAAAAAAA
CCCCCCCCCCCC,        SSSSS         ZZZZZ

NNNNNNNNNNNNNNNNNNNNNNNNNNNNNN
CCCCCCCCCCCCCCCCCCCCCCCCCCCCCC
AAAAAAAAAAAAAAAAAAAAAAAAAAAAAA
CCCCCCCCCCCC,        SSSSS         ZZZZZ
```

The user can then glance quickly at the printer to see if the labels are properly lined up. The screen will ask:

    Check alignment again? :   :

If the labels are not properly aligned, the user can adjust, and answer Y (yes) to this question. The command file will then print two more fake labels. When the user is satisfied with the label alignment, he answers N (no) to the question about checking the alignment, and the command file starts printing the labels.

Finally, another inconvenience with labels is that the printer occasionally gets them out of alignment while printing. This error might entail reprinting all of the labels over again, starting at the top. Our command file can handle this situation pretty well. As soon as the LABELS program starts printing the labels, it displays this message on the screen:

    If printer devours labels, press Esc key, then
    type DO LABELS and press the RETURN key.

If something goes wrong while the labels are being printed, the user can press the Esc key, which brings up the dot prompt. The LABELS command file will return to where it left off while printing. Then the user can type in DO LABELS. The command file will first allow him to readjust and test the label alignment and then continue printing labels from the one *before* where it last left off (because that label was probably ruined).

There is one slight disadvantage to this feature, though. The command file sets the console off while printing labels so that the labels do not appear on the screen. If the user happens to press Esc while the console is off, the command DO LABELS will not appear on the screen while he is typing it. But, nonetheless, if the command is typed in properly, the LABELS program will still start printing labels again from where it left off. There appears to be no more elegant way to handle this, other than avoiding SET CONSOLE OFF within the command file.

Since the LABELS command file is called from the REPORTS program, the labels it prints will be in the order specified by the user. Also, it will print labels for only those records that match the requested search criterion. The command file is designed to handle single-column mailing labels, three inches across and one inch tall.

The pseudocode for the LABELS program is presented in Figure 6.4. The code for the LABELS command file begins like this:

```
* * * * * * * * * * * * * * * * * * * * * * * * * * * * * LABELS.CMD
* * * * * * * * * * * * * * * * * * * Print multiple mailing labels.
SET CONSOLE ON
SET PRINT OFF
```

The usual comments are at the top, and the command file immediately sets the console on and the printer off. This is just in case the user interrupts printing by pressing Esc while the printer was still set on and/or the console was still set off.

Next, the command file needs to decide whether it should start at the top of the database or at some other point where it previously left off. These lines handle that job:

```
** If just starting, start at beginning of file.
IF TYPE(START) = "U"
   STORE "TOP" TO START
ENDIF (type = u)
```

The IF clause checks to see if the memory variable START already exists. If not, then TYPE(START) will be U (undefined), which means that the command file should start printing labels from the top of the database. The word "TOP" is therefore assigned to the memory variable START. Later in the command file, the command GOTO &START will be used to position the record pointer to the first label to be printed.

> Set the printer off and the console on
>
> If just starting to print labels,
>   start at top of the data file
>
> Clear the screen
>
> Ask user how many copies of each label, store to NO:LABELS
>
> Ask user if they want to check the label alignment
>
> As long as user keeps requesting labels,
>   print two fake labels
>   ask user if another alignment check is needed
>
> Prepare to print real labels
>
> Go to appropriate record number (START)
> Display instructions on the screen for
>   handling printing problems
>
> Set the printer on
> Begin loop through data file (until end of file)
>   If label meets search criterion
>   Print the amount of copies of the label
>   the user requested (NO:LABELS)
>
>   Record record number of last label printed
> Skip to next record and continue loop (while not EOF)
>
> When done, set print off
> Release memory variables
> Return to REPORTS command file

Figure 6.4: Pseudocode for the LABELS command file.

If the memory variable START already exists, it will be because the user started printing labels, but interrupted printing. In that case, TYPE(START) will be C (character data), and it will contain the record number of the label to start printing at, as we'll see in a moment.

Next, the command file asks how many copies of each label to print in the routine below.

```
** First, ask user how many copies of each label.
ERASE
STORE 1 TO NO:LABELS
2,2 SAY "How many copies of each label? ";
    GET NO:LABELS PICTURE "99"
READ
```

Notice that the user's answer is stored to the variable NO:LABELS.

The next step is to ask the user if he wants to check the alignment of the labels in the printer. These lines handle that job:

```
****** Next, ask user if they want to check the
****** alignment of the labels in the printer.
STORE " " TO ALIGN
4,4 SAY "Check alignment of labels first? ";
   GET ALIGN
READ
```

Now, as long as the user keeps requesting an alignment check (the variable ALIGN is "Y"), the command file prints two fake labels, and asks again if the alignment is correct. The DO WHILE clauses below handle the alignment check:

```
*** If alignment requested, print two false labels.
DO WHILE !(ALIGN) = "Y"
   SET PRINT ON
   SET CONSOLE OFF
   STORE 1 TO COUNT
   DO WHILE COUNT < 3
      ? "NNNNNNNNNNNNNNNNNNNNNNNNNNNNNN"
      ? "CCCCCCCCCCCCCCCCCCCCCCCCCCCCCC"
      ? "AAAAAAAAAAAAAAAAAAAAAAAAAAAAAA"
      ? "CCCCCCCCCCCC,      SSSSS      ZZZZZ"
      ?
      ?
      STORE COUNT+1 TO COUNT
   ENDDO (while count < 3)

   ******** Check for permission to continue.
   SET CONSOLE ON
   SET PRINT OFF
   STORE " " TO ALIGN
   @ 6,5 SAY "Check alignment again?" GET ALIGN
   READ

ENDDO (while align = Y)
```

Once the user is satisfied with the alignment of the labels in the printer, the command file can begin printing. First, the program needs to position the record number pointer to the starting place in the command file (stored in the variable START). These lines will accomplish the task:

```
********************** Position the record number pointer.
GOTO &START
```

Then the program clears the screen and displays instructions for interrupting the printing process.

```
*************************** Display instructions.
ERASE
? "If printer devours labels, press Esc key, then"
? "type DO LABELS and press the RETURN key."
```

Next, the program must set the printer on and begin the loop through the data file with these lines:

```
SET PRINT ON
DO WHILE .NOT. EOF
```

Then the program checks that the label meets the search criterion specified in the REPORTS program:

```
******* Make sure label meets search condition.
IF &SEARCH = CONDITION
```

If it does, the program will print NO:LABELS copies of the mailing label with these lines:

```
    STORE 1 TO COUNT
    ******* Print multiple copies of this label.
    DO WHILE COUNT < = NO:LABELS
       SET CONSOLE OFF
       ? TRIM(FNAME),LNAME
       ? COMPANY
       ? ADDRESS
       ? TRIM(CITY) + ", " + STATE,ZIP
       ?
       ?
       SET CONSOLE ON
       STORE COUNT + 1 TO COUNT
    ENDDO (while count < = no:labels)
ENDIF (search = condition)
```

The program then stores the record number of the label just printed to the memory variable START. These lines will take care of this task:

```
*********** Keep track of last label printed.
STORE STR(#,4) TO START
```

Next, the program skips to the next record in the data file, and closes the main DO WHILE loop (do while .not. eof):

```
SKIP
ENDDO (while not eof)
```

When done printing the labels, the command file sets the printer off, releases the memory variables, and returns control to the REPORTS command file.

```
*************************** Done printing labels.
SET PRINT OFF

RELE NO:LABELS,ALIGN,COUNT,START
RETURN
```

The full LABELS command file is presented in Figure 6.5.

```
************************************** LABELS.CMD
***************** Print multiple mailing labels.
SET CONSOLE ON
SET PRINT OFF

** If just starting, start at beginning of file.
IF TYPE(START)="U"
   STORE "TOP" TO START
ENDIF (type= u)

** First, ask user how many copies of each label.
ERASE
STORE 1 TO NO:LABELS
@ 2,2 SAY "How many copies of each label? ";
   GET NO:LABELS PICTURE "99"
READ

****** Next, ask user if they want to check the
****** alignment of the labels in the printer.
STORE " " TO ALIGN
@ 4,4 SAY "Check alignment of labels first? ";
   GET ALIGN
READ

*** If alignment requested, print two false labels.

DO WHILE !(ALIGN) = "Y"
   SET PRINT ON
   SET CONSOLE OFF
   STORE 1 TO COUNT
   DO WHILE COUNT < 3
      ? "NNNNNNNNNNNNNNNNNNNNNNNNNNNNNN"
      ? "CCCCCCCCCCCCCCCCCCCCCCCCCCCCC"
      ? "AAAAAAAAAAAAAAAAAAAAAAAAAAAA"
      ? "CCCCCCCCCCC,    SSSSS    ZZZZZ"
      ?
      ?
      STORE COUNT+1 TO COUNT
   ENDDO (while count < 3)

   ******** Check for permission to continue.
```

Figure 6.5: *The LABELS.CMD command file.*

```
      SET CONSOLE ON
      SET PRINT OFF
      STORE " " TO ALIGN
      @ 6,5 SAY "Check alignment again?" GET ALIGN
      READ

ENDDO (while align = Y)

************** Position the record number pointer.
GOTO &START

************************* Display instructions.
ERASE
? "If printer devours labels, press Esc key, then"
? "type DO LABELS and press the RETURN key."
SET PRINT ON
DO WHILE .NOT. EOF

      ******* Make sure label meets search condition.
      IF &SEARCH=CONDITION
         STORE 1 TO COUNT

         ******* Print multiple copies of this label.
         DO WHILE COUNT <= NO:LABELS
            SET CONSOLE OFF
            ? TRIM(FNAME),LNAME
            ? COMPANY
            ? ADDRESS
            ? TRIM(CITY)+", "+STATE,ZIP
            ?
            ?
            SET CONSOLE ON
            STORE COUNT+1 TO COUNT
         ENDDO (while count <= no:labels)
      ENDIF (search=condition)

      ************ Keep track of last label printed.
      STORE STR(#,4) TO START

SKIP
ENDDO (while not eof)

************************** Done printing labels.
SET PRINT OFF

RELE NO:LABELS,ALIGN,COUNT,START
RETURN
```

Figure 6.5: The LABELS.CMD command file (continued).

Creating a MailMerge File

With the help of WordStar's MailMerge option, we can use data from the mailing system to create form letters. The main task here is to transfer the data from MAIL.DBF to another data file that MailMerge can read. MailMerge files should have each field enclosed in quotes, with no trailing blanks, and commas between fields, as shown below:

"field 1", "field 2", "field 3", "field 4"
"field 1", "field 2", "field 3", "field 4"

The DELIMITED option, used with the COPY command, can set up such a data file.

We'll create a command file called MMERGE.CMD to transfer data from the MAIL.DBF data file to a MailMerge file. The user can select a name for the MailMerge file, and the data sent to it will be in the order specified in the REPORTS program, and will include only records that meet the user's search criterion. Pseudocode for the MMERGE.CMD command file is displayed in Figure 6.6.

The first lines of the MMERGE program will be the usual identifying comments and the command to clear the screen:

```
***************************** MMERGE.CMD
********************* Create a WordStar MailMerge file.
ERASE
```

Next the command file asks the user for a filename for the MailMerge file. It stores the user's answer to a memory variable called MFILE:

```
************************** Get name of MailMerge file.
? " Enter name of MailMerge file"
ACCEPT " (Include drive spec, e.g. B:MM.DAT) " TO MFILE
```

This brief message displays on the screen while the records are being copied:

```
ERASE
? "Creating MailMerge file &MFILE"
```

Clear the screen

Ask user for name of MailMerge file to create

Copy records that meet search criterion to the MailMerge
    file in MailMerge readable form

Release memory variables
Return to main menu

Figure 6.6: *Pseudocode for the MMERGE.CMD command file.*

The next line sends data from the MAIL.DBF file to the MailMerge file. The DELIMITED WITH " option assures that the fields will be surrounded by quotation marks and separated with commas. The FOR &SEARCH=CONDITION makes sure that only records that match the user's search criterion are copied. Since the REPORTS program already assigned an index file, the data will be sent to the MailMerge file in sorted order:

   COPY TO &MFILE DELIMITED WITH " FOR &SEARCH = CONDITION

When the copy procedure is done, the program displays a brief message, releases memory variables, and returns to the main menu:

```
******************* Done. Return to print menu.
?
?
? " MailMerge file &MFILE completed..."
?
RELEASE MFILE
RETURN
```

Figure 6.7 shows the entire MMERGE.CMD command file.

Figure 6.8 shows a WordStar document file that is capable of printing form letters from the file created by MMERGE. It assumes that the name of the file is MM.DAT and is stored on the disk in drive B (.DF B:MM.DAT).

```
********************************* MMERGE.CMD
************ Create a WordStar MailMerge file.
ERASE

****************** Get name of MailMerge file.
? " Enter name of MailMerge file"
ACCEPT "(Include drive spec, e.g. B:MM.DAT)" TO MFILE
ERASE
? "Creating MailMerge file &MFILE"

COPY TO &MFILE DELIM WITH " FOR &SEARCH = CONDITION

******************** Done. Return to print menu.
?
?
? " MailMerge file &MFILE completed..."
?
RELEASE MFILE
RETURN
```

Figure 6.7: The MMERGE.CMD command file.

```
.OP
.DF B:MM.DAT
.RV LNAME,FNAME,COMPANY,ADDRESS,CITY,STATE,ZIP,PHONE,KEYWORD

&FNAME& &LNAME&
&COMPANY&
&ADDRESS&
&CITY&, &STATE& &ZIP&

Dear &FNAME&,

  Our records indicate that your membership expires next month. If you would like to continue being in our wonderful club, send us a check for $10.00 and we won't delete you from our database.

                    Sincerely,


                    Terri Nichols, President

.PA
```

Figure 6.8: Sample WordStar document for printing form letters.

To create such a letter, load a disk with the WordStar and MailMerge programs on it and call up WordStar by typing WS and pressing RETURN. Create a document file (D) and store it on the disk in drive B with a valid file name (e.g. B:FORM.LET). Then, type in the dot commands *exactly* as they appear in Figure 6.8. (However, be sure to use the correct file name in the .DV command.)

When you're done creating the form letter, save it with the ^KD command, and when the WordStar menu reappears, select M to print a MailMerge file. When WordStar asks for the name of the file to print, type in the name of the *document* file (i.e. B:FORM.LET). Make sure the printer is ready, and off you go. The WordStar program will print a form letter for each name in the MailMerge file. Figure 6.9 shows a sample form letter created by WordStar.

Summary

In this chapter we've discussed several techniques in dBASE II for creating custom reports, including general reports formatted for the

> Rocco Moe
> ABC Company
> P.O. Box 3470
> Wilmington, DE 01234
>
> Dear Rocco,
>
> Our records indicate that your membership expires next month. If you would like to continue being in our wonderful club, send us a check for $10.00 and we won't delete you from our database.
>
> Sincerely,
>
> Terri Nichols, President

Figure 6.9: Sample form letter created by the WordStar program.

screen and printer, mailing labels, and data files that can be used to print form letters using WordStar's MailMerge option. In the next chapter we'll discuss command files for editing and deleting data from the database.

CHAPTER 7
CUSTOM COMMAND FILES FOR EDITING AND DELETING

dBASE II provides the EDIT, DELETE, and PACK commands for handling changes to, and deletions from, the database. These commands require some knowledge of locating data by record number, as well as familiarity with control-key commands. In a menu-driven system, editing and deleting can be handled by a user who is unfamiliar with the commands and syntax for locating and modifying records. Furthermore, instructions for managing the cursor can be displayed on the screen so that the less sophisticated user need not memorize them in order to edit a database.

Automating the Editing Process

If a user can type in readily available information for locating a record to be edited, i.e., a name from the mailing list, the editing process is simple. We can create a command file which asks the user for such simple information as a name:

    Edit whom? (last name, or just <RET> to exit) :

All the user has to do is type in the last name Smith, and press RETURN. If Smith is not on the database, the screen displays this message:

    There is no Smith on the database

        Press any key to try again . . .

On the other hand, if there are several Smiths on the database, the screen displays them all:

00005	Smith Andy	ABC Company	123 A St.
00096	Smith Henrietta	XTZ Corp	345 B St.
00198	Smith Manny	Data Ventures	5328 Bragg St.
01234	Smith Zeppo	Motown Inc.	P.O. Box 1182

        Which one? (by number) :

In this case, the user can specify the exact Smith to edit by typing the correct record number from those displayed on the left side of the screen. Then, a custom edit screen appears with the data the user wishes to edit.

If there is only one Smith on the database, the command file immediately displays a custom edit screen, complete with instructions, as shown in Figure 7.1.

When the user is done editing the record, the screen clears and this prompt appears again:

    Edit whom? (last name, or just <RET> to exit) :

If he wishes to edit another record, the user can specify the name; if he wishes to return to the main menu, he can press RETURN.

In our mailing list system example, editing is handled by the EDIT command file and the MSCREEN1.FMT format file developed in Chapter 4. The logical flow of the EDIT program is presented in pseudocode in Figure 7.2.

Now we are ready to develop the EDIT command file based upon the logic of our pseudocode. We can also take advantage of the

Custom Command Files for Editing and Deleting

```
Cursor Movement: (The ^ symbol means 'hold down the CTRL key . . .')
^E up : ^X down : ^D right : ^S left : ^G delete : ^V Insert

Last Name      :Smith                  : First Name :Samuel :
Company        :ABC Company            :
Address        :123 A St.              :
City           :San Diego              : State :CA     : Zip :92122  :
Phone number   :(619)555-1212:
Keyword        :EXPIRES 10/84          :
```

Figure 7.1: Custom edit screen for the mailing system.

```
Set up a looping variable
As long as the user does not request to exit this program

   Clear the screen
   Ask user for the name of the individual to edit
   Translate name to uppercase
   Find that individual
   Count how many people on the database have the requested
      last name

   If the user did not type in a name for editing,
      just clear the screen and return to the main menu

   If the requested last name is not on the database,
      inform user that nobody has that name,
      then allow him to try again

   If one person has the requested last name,
      edit that record using the custom screen

   If several people have the requested last name,
      display them and get further information,
      then edit, using the custom screen

   Repeat the edit process (while user does not request to exit)

   When the user is done editing,
      release memory variables and
      return to the main menu
```

Figure 7.2: Pseudocode for the EDIT command file.

NAMES index file and the WHILE command to speed the process of locating the record the user wishes to edit.

The first step is to type in the comments identifying the name and function of this command file. These first lines handle that job:

```
*********************************** EDIT.CMD
************* Edit MAIL data using custom screen.
```

Next, we will set up a loop that keeps asking for new names to be edited, as long as the user doesn't press RETURN. These are the tasks that the program must accomplish within that loop: clear the screen, ask for the name of the individual to edit and wait for a response, then clear the screen again. These lines handle those jobs:

```
********** First, get last name of person to edit.
STORE "X" TO SEARCH
DO WHILE SEARCH # " "
    ERASE
    ACCEPT " Edit whom? (last name) " TO SEARCH
    ERASE
```

Notice that the looping condition is DO WHILE SEARCH # " ". To get the loop started, we need to store a *non-blank*, which is

1. something other than a blank,
2. any letter from the alphabet, or
3. any character other than a blank

to the memory variable SEARCH. Above, we've randomly selected the letter X as a non-blank character.

Next, the command file translates the user's input to uppercase, so the FIND will work properly with the index. (Recall that we indexed on the !(LNAME) and the !(FNAME)). Then the command file counts how many individuals on the database have that last name so it can decide how to handle the edit. The lines below perform that task:

```
********* Translate to uppercase, then count how
********* many individuals have that last name.
STORE !(SEARCH) TO SEARCH
FIND &SEARCH
COUNT WHILE !(LNAME) = SEARCH TO HOWMANY
```

Depending upon how many users on the database have the requested last name, the command file must decide how to proceed. We'll add a

DO CASE clause below to make these decisions:

    ****** Proceed with edit, depending on how many
    ****** individuals have the requested last name.
DO CASE

If the user does not specify a name to edit, the command file does nothing except clear the screen, then return to the main menu. The first CASE statement below will be true (SEARCH=" ") if the user does not enter a name. So the CASE statements below will be skipped over, the ENDDO loop will not repeat, and the command file will return to the main menu. The first CASE statement appears below:

    ******** If no name entered, just clear screen.
CASE SEARCH=" "
   ERASE

If the FIND and COUNT commands determined that nobody on the database has the last name that the user requested, the command file should warn and allow him to try again. The CASE statement below takes care of that job:

    ******** If nobody has that last name, warn user.
CASE HOWMANY = 0
   ? "There is no &SEARCH on the database"
   ?
   ? "Press any key to try again . . . ."
   WAIT

If one person on the database has the last name the user requested, the command file can simply present the data for that individual on the screen ready for editing. Note that the MSCREEN1.FMT format file, coupled with the READ command, is used to display the data for editing. The next CASE statement takes care of this situation:

    ******* If one person has that last name, edit
    ******* using the MSCREEN1 format.
CASE HOWMANY = 1
   FIND &SEARCH
   SET FORMAT TO MSCREEN1
   READ
   SET FORMAT TO SCREEN

This CASE option positions the record pointer to the individual to be edited (FIND &SEARCH), sets the screen to the custom MSCREEN1 format (SET FORMAT TO MSCREEN1), allows the user to make changes (READ), then sets the format back to the normal dBASE screen (SET FORMAT TO SCREEN).

Of course, if several people on the database have the requested last name, the command file will need further information. So, it will display all individuals with the requested last name, along with their record numbers, and then ask the user to supply the record number of the individual to edit. The next lines in the command file handle that task:

```
******* If several people have that last name,
******* display them and get further information.
CASE HOWMANY > 1
   FIND &SEARCH
   LIST WHILE !(LNAME) = SEARCH;
      TRIM(FNAME),LNAME,COMPANY,ADDRESS
   ?
   ACCEPT "Which one? (by number) " TO RECNO

   *********** If user types in a number,
   ***** edit that record using MSCREEN1.

   IF VAL(RECNO)>0
      GOTO &RECNO
      SET FORMAT TO MSCREEN1
      READ
      SET FORMAT TO SCREEN
   ENDIF (value of recno > 0)
```

As a precaution, the command file first checks to make sure that the user types in a reasonable record number [IF VAL(RECNO) > 0] prior to attempting to go to that record. If the record number that the user supplied is greater than zero, the command file goes to that record, sets the screen to the custom MSCREEN1 format, and allows the user to make changes. Then, the command file sets the screen back to the normal dBASE II screen.

The DO CASE clause is now complete, because it will check for all possible situations. So the next lines just close the DO CASE clause, and the DO WHILE SEARCH # " " loop. These lines handle that job:

```
   ENDCASE
ENDDO (while search # " ")
```

The DO WHILE loop will quit repeating "Edit whom?" as soon as the user presses RETURN, so the remaining lines in this program simply clear the memory variables and return to the main menu. These lines are presented below:

```
****** If no last name entered to edit clear memory
****** variables and return to main menu.

RELEASE SEARCH,HOWMANY
RETURN
```

Custom Command Files for Editing and Deleting

Figure 7.3 shows the complete EDIT command file. Notice the use of the FIND, COUNT WHILE, and LIST WHILE commands to speed processing. The MAIN MENU program, MAIL, has already defined the NAMES.NDX index file as primary, so the FIND command will work here. To test the EDIT command file after keying it in, be sure to DO MAIL and select the option to edit names and addresses, so that the MAIL command file can first set up the approriate USE MAIL INDEX NAMES,ZIPS command for defining the database to be edited.

```
****************************************** EDIT.CMD
************ Edit MAIL data using custom screen.

********* First, get last name of person to edit.
STORE "X" TO SEARCH
DO WHILE SEARCH # " "
   ERASE
   ACCEPT " Edit whom? (last name) " TO SEARCH
   ERASE

   ********  Translate to uppercase, then count how
   ********  many indiviuduals have that last name.
   STORE !(SEARCH) TO SEARCH
   FIND &SEARCH
   COUNT WHILE !(LNAME) = SEARCH TO HOWMANY

   ****** Proceed with edit, depending on how many
   ****** individuals have the requested last name.

   DO CASE
      ******** If no name entered, clear screen.
      CASE SEARCH=" "
         ERASE

      ******** If nobody has that last name, warn user.
      CASE HOWMANY = 0
         ? "There is no &SEARCH on the database"
         ?
         ? "Press any key to try again...."
   ****** Proceed with edit, depending on how many
   ****** individuals have the requested last name.

   DO CASE
      ******** If no name entered, clear screen.
      CASE SEARCH=" "
         ERASE
```

Figure 7.3: *The EDIT.CMD command file.*

```
******* If nobody has that last name, warn user.
CASE HOWMANY = 0
    ? "There is no &SEARCH on the database"
    ?
    ? "Press any key to try again...."
    WAIT

******* If one person has that last name, edit
******* using the MSCREEN1 format.
CASE HOWMANY=1
    FIND &SEARCH
    SET FORMAT TO MSCREEN1
    READ
    SET FORMAT TO SCREEN

******* If several people have that last name,
******* display them and get further information.
CASE HOWMANY > 1
    FIND &SEARCH
    LIST WHILE !(LNAME)=SEARCH;
        TRIM(FNAME),LNAME,COMPANY,ADDRESS
    ?
    ACCEPT "Which one? (by number) " TO RECNO
    ************* If user types in number,
    ***** edit that record using MSCREEN1
    IF VAL(RECNO)>0
        GOTO &RECNO
        SET FORMAT TO MSCREEN1
            READ
            SET FORMAT TO SCREEN
        ENDIF (value of recno > 0)
ENDCASE

ENDDO   (while search # " ")

****** If no last name entered to edit, release memory
****** variables and return to main menu.
RELEASE SEARCH,HOWMANY
RETURN
```

Figure 7.3: *The EDIT.CMD command file (continued).*

Deleting Records from the Database

The command file to delete records from the database is almost identical to the editing command file. It first asks the user:

Delete whom? (last name, or just <RET> to exit) :

and allows him to type in a name or press RETURN to exit. As with the editing program, if the user types in the name of an individual who does not exist on the database, the screen informs him of the error and allows him to try again. If the user types in a name that dBASE recognizes, and only one individual has that name, the command file briefly displays this message:

Deleting (whomever user requested)

Then the user can specify more names to delete.

If several people on the database have the last name requested by the user, the command file displays all individuals with the requested last name and asks for further information.

As a safety precaution, the command file displays all individuals who are to be permanently deleted from the database prior to returning to the main menu. For example, if the user requested that four individuals be deleted from the database, the screen would display them all, with record numbers in the left column, and ask for permission to delete them permanently, as shown below:

00999	*Zach Anton	IBM CO.	123 A St.
02345	*Muriel Duvall	Sierra Computers	301 Grape Vn.
00055	*Rick Rosiello	Raydonics	311 Pasadena Blvd.
01234	*Anna Tumeo	Logicon, Inc.	P.O. Box 2802

Delete all these people? (Y/N) :

The user can double-check the names to be deleted, and if he spots one that should be retained, he can answer N (no) to the question about deleting all of them. If so, the screen will display the prompt:

Recall whom? (left-column number) :

The user can then type in the individual's record number, which is readily displayed on the screen. For instance, suppose the user decides not to delete Muriel Duvall. He can type in the appropriate record number (2345 in this example) in response to the prompt on the screen. The command file will eliminate Muriel from consideration for deletion and redisplay the remaining names and record numbers to be deleted, as shown below:

00999	*Zach Anton	IBM CO.	123 A St.
00055	*Rick Rosiello	Raydonics	311 Pasadena Blvd.
01234	*Anna Tumeo	Logicon, Inc.	P.O. Box 2802

Delete all these people? (Y/N) :

The user can double-check again, and recall anybody he desires. If the user decides to go ahead and delete all these people, by typing in Y (yes), the screen will display the prompt:

   Deleting requested names . . . . .

and then pack the database (including the index files) so that these individuals will be deleted permanently.

The DELNAMES command file handles all of these aspects of deleting names from the database. Its pseudocode is very similar to that of the EDIT command file, except for the routine to double-check prior to deleting names from the database permanently. Figure 7.4 shows the pseudocode for the DELNAMES command file.

The code for asking whom to delete is virtually identical to the logic for asking whom to edit, so we'll present those lines in their entirety below:

```
* * * * * * * * * * * * * * * * * * * * * * * * * * * DELNAMES.CMD
* * * * * * * * * * * * * * * Delete individuals from the database.

* * * * * * * * * First, get last name of person to delete.
STORE "X" TO SEARCH
DO WHILE SEARCH # " "
   ERASE
   ACCEPT " Delete whom? (last name) " TO SEARCH
   ERASE

      * * * * * * * * Translate to uppercase, then count how
      * * * * * * * * many individuals have that last name.
   STORE !(SEARCH) TO SEARCH
   FIND &SEARCH
   COUNT WHILE !(LNAME) = SEARCH TO HOWMANY

      * * * * * * Proceed with deletion, depending on how many
      * * * * * * individuals have the requested last name.
   DO CASE
         * * * * * * * * If no name entered, just clear screen.
      CASE SEARCH = " "
         ERASE

         * * * * * * * * If nobody has that last name, warn user.
      CASE HOWMANY = 0
         ? "There is no &SEARCH on the database"
         ?
         ? "Press any key to try again . . . ."
         WAIT

         * * * * * * * If one person has that last name, delete.
      CASE HOWMANY = 1
         FIND &SEARCH
```

Set up a looping variable
As long as the user does not request to exit this program

    Clear the screen
    Ask user for the name of the individual to delete
    Translate name to uppercase
    Find that individual
    Count how many people on the database have the requested
       last name

    If the user did not type in a name for deleting
       Double-check prior to deleting permanently

    If nobody has the requested last name,
       Inform user that nobody has that name,
       then allow him to try again

    If one person has the requested last name,
       delete that individual, informing user of the deletion

    If several people have the requested last name,
       display them and get further info,
       then delete the specified name (if any)

Repeat the deletion question while user does not request exit

When the user is done specifying names to delete

    Display which names are to be deleted
    Ask user for permission to delete all
    While user does not provide permission
       Ask who not to delete
       Recall the name not to be deleted
       Redisplay remaining names to be deleted

    When user stops specifying names to recall
       Delete all people requested

    Release memory variables
    Return to the main menu

Figure 7.4: Pseudocode for the DELNAMES command file.

```
        ? "Deleting ",TRIM(FNAME),LNAME
        DELETE

    ******* If several people have that last name,
    ******* display them and get further information.
    CASE HOWMANY > 1
    FIND &SEARCH
    LIST WHILE !(LNAME)=SEARCH;
        TRIM(FNAME),LNAME,COMPANY,ADDRESS
    ?
    ACCEPT "Which one? (by number) " TO RECNO
    IF VAL(RECNO)>0
        GOTO &RECNO
        DELETE
    ENDIF (value of recno > 0)
ENDCASE

ENDDO (while search # " ")
```

The remaining lines in the DELNAMES command file check for permission to delete the requested individuals permanently from the database prior to actually deleting them. The first step here is to count how many individuals are going to be deleted. The COUNT FOR * command below handles that job:

```
************************ Before packing the database
************************ and returning to the main menu
************************ get permission to pack.
COUNT FOR * TO NO:DELS
```

Next, the command file assumes that there will be records to recall (by storing an N to the memory variable PACKEM), displays the name, company, and address of the individuals to be deleted, and asks if anyone should be recalled in the lines below:

```
STORE "N" TO PACKEM
DO WHILE !(PACKEM) # "Y" .AND. NO:DELS > 0
    ERASE
    DISPLAY ALL FOR * TRIM(FNAME),LNAME,COMPANY,ADDRESS
    ?
    ACCEPT "Delete all these people? (Y/N) " TO PACKEM
```

If the user opts to recall a name, the command file asks whom to recall, then recalls that individual, and subtracts 1 from the number of people to to be deleted (NO:DELS):

```
    ***************** If not OK to pack everyone,
    ***************** find out who to recall.
    IF !(PACKEM) # "Y"
        ?
```

```
        ACCEPT "Recall whom (left-column number) " TO SAVE
        IF VAL(SAVE)>0
            RECALL RECORD &SAVE
            STORE NO:DELS-1 TO NO:DELS
        ENDIF (val(save>0))
      ENDIF (packem # "Y")
    ENDDO (while packem # Y)
```

As soon as the user gives permission to delete all names, the command file performs the pack. Since both the NAMES and ZIPS index files are active, the index files will also have the requested names deleted. These lines handle that job:

```
*********** When OK to pack, do so if there are names to delete.
ERASE
IF NO:DELS > 0
    ? "Deleting requested names . . . . ."
    PACK
ENDIF (number of names to delete > 0).
```

At this point, the only remaining job is to release the memory variables and return to the main menu. The last few lines handle that task:

```
RELEASE PACKEM, SEARCH, HOWMANY, NO:DELS
?
"Returning to main menu . . ."
RETURN
```

The entire DELNAMES command file is presented in Figure 7.5.

```
************************************* DELNAMES.CMD
************ Delete individuals from the database.

********* First, get last name of person to delete.
STORE "X" TO SEARCH
DO WHILE SEARCH # " "
    ERASE
    ACCEPT " Delete whom? (last name) " TO SEARCH
    ERASE

    ******** Translate to uppercase, then count how
    ******** many indiviuduals have that last name.
STORE !(SEARCH) TO SEARCH
FIND &SEARCH
COUNT WHILE !(LNAME) = SEARCH TO HOWMANY

    ****** Proceed with deletion, depending on how many
    ****** individuals have the requested last name.
```

Figure 7.5: *The DELNAMES.CMD command file.*

```
    DO CASE
       ******* If no name entered, just clear screen.
       CASE SEARCH=" "
            ERASE

       ******* If nobody has that last name, warn user.
       CASE HOWMANY = 0
            ? "There is no &SEARCH on the database"
            ?
            ? "Press any key to try again...."
            WAIT

       ******* If one person has that last name, delete.
       CASE HOWMANY=1
            FIND &SEARCH
            ? "Deleting ",TRIM(FNAME),LNAME
            DELETE

       ******* If several people have that last name,
       ******* display them and get further information
       CASE HOWMANY > 1
            FIND &SEARCH
            LIST WHILE !(LNAME)=SEARCH;
                TRIM(FNAME),LNAME,COMPANY,ADDRESS
            ?
            ACCEPT "Which one? (by number) " TO RECNO
            IF VAL(RECNO)>0
                GOTO &RECNO
                DELETE
            ENDIF (value of recno > 0)
    ENDCASE

ENDDO (while search # " ")
*************************** Before packing the database
*************************** and returning to the main menu
*************************** get permission to pack.
COUNT FOR * TO NO:DELS
STORE "N" TO PACKEM
DO WHILE !(PACKEM) # "Y" .AND. NO:DELS > 0
    ERASE
    DISPLAY ALL FOR * TRIM(FNAME),LNAME,COMPANY,ADDRESS
    ?
    ACCEPT "Delete all these people? (Y/N) " TO PACKEM

    ***************** If not OK to pack everyone,
    ***************** find out who to recall.
    IF !(PACKEM) # "Y"
       ?
       ACCEPT "Recall whom (left-column number) " TO SAVE
       IF VAL(SAVE)>0
            RECALL RECORD &SAVE
            STORE NO:DELS-1 TO NO:DELS
       ENDIF (val(save>0))
    ENDIF (packem # "Y")

ENDDO (while packem # Y)
```

Figure 7.5: The DELNAMES.CMD command file (continued).

```
*********** When OK to PACK, do so if there are names to delete.
ERASE
IF NO:DELS > 0
   ? "Deleting requested names....."
   PACK
ENDIF (number of names to delete > 0).

***** Release memory variables and return to main menu.
RELEASE PACKEM,SEARCH,HOWMANY,NO:DELS
?
? "Returning to main menu..."
RETURN
```

Figure 7.5: *The DELNAMES.CMD command file (continued).*

Summary

In this chapter, we've covered user-friendly techniques for handling changes to, and deletions from, the database. When editing the database, the user simply types in the last name of the individual that he wishes to edit. If no such individual exists, the command file tells him so and allows him to try again. If one individual has the requested last name, the command file allows the user to edit the appropriate record immediately, using a custom screen similar to the one used for adding new individuals to the database.

If the user enters a name for which there are several individuals on the database (Smith, for example), the command file displays all the Smiths along with their record numbers. The user can then specify exactly which Smith he wants to edit by typing in the appropriate record number as displayed on the screen. This frees the user from having to search the database for record numbers, and allows him to perform edits in a more natural fashion, based upon a name rather than a number.

The procedure for deleting individuals is similar to the procedure used for editing. The user enters the last name of the individual to delete and the command file handles the deletion process from there. As an added safety feature, the command file displays all individuals that have been marked for deletion prior to packing the database. This gives the user a chance to change his mind prior to deleting any records permanently.

In the next chapter, we'll discuss a technique that allows the user to look up information for an individual based upon last and first name. We'll also develop a program that helps the user locate duplicate names and addresses on the database.

CHAPTER 8
ADDITIONAL OPTIONS

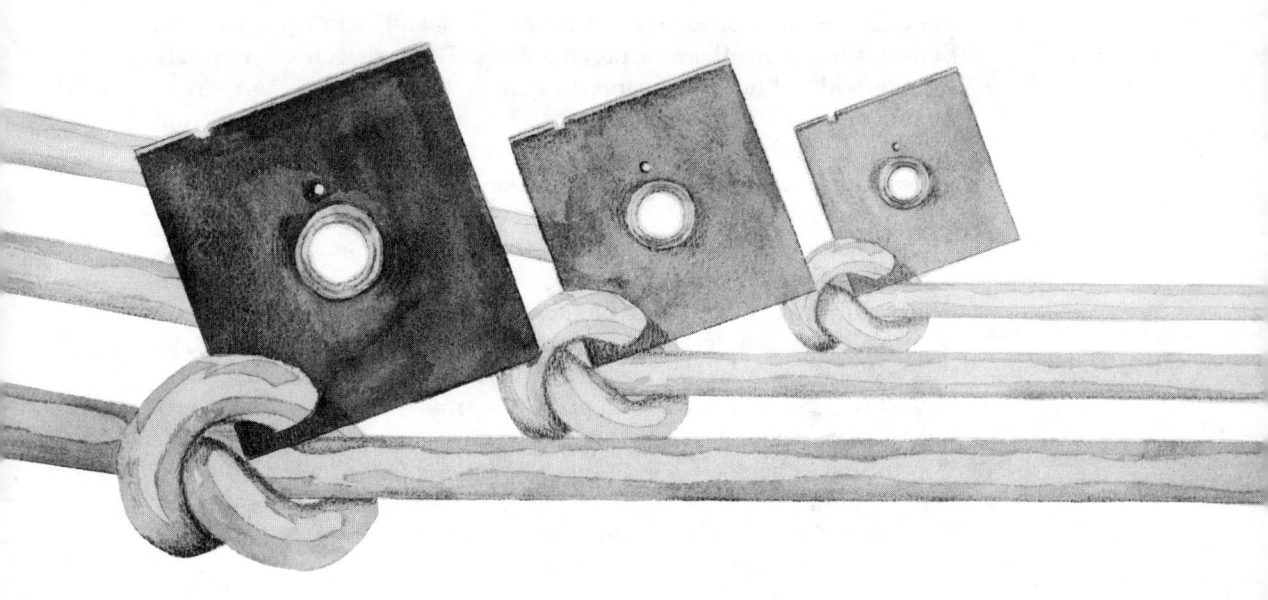

There are two more options we've included in the mailing system that we have not written command files for yet. These are the options to do a quick lookup, and to check the database for duplicate records. We'll design and develop those command files now.

Quick Lookup of a Single Record

The quick lookup feature is something like an electronic Rolodex. The user selects the menu option, types in a last name and either a first name or first initial, and the program displays data for that individual on the screen or printer, as shown below:

```
Last name   :  Cusey
First name  :  Julie
Company     :  Deluxe Banking
Address     :  8652 Bragg St.
City        :  La Jolla
State       :  CA
Zip code    :  92122
Phone       :  (619) 123-5555
Keyword     :  Manager, Banking
```

The lookup feature is faster when the FIND command is used to look up the name in the NAMES.NDX index file. Recall that the NAMES index was created with this command:

INDEX ON !(LNAME) + !(FNAME) TO NAMES

Therefore, the NAMES.NDX index file contains the last and first names of all the individuals on the database, all in uppercase and in sorted order (indexes are *always* in sorted order). Therefore, the data in the index file look something like this:

ADAMS	ANDY
BLOMGREN	LYNEA
BREWER	ADOLPH
CAPUSHNIAK	IGOR
DANIELS	KAREN
DANIELS	MARY
EDWARDS	EDWARD

Notice that all the last names have spaces after them. Since the LNAME field was assigned a length of 20 characters when the database was created, the LNAME field in the index file also has a length of 20 characters. When a user requests a first and last name to look up, the command file will have to make certain that the variable storing the last name to look for is also padded to a length of 20 characters.

Here is the lookup scenario from the user's point of view. First, he selects main menu option 3 to do a quick lookup. The screen will display:

Enter last name name :   :
Enter first name   :   :

Send data to printer? :   :

When the user fills in a last and first name, and this person is listed on the database, the screen (or printer) quickly displays the information for that person, as shown below:

Last name   : Daniels
First name   : Karen
Company   : La Jolla Bank
Address   : 1234 Prospect St.
City   : La Jolla
State   : CA
Zip code   : 92138

Additional Options 109

```
Phone    : (213)555-1212
Keyword  : Loan Officer
```

Press any key to return to main menu . . . .

If the requested name does not exist, then a message like this appears on the screen:

Karen Daniels does not exist!

At this point, the user can try to find another name. The pseudocode for the LOOKUP program appears in Figure 8.1.

We will begin creating this command file by putting the usual comments at the top of the command file. Then the program will set up the memory variables LLOOK (to hold the last name), FLOOK (to hold the first name), and LP (to determine whether or not the output will be sent to the printer). These lines take care of those tasks:

```
* * * * * * * * * * * * * * * * * * * * * * * * * * * * * * * * LOOKUP.CMD
* * * Quick lookup of an individual by first and last name.

* * * First, store 20 blanks to LLOOK and FLOOK,
* * * and a blank to variable LP.
STORE "                    " TO LLOOK,FLOOK
STORE " " TO LP
```

Set up blank memory variables
Clear the screen

Ask user for first and last name
Ask user if data should be sent to the printer

Store uppercase of first and last name to search variable

Find that person

If that person found
   Display data (on screen or printer)

If not found
   Display error message

Pause so user can read the screen

Release memory variables

Return to main menu

Figure 8.1: *Pseudocode for the LOOKUP command file.*

Note that there are *exactly* 20 spaces between the quotation marks on the line which reads:

```
STORE "                    " TO LLOOK,FLOOK
```

This length must exactly match the length assigned to the field when the database was created.

The next commands ask the user who they want to look up and whether or not the data should be sent to the printer, as below:

```
*** Find out who the user wants to look up.
ERASE
2,2 SAY "Enter last name name " GET LLOOK
3,2 SAY "Enter first name     " GET FLOOK
7,2 SAY "Send data to printer?" GET LP
READ
```

Next the program creates a variable to use with the FIND command to perform the search. The memory variable is called SEARCH and it contains the last name that the user requested to search on, plus the first name with the blanks trimmed off. The uppercase function (!) ensures that all characters will be in uppercase to match the contents of the index file.

```
*********** Link first and last name; make all uppercase.
STORE !(LLOOK) + !(TRIM(FLOOK)) TO SEARCH
```

The TRIM function allows the user extra flexibility. For example, if the user types in Daniels as the last name to look up, and only the first initial K instead of the whole first name, the program will still find Karen Daniels.

Next, the command file must attempt to find the specified individual, using the FIND command and the SEARCH variable, as the lines below indicate:

```
********** Find that individual.
FIND &SEARCH
ERASE
```

If the command file finds that individual, it displays the data. Furthermore, if the user requests that the report be sent to the printer, it sets the printer on first. If the requested name is not found, it displays an error message. The DO CASE clause below handles these tasks:

```
********* If found, display. Otherwise, present message.
DO CASE
```

```
        CASE # > 0
        IF !(LP)="Y"
            SET PRINT ON
        ENDIF (lp=Y)
     ? "Last name :",LNAME
     ? "First name :",FNAME
     ? "Company   :",COMPANY
     ? "Address   :",ADDRESS
     ? "City      :",CITY
     ? "State     :",STATE
     ? "Zip code  :",ZIP
     ? "Phone     :",PHONE
     ? "Keyword   :",KEYWORD
        ?
        EJECT
        SET PRINT OFF
        CASE # = 0
           ?
           ? TRIM(FLOOK),TRIM(LLOOK),"does not exist!"
        ENDCASE
```

Note that if the FIND command finds the requested data, it sets the record number pointer (#) to the number of that record. Otherwise, it sets the record number pointer to 0. Hence the two cases in the DO CASE clause: 1) CASE # > 0 (which means the name was found), and 2) CASE # = 0 (which means the name was not found).

Next, the command file should pause to allow the user time to look at the screen. The next lines perform that simple job:

```
        ************* Pause before returning to menu.
        ?
        ?
        ?"Press any key to return to main menu. . . ."
        ?
        WAIT
```

Then, the program releases the memory variables and returns to the main menu with these lines:

```
        ************* Release memory variables.
        RELEASE LLOOK,FLOOK,LP,SEARCH
        RETURN
```

The entire LOOKUP command file is displayed in Figure 8.2. As usual, DO MAIL (the MAIN MENU program) and select menu option 3 to test the LOOKUP command file.

```
*************************************** LOOKUP.CMD
************ Quick lookup by first and last name.

*** First, store 20 blanks to LLOOK and FLOOK,
*** and a blank to variable LP.
STORE "                    " TO LLOOK,FLOOK
STORE " " TO LP

*** Find out who user wants to look up.
ERASE
@ 2,2 SAY "Enter last name name " GET LLOOK
@ 3,2 SAY "Enter first name     " GET FLOOK
@ 7,2 SAY "Send data to printer?" GET LP
READ

****** Link first and last name; make all uppercase.
STORE !(LLOOK) + !(TRIM(FLOOK)) TO SEARCH

********** Find that individual.
FIND &SEARCH
ERASE

* If found, display.  Otherwise, present message.
DO CASE

CASE # > 0

   IF !(LP)="Y"
      SET PRINT ON
   ENDIF (lp=Y)
   ? "Last name   :",LNAME
   ? "First name  :",FNAME
   ? "Company     :",COMPANY
   ? "Address     :",ADDRESS
   ? "City        :",CITY
   ? "State       :",STATE
   ? "Zip code    :",ZIP
   ? "Phone       :",PHONE
   ? "Keyword     :",KEYWORD
   ?
   EJECT
   SET PRINT OFF

CASE # = 0
   ?
   ?  TRIM(FLOOK),TRIM(LLOOK),"does not exist!"

ENDCASE

************** Pause before returning to menu.
?
?
? "Press any key to return to main menu...."
?
WAIT

************** Release memory variables.
RELEASE LLOOK,FLOOK,LP,SEARCH

RETURN
```

Figure 8.2: The LOOKUP.CMD command file.

If you wish to have the quick look up program work with either a last name, or a first and last name search, you should modify the program slightly. The line which concatenates the LLOOK and FLOOK variables:

```
STORE !(LLOOK)+!(TRIM(FLOOK)) TO SEARCH
```

should be modified so that the first name is linked to the last name only if the user requests a look up based on both first and last name. Replace the existing line with the routine below:

```
STORE !(LLOOK) TO SEARCH
***** Add first name, if user enters one.
IF FLOOK # " "
    STORE SEARCH + !(TRIM(FLOOK)) TO SEARCH
ENDIF (flook # " ")
```

Also, on a large database, you might want to be sure that just in case several people have the same first and last name, the user has a chance to see them all. At present, the first person found on the database is displayed with the routine below:

```
CASE # > 0
    IF ! (LP)="Y"
ENDIF (1p=y)
? "Last name    :    ",LNAME
? "First name   :    ",FNAME
? "Company      :    ",COMPANY
? "Address      :    ",ADDRESS
? "City         :    ",CITY
? "State        :    ",STATE
? "Zip code     :    ",ZIP
? "Phone        :    ",PHONE
? "Keyword      :    ",KEYWORD
?
```

To have the lookup program display several people with the same name, you can put this routine in a loop, as shown below:

```
CASE # > 0
    ** Display all individuals with requested name.
    DO WHILE !(LNAME)+!(TRIM(FNAME)) = SEARCH .AND. .NOT. EOF
        ERASE
        IF !(LP)="Y"
            SET PRINT ON
        ENDIF (1p=y)
        ? "Last name    :    ",LNAME
        ? "First name   :    ",FNAME
```

```
            ? "Company    :  ",COMPANY
            ? "Address    :  ",ADDRESS
            ? "City       :  ",CITY
            ? "State      :  ",STATE
            ? "Zip code   :  ",ZIP
            ? "Phone      :  ",PHONE
            ? "Keyword    :  ",KEYWORD
            ?
            ?
            EJECT
            SKIP
            SET PRINT OFF
            ***** If next name matches search, ask user what to do.
            IF !(LNAME) + !(TRIM(FNAME)) = SEARCH
                ? "Press any key to see next, or X to exit"
                WAIT TO MORE
                ***** If user wants to exit, get out of loop.
                IF !(MORE) = "X"
                    GO BOTT
                ENDIF (more = x)
            ENDIF (name = search)
        ENDDO (name = search and not eof)
```

Quick Check for Duplicates

In *Understanding dBASE II*, I provided a program to check for and display possible duplicates on a database. The mailing system we are developing now will accomplish the same task in a similar way, but it will take advantage of the existing NAMES index file. This lets the user avoid reindexing in order to perform the search, and will speed up the search for duplicates considerably.

The basic logic for checking for duplicates is first to sort all the names and addresses into alphabetical order by first and last name. The NAMES index file already takes care of that task. Then, the command file must read adjacent pairs of names from the sorted order. Obviously, if two names are identical, they will be adjacent to each other in sorted order. If the command file detects two identical names, it can then further check to see if the addresses and cities for the two common names are also identical. If so, it can inform the user of this fact. Otherwise, it just goes on and compares the next pair of names, until all the names and addresses in the database have been checked.

The checking-for-duplicates command file also allows the user to display possible duplicates on the printer rather than on the screen. It displays its data on a report that looks like this:

Possible Duplications . . .

Record # 123 is Smith Arnold 123 A St. San Diego
Record # 932 is Smith Arnold 123 A St. San Diego

Record # 39 is Waldo Nancy 234 Grape St. La Jolla
Record # 321 is Waldo Nancy 234 Grape St. La Jolla

The command file does not delete any records. Rather, it informs the user of the possibility of duplication. This allows the user further investigation of the possible duplicates prior to deleting them through the delete option from the main menu.

If the command file does not find any duplicates, it presents this message:

No duplicates found!
Press any key to return to main menu . . .

The user can then press any key to return to the main menu.

The DUPES command file handles the task of checking for duplicates. The logical flow of the program is displayed in Figure 8.3.

The MAIL command file has already set up the NAMES index as the primary index file, so the DUPES command file need not create a new index. Instead, it will clear the screen and ask the user if he wishes to have the possible duplicates displayed on the screen. It will store the user's answer to a memory variable called YN (yes/no). These first lines of the command file handle that job:

```
* * * * * * * * * * * * * * * * * * * * * * * * * * * * * * DUPES.CMD
* * * * * * * * * * * * * * * * * * * * * * * * Check for duplicates.
ERASE

* * * * * * * * * * * * * * * * * * * * * * * * Ask about hardcopy.
STORE " " TO YN
2,2 SAY "Do you want a hardcopy of duplicates ";
  GET YN
READ
```

If the user types in Y (or y) to this question, the command file will set the printer on, as displayed in the lines below:

```
* * * * * * * * * * * * * * * * * * * * * If yes, set printer on.
IF !(YN) = "Y"
  SET PRINT ON
ENDIF (yn = Y)
```

Advanced Techniques in dBASE II

Clear the screen

Ask about hardcopy

If user wants hardcopy, set printer on

Clear the screen
Set duplicates counter to 0

Print report heading and 2 blank lines

Loop through and compare pairs, starting at record 1
    Store name, address, and city to variable 1
    Skip down a record
    If not at the end of the file,
    Store name, address, and city to variable 2
    If the two are identical
        Skip back a record,
        Display that record's data
        Skip forward a record
        Display that record's data
        Print two blank lines
        Increment duplicates counter by 1

    Set memory variables back to blanks
Continue checking (until the end of the file)

Set the printer off

If no duplicates found, tell user
If duplicates not going to printer, pause

Release memory variables
Return to the main menu

Figure 8.3: *Pseudocode for the DUPES command file.*

Next the command file will clear the screen and print the heading of the report, followed by two blank lines. It will also set the memory variable, which counts how many duplicates are found (DUPCOUNT) to zero, as below:

```
******************* Print duplicates report.
ERASE
STORE 0 TO DUPCOUNT

? "Possible Duplications . . . . . . ."
?
?
```

The command file now must be sure that it is starting at the top of the database, then needs to set up a loop through all the records. These lines take care of that job:

```
*************** Loop through and compare pairs.
GO TOP
DO WHILE .NOT. EOF
```

Now, for each record in the database, the program file stores data for the current record into a memory variable, which we'll call AD1, as shown in the next line:

```
STORE LNAME + ADDRESS + CITY TO AD1
```

Then, the program skips to the next record to make the comparison. However, for the command file to work properly, it must also make sure that it has not skipped off the end of the database. If it has not, it stores the last name, address, and city of the current record to a memory variable called AD1, as shown in the next lines:

```
SKIP 1
IF .NOT. EOF
    STORE LNAME + ADDRESS + CITY TO AD1
ENDIF (not eof)
```

Now it checks to see if the two adjacent records are identical in last name, address, and city (using uppercase equivalents for better accuracy). If the records are identical, it must skip back a record, display data for that record, then skip forward again and display the data for that record. Then it should print a couple of blank lines and increment the duplicates counter (DUPCOUNT) by one. The lines within the IF clause below perform that task:

```
************* Report duplicates.
IF !(AD1) = !(AD2)
    SKIP -1
    ? "Record # " + STR(#,3) + " is ",TRIM(LNAME),;
        TRIM(FNAME),TRIM(ADDRESS),CITY
    SKIP 1
    ? "Record # " + STR(#,3) + " is ",TRIM(LNAME),;
        TRIM(FNAME),TRIM(ADDRESS),CITY
    ?
    ?
    STORE DUPCOUNT + 1 TO DUPCOUNT
ENDIF (ad1 = ad2)
```

Prior to performing the next comparison, the command file resets the comparison memory variables (AD1 and AD2) to blanks. This line takes care of that job:

    STORE " " TO AD1,AD2

Then the loop simply continues (until the end of the file has been encountered), and continues checking for duplicates. We just need to add a line to close the DO WHILE loop now:

    ENDDO (while not eof)

Once all of the records have been checked for duplication, the command file will turn off the printer with the lines below:

```
* * * * * * * * * * * * * * * * * * * * * * * * * * * * * Done with program.
SET PRINT OFF
```

If no duplicate records were found, the command file should inform the user so that he knows the program did perform the search. Since the DUPCOUNT memory variable has been counting duplicates, the command file can decide whether or not duplicates were found by simply checking to see if DUPCOUNT is zero. The next lines in the command file inform the user if no duplicates were found, and gives him a chance to read the screen prior to returning to the main menu:

```
* * * * * * * * * * * * * If no duplicates found, tell user.
IF DUPCOUNT = 0
   ERASE
   ? "No duplicates found!"
   ? "Press any key to return to main menu . . ."
   ?
   WAIT
ENDIF (dupcount = 0)
```

If the command file did find and display duplicates, but the data were not printed on the printer, the command file should pause to allow the user to read the duplicates from the screen prior to returning to the main menu. These lines handle that situation:

```
* * * * * * If duplicates not going to printer, pause.
IF !(YN) # "Y" .AND. DUPCOUNT > 0
   ?
   ?
   ? "Press any key to return to main menu."
   ?
   WAIT
ENDIF (yn # Y and dupcount > 0)
```

The only remaining task is to release the memory variables and return to the main menu, as displayed in the lines below:

```
*********** Return to main menu.
RELE AD1,AD2,YN,DUPCOUNT
RETURN
```

Figure 8.4 displays the entire DUPES command file. Remember to DO MAIL and select the Check for Duplicates option from the main menu to test the command file.

```
************************************* DUPES.CMD
************************** Check for duplicates.
ERASE

************************** Ask about hardcopy.
STORE " " TO YN
@ 2,2 SAY "Do you want a hardcopy of duplicates ";
   GET  YN
READ

********************* If yes, set printer on.
IF !(YN)="Y"
    SET PRINT ON
ENDIF (yn=Y)

******************** Print duplicates report.
ERASE
STORE 0 TO DUPCOUNT

? "Possible Duplications......."
?
?

**************** Loop through and compare pairs.
GO TOP
DO WHILE .NOT. EOF

    STORE LNAME+ADDRESS+CITY TO AD1
    SKIP 1
    IF .NOT. EOF
       STORE LNAME+ADDRESS+CITY TO AD2
    ENDIF (not eof)

    ************* Report duplicates.
    IF !(AD1)=!(AD2)
       SKIP -1
       ? "Record # "+STR(#,3)+" is ",TRIM(LNAME),;
          TRIM(FNAME),TRIM(ADDRESS),CITY
       SKIP 1
       ? "Record # "+STR(#,3)+" is ",TRIM(LNAME),;
          TRIM(FNAME),TRIM(ADDRESS),CITY
       ?
```

Figure 8.4: The DUPES.CMD command file.

```
           ?
           STORE DUPCOUNT+1 TO DUPCOUNT
       ENDIF (ad1=ad2)

       STORE " " TO AD1,AD2

   ENDDO (while not eof)

   ***************************** Done with program.
   SET PRINT OFF

   ************* If no duplicates found, tell user.
   IF DUPCOUNT = 0
      ERASE
      ? "No duplicates found!"
      ? "Press any key to return to main menu..."
      ?
      WAIT
   ENDIF (dupcount = 0)

   ****** If duplicates not going to printer, pause.
   IF !(YN) # "Y" .AND. DUPCOUNT > 0
      ?
      ?
      ? "Press any key to return to main menu."
      ?
      WAIT
   ENDIF (yn # Y)

   ************ Return to main menu.
   RELE AD1,AD2,YN,DUPCOUNT
   RETURN
```

Figure 8.4: The DUPES.CMD command file (continued).

Summary

Now you have learned about the design and development of our sophisticated mailing list system. Starting with the next chapter, we'll design and develop another command file: an inventory system that requires multiple database files as well as multiple index files. This will pose a more complex programming problem, of course, but we will be able to transfer many of the techniques we've developed with the mailing system to the inventory system, which will help make that goal a bit easier to accomplish.

CHAPTER 9
A CUSTOM INVENTORY SYSTEM

In this chapter, we'll begin developing an inventory system. In the process of developing the programs, we'll discuss some new programming techniques, including:

1. Checking for valid user entries.
2. Checking for duplicate entries.
3. Updating a master file from transaction files.
4. Automatically calculating data and displaying the results.
5. Automatically filling in certain fields on a record.
6. Searching for data within a range of dates.

We'll begin by discussing the design of inventory systems.

Inventory systems generally require the use of several data files. One file, usually referred to as the *master file,* keeps track of the quantity of each item presently in stock. In addition, it may also keep track of the cost of each item, the reorder point, the quantity on order, the location of the item in the warehouse, and the name and address of the vendor the item is purchased from. This allows the user of the system to locate an item quickly, get a listing of goods which need to be ordered, automatically create and print new orders, etc.

Most businesses also like to keep track of each individual transaction that occurs within the business. Individual transactions are generally maintained on separate data files called *transaction files*. One file might keep track of individual sales transactions (i.e., to whom items were sold, on what date, for how much, etc.) and invoice or receipt numbers. Incoming stock may also be recorded on a second transaction file to maintain an ongoing history of all goods received. We can envision the relationship among the master file and the two transaction files as displayed in Figure 9.1.

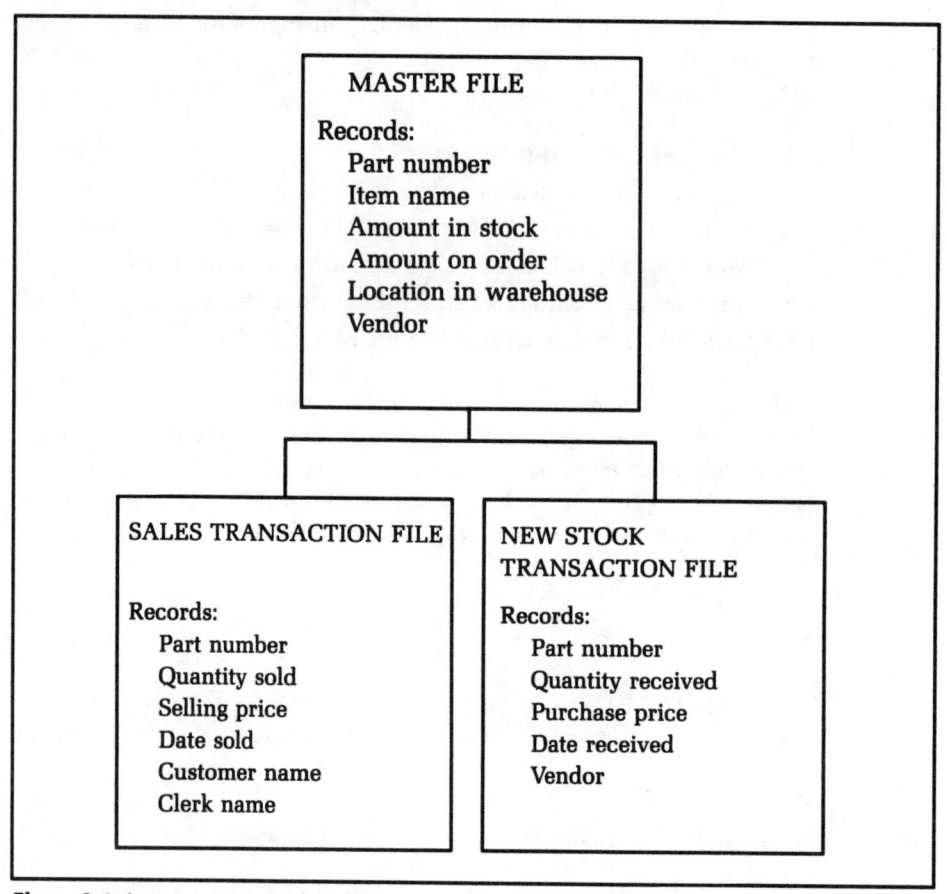

```
                    MASTER FILE
                Records:
                    Part number
                    Item name
                    Amount in stock
                    Amount on order
                    Location in warehouse
                    Vendor

    SALES TRANSACTION FILE        NEW STOCK
                                  TRANSACTION FILE
    Records:                      Records:
        Part number                   Part number
        Quantity sold                 Quantity received
        Selling price                 Purchase price
        Date sold                     Date received
        Customer name                 Vendor
        Clerk name
```

Figure 9.1: *Inventory system data files.*

The transaction files maintain a history of all individual transactions involving the sales and receipt of goods while the master file maintains the current status of goods in stock at any given moment. The master file keeps track of the current inventory through information supplied directly from the two transaction files. In a sense, the master file is an ongoing summary of all events that have been recorded on the two transaction files.

Whenever you design a system involving multiple, related data files such as these, it is very important to define a *key field* that can be used to relate the information in the various files to one another. A key field has the following characteristics:

1. It is unique to every record on the master file.
2. It exists on the master file *and* the transaction files with the same field name, type, and width.

The key field in most software systems is an identifying code. In an inventory system such as this, a part number is usually used as the key field. A store keeps track of each item of stock by using a part number, just like the government keeps track of people with social security numbers. Drivers licence numbers, bank account numbers, and credit card numbers are all key fields on various computers.

Without key fields, data are difficult to manage. For example, if the government didn't use social security numbers, it would have to record my tax payment by searching through all the people who have the name Alan Simpson. By simply keying in my social security number instead, they can save time and avoid costly errors. Thus, by assigning each individual a unique code, and using that code as a key field, the government's job becomes much easier.

Even on a scale as small as our inventory system, key fields are necessary, as we will see while developing our system.

Inventory System Goals

The inventory system will be designed to allow a small business to keep track of all goods in stock and on order. Whenever the store decides to carry a new item, they can assign the new item a unique part number and add it to the inventory master database. The system will also provide the user with the ability to print reports of all goods in stock, items which need to be reordered, and items on order, as well as to produce orders automatically.

The system will also allow the user to keep track of all individual sales transactions: the items sold, to whom they were sold, who sold them, the date of the sale, and the number of the invoice. Similarly, the user can keep track of all incoming goods as the stock is replenished. The individual transactions from the sales and goods received will be used to update the status of the current stock automatically.

Inventory System Database Design

Three data files will be used to manage the inventory. First will be the master file, called MASTER.DBF. Its structure, as well as a brief description of each field's contents, are displayed below:

STRUCTURE FOR FILE: B:MASTER .DBF

FLD	NAME	TYPE	WIDTH	DEC	CONTENTS
001	PART:NO	C	005		Part number (key field)
002	TITLE	C	020		Item description
003	QTY	N	004		Quantity in stock
004	COST	N	009	002	Purchase price
005	REORDER	N	004		Reorder point
006	ON:ORDER	N	004		Quantity on order
007	LOCATION	C	005		Location in warehouse
008	VENDOR	C	025		Vendor name
009	VENDOR:ADD	C	025		Vendor address
010	VENDOR:CSZ	C	025		Vendor city, state, zip
011	DATE	C	008		Date of last update
012	ORDER:DATE	C	008		Date of last order
013	NEW:ORDER	N	004		Quantity to order

You can create this data file from the information above by using the dBASE CREATE command, and filling in the field names, types, widths, and decimal places shown.

To keep the data file in part number order, as well as to speed up the process of looking up and updating items, an index file called MASTER.NDX will be maintained. Once you create the MASTER.DBF data file, you can create the MASTER index file by typing in these commands:

```
USE MASTER
INDEX ON PART:NO TO MASTER
```

Remember to set the default to the appropriate disk drive before you create and index the file. (In the examples in the book, we'll use drive B as the default drive.)

Next, we'll create a data file to keep track of individual sales transactions. In the MASTER.DBF data file just created, notice that the key field is named PART:NO. It is a character (C) type, and is five spaces wide. Since this will be the key field used for updating the master file, the sales transactions file must have an identical field. The name of the sales file is SALES.DBF, and it has this structure:

STRUCTURE FOR FILE: B:SALES .DBF

FLD	NAME	TYPE	WIDTH	DEC	CONTENTS
001	PART:NO	C	005		Part number (key field)
002	INVOICE:NO	N	006		Invoice number
003	CLERK	C	012		Salesman's name (or code)
004	CUSTOMER	C	012		Customer name
005	QTY	N	004		Quantity sold
006	PRICE	N	009	002	Selling Price
007	DATE	C	008		Date sold
008	POSTED	L	001		Posted to master yet?

Field number eight above, POSTED, is a special field that will be used to determine whether or not a given transaction has already been recorded on (or posted to) the master inventory file. This is to keep any transactions from being posted twice by accident. Notice that its type is L (logical). A logical field can either be .T. (true), or .F. (false). We'll design our system so when dBASE updates the master file, the POSTED field becomes .T. (true) for the records which have been updated.

To speed the updating process, the SALES file will also be indexed on part number, using an index file called SALES.NDX. You can now create the SALES file on the same disk as the MASTER file, using the field names, types, widths, and decimal places shown above. Then, use the commands:

USE SALES
INDEX ON PART:NO TO SALES

to create the SALES.NDX index file.

The third file in the system will be used to keep track of orders received to replenish the stock. Again, since the master file will be receiving information from this file, it should have the key field PART:NO. The name of the data file will be NEWSTOCK.DBF, and it will have this structure:

STRUCTURE FOR FILE: B:NEWSTOCK.DBF

FLD	NAME	TYPE	WIDTH	DEC	CONTENTS
001	PART:NO	C	005		Part number (key field)

002	QTY	N	004			Quantity received
003	COST	N	009	002		Purchase price
004	DATE	C	008			Date received
005	VENDOR	C	025			Vendor name
006	POSTED	L	001			Posted to master file?

Once again, you can use the CREATE command to create the NEWSTOCK file as shown, and index it on PART:NO to an index file called NEWSTOCK.NDX using these commands:

```
USE NEWSTOCK
INDEX ON PART:NO TO NEWSTOCK
```

The overall database for our inventory now consists of six files; three data (.DBF) files, and three index (.NDX) files, as shown below:

Data files   *Index Files*
MASTER.DBF   MASTER.NDX
SALES.DBF   SALES.NDX
NEWSTOCK.DBF   NEWSTOCK.NDX

Having designed the database for the inventory, next we need to design the software structure. Obviously this is going to be a fairly large system, so some preplanning is strongly recommended.

Inventory System Software Design

The design of the inventory system will allow the various major tasks to be performed by separate individuals. That is, the store manager will manage the master inventory, place orders, check the status of goods, and so forth. Sales clerks will handle individual sales transactions at the point of sale. A stock room clerk will keep track of incoming stock.

In a sense, we will develop three separate, though related, systems. The overall structure of these systems is shown in Figure 9.2.

The IMENU.CMD command file will be the overall inventory system menu. Based on the user's choice, it will branch to either 1) MMENU.CMD, the main menu for managing the master file, 2) SMENU.CMD, the menu for handling individual sales transactions, or 3) NMENU.CMD, the menu for handling incoming stock. Each of the submenus in Figure 9.2 will further refer to other command files, but we'll cross those bridges when we come to them.

```
             ┌─────────────────────────────┐
             │        IMENU.CMD            │
             │ Inventory System Main Menu  │
             │                             │
             │ 1. Manage Master Inventory  │
             │ 2. Record Sales Transactions│
             │ 3. Record New Stock         │
             │ 4. Exit                     │
             └─────────────────────────────┘
```

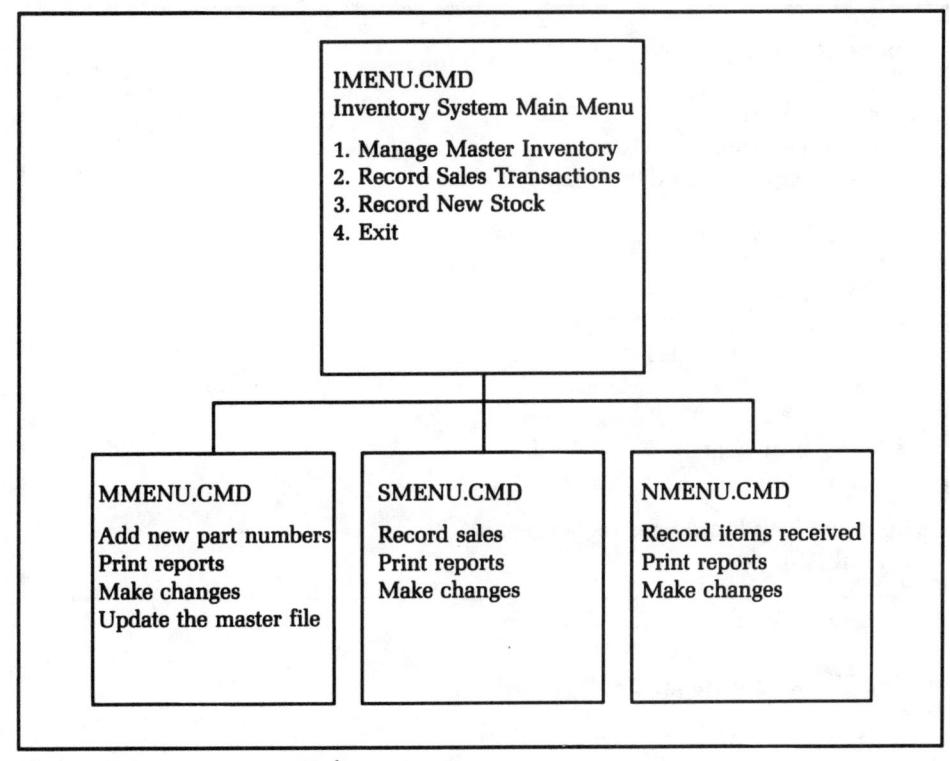

┌──────────────────────┐ ┌──────────────────┐ ┌──────────────────────┐
│   MMENU.CMD   │ │   SMENU.CMD   │ │   NMENU.CMD   │
│   │ │   │ │   │
│ Add new part numbers │ │ Record sales   │ │ Record items received│
│ Print reports   │ │ Print reports   │ │ Print reports   │
│ Make changes   │ │ Make changes   │ │ Make changes   │
│ Update the master file│ │   │ │   │
└──────────────────────┘ └──────────────────┘ └──────────────────────┘

Figure 9.2: *Inventory systems software structure.*

Inventory System Main Menu

Let's begin developing the inventory system with the overall main menu. We'll develop each of the submenu command files in later chapters.

The main menu for the inventory program asks the user for two pieces of information. First, it asks the user for today's date (if necessary), and uses that date throughout various procedures in the system. Then it asks the user which file to work with; 1) the master file, 2) the sales transactions file, or 3) the incoming goods file. Then it branches to the appropriate command file based upon the user's request. Figure 9.3 shows the pseudocode for the inventory system main menu.

We can now develop the command file. Our first job, as usual, is to put some identifying comments at the top of the program, and set up

> Set parameters
> Clear the screen
> If no date available
>   Ask user for today's date
>   Set dBASE system date to today's data
>
> Set up loop for main menu
>   Clear the screen
>   Display options:
>   1. Master Inventory
>   2. Record Sales
>   3. Record New Stock
>   4. Exit
>   Wait for answer
>   Branch to appropriate program
>
> Continue loop (until user requests exit)
> Quit dBASE

Figure 9.3: *Pseudocode for IMENU.CMD command file.*

the dBASE parameters, as displayed below:

```
******************************* IMENU.CMD
************* Main menu for the inventory system.
SET TALK OFF
SET DEFA TO B
```

Next, the program will clear the screen, check to see if it should ask for today's date, and then ask for the date if necessary. Add these lines to the command file:

```
************ Set up system date (if necessary).
ERASE
STORE DATE() TO T:DATE
IF VAL(T:DATE)< = 1
   @ 5,5 SAY "Enter today's date ";
     GET T:DATE PICTURE "99/99/99"
   READ
     SET DATE TO ө:DATE
ENDIF (t:date = 0)
```

Notice that the command file first stores dBASE's built-in date [DATE( )] to a variable called T:DATE. Then it checks to see if the value (VAL) of that date is less than or equal to 1. (Since some systems automatically default to a date of 01/01 if no other date is available, it's best to double-check on the date if the month is less than or equal to one.) The screen asks for today's date using the template " / / ", and then sets dBASE's internal date at the same date.

Next, we must set up a loop for clearing the screen, displaying the menu, and waiting for a response from the user. We've already written this routine in other command files. For the inventory system, the code is:

```
* * * * * * * * * * * * * * * *  Set up loop for main menu.
STORE " " TO ICHOICE
DO WHILE ICHOICE # "4"
ERASE
TEXT

         Inventory System Main Menu

     1. Master Inventory
     2. Record Sales
     3. Record New Stock

     4. Exit

ENDTEXT
* * * * * * * * * * * * * * * * * *  Get response from user.
@ 10,18 SAY "Enter choice ";
   GET ICHOICE PICTURE "9"
READ
```

Next, the program branches to the appropriate command file based upon the user's request. Add the DO CASE clause to the program as shown below:

```
DO CASE

    CASE ICHOICE = "1"
       DO MMENU

    CASE ICHOICE = "2"
       DO SMENU

    CASE ICHOICE = "3"
       DO NMENU

ENDCASE
```

Next, we need to close the DO WHILE loop, and tell dBASE to quit should the user decide to exit. Let's add these two lines to handle that job:

```
ENDDO (while ichoice # 4)
QUIT
```

The entire IMENU command file is displayed if Figure 9.4.

```
**************************************** IMENU.CMD
************* Main menu for the inventory system.
SET TALK OFF
SET DEFA TO B

************ Set up system date (if necessary).
ERASE
STORE DATE() TO T:DATE
IF VAL(T:DATE)<=1
   @ 5,5 SAY "Enter today's date ";
     GET T:DATE PICTURE "99/99/99"
   READ
   SET DATE TO &T:DATE
ENDIF (t:date = 0)

**************** Set up loop for main menu.
STORE " " TO ICHOICE
DO WHILE ICHOICE # "4"
   ERASE
   TEXT

                  Inventory System Main Menu

              1. Master Inventory
              2. Record Sales
              3. Record New Stock

              4. Exit

   ENDTEXT
   ******************** Get response from user.
   @ 10,18 SAY "Enter choice ";
      GET ICHOICE PICTURE "9"
   READ

   DO CASE

      CASE ICHOICE = "1"
           DO MMENU

      CASE ICHOICE = "2"
           DO SMENU

      CASE ICHOICE = "3"
           DO NMENU

   ENDCASE

ENDDO (while ichoice # 4)
QUIT
```

Figure 9.4: *The IMENU.CMD command file.*

Summary

In this chapter, we've designed the inventory system that we'll be developing throughout the following chapters. Three databases were created to maintain records of the current stock (MASTER.DBF), individual sales transactions (SALES.DBF) and new stock received (NEWSTOCK.DBF). A field named PART:NO will be used as a key field for updating the current stock based upon changes in the SALES and NEWSTOCK databases.

We've also developed the MAIN MENU program for the overall inventory system: IMENU.CMD. In the following chapter, we'll design and develop the command files used to manage, and get information from, the master inventory file.

CHAPTER 10
THE MASTER INVENTORY FILE

As discussed in the previous chapter, the master file for the inventory system keeps track of the current status of goods in stock. The data file is called MASTER.DBF, and it has this structure:

STRUCTURE FOR FILE: B:MASTER .DBF

FLD	NAME	TYPE	WIDTH	DEC
001	PART:NO	C	005	
002	TITLE	C	020	
003	QTY	N	004	
004	COST	N	009	002
005	REORDER	N	004	
006	ON:ORDER	N	004	
007	LOCATION	C	005	
008	VENDOR	C	025	
009	VENDOR:ADD	C	025	
010	VENDOR:CSZ	C	025	
011	DATE	C	008	
012	ORDER:DATE	C	008	
013	NEW:ORDER	N	004	

Furthermore, it has already been indexed on the PART:NO field to an index file named MASTER.NDX. In this chapter, we'll design and develop command files to manage data on the master file.

Master File Software Design

Recall from the previous chapter that the user enters the inventory system through the IMENU command file, which presents these options:

    Inventory System Main Menu

1. Master Inventory
2. Record Sales
3. Record New Stock
4. Exit

If the user selects option 1, IMENU.CMD branches to MMENU.CMD, which is the submenu for handling the master file. MMENU.CMD, in turn, presents these additional options to the user:

    Inventory Master File Menu

1. Add New Part Numbers
2. Print Reports
3. Make Changes
4. Update from Sales and New Stock
5. Return to Main Menu

The structure of the command files used to manage the master inventory file is displayed in Figure 10.1.

Master File Menu

Let's begin by developing the MMENU command file. This is a menu program with the same basic structure as previous menu programs, so we can bypass the pseudocode and the tutorial. The MMENU command file is displayed in Figure 10.2. Viewing the figure, you'll notice how similar to previous menu programs MMENU.CMD is.

```
                    From IMENU.CMD
                           ↓
                    ┌─────────────────────┐
                    │ MMENU.CMD           │
                    │ Master File Menu    │
                    │ 1. Add New Part Numbers │
                    │ 2. Print Reports    │
                    │ 3. Make Changes     │
                    │ 4. Update           │
                    │ 5. Return to Main Menu │
                    └─────────────────────┘
```

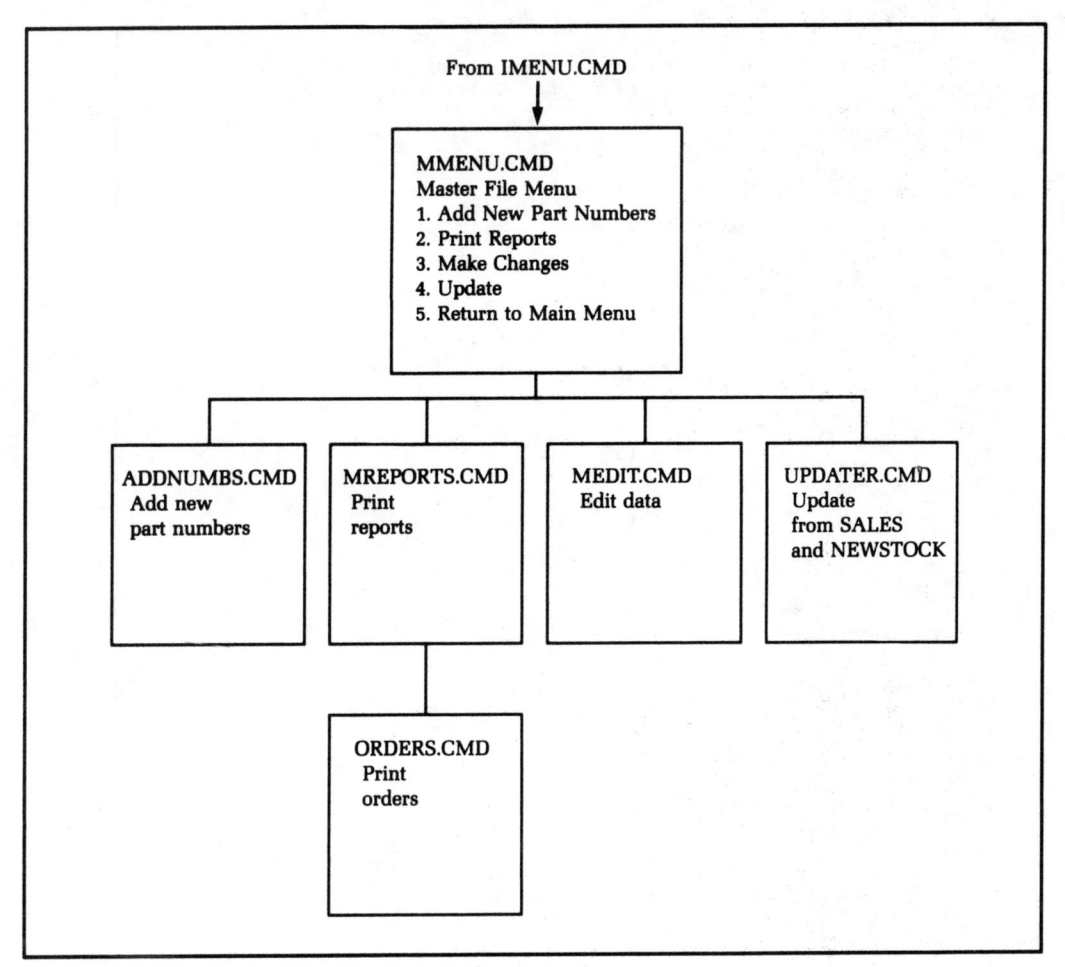

Figure 10.1: Software structure for managing the master inventory.

Adding Unique Part Numbers

The first option from the master file menu is to add new part numbers. This job is handled by the ADDNUMBS.CMD command file. When the user selects option 1, the screen asks the user to:

    Enter part number :   :

Recall that each part number must be unique because it is a key field. The ADDNUMBS command file will then check that the part number

```
***************************************** MMENU.CMD
********************* Inventory master file menu.
STORE " " TO MCHOICE
DO WHILE MCHOICE # "5"
   ERASE
   TEXT

        Inventory Master File Menu

        1. Add New Part Numbers
        2. Print Reports
        3. Make Changes
        4. Update from Sales and New Stock

        5. Return to Main Menu

   ENDTEXT

   @ 12,10 SAY "Enter Choice (1-5)";
      GET MCHOICE PICTURE "9"
      READ

   DO CASE

      CASE MCHOICE = "1"
           DO ADDNUMBS

      CASE MCHOICE = "2"
           DO MREPORTS

      CASE MCHOICE = "3"
           DO MEDIT

      CASE MCHOICE = "4"
           DO UPDATER

      ENDCASE
ENDDO (while mchoice # 5)

RELEASE MCHOICE
RETURN
```

Figure 10.2: The MMENU.CMD command file.

is new. If not, it will tell the user:

> X-999 already exits!

(where X-999 is the existing number) and give a warning beep. Then the user can try another number. If the user types in a unique part number, he can add the additional data to the master file using the custom screen displayed in Figure 10.3.

As discussed previously, the easiest way to create this custom screen is to use ZIP or SED to draw it on the screen. The name of the screen

```
┌─────────────────────────────────────────────────────────────┐
│ Cursor Control:  ^E up : ^X down : ^D right : ^S left : ^G delete │
├─────────────────────────────────────────────────────────────┤
│ Part Number          :X-999:        Date :10/30/84:         │
│ Title                :                    :                 │
│ Quantity in Stock :     :           Unit Cost :     . :     │
│ Quantity on Order :     :           Reorder Point :     :   │
│ Storage Location :      :                                   │
│ Vendor Name :           :                                   │
│ Vendor Address :        :                                   │
│ Vendor City, State, Zip :                :                  │
└─────────────────────────────────────────────────────────────┘
```

Figure 10.3: *Custom data entry screen of the MASTER file.*

will be ISCREEN1.FMT. Figure 10.4 shows how you can draw the screen with SED.

Figure 10.5 shows the dBASE command file for ISCREEN1.FMT as generated by SED.

Once the ISCREEN1.FMT file is created, we can begin developing the ADDNUMBS.CMD command file. Our pseudocode is displayed in Figure 10.6.

Now let's write the file. The first step is to add the leading comments, and define MASTER.DBF with the MASTER.NDX index file as the file to use:

```
* * * * * * * * * * * * * * * * * * * * * * * * * * ADDNUMBS.CMD
* * * * * * * * * * * * * * * Add new items to the master file.
USE MASTER INDEX MASTER
```

```
┌─────────────────────────────────────────────────────────────┐
│ Cursor Control:  ^E up : ^X down : ^D right : ^S left : ^G delete │
├─────────────────────────────────────────────────────────────┤
│ Part Number          <PART:NO       Date <DATE!"99/99/99"   │
│ Title                <TITLE                                 │
│ Quantity in Stock <QTY              Unit Cost <COST         │
│ Quantity on Order <ON:ORDER         Reorder Point <REORDER  │
│ Storage Location <LOCATION                                  │
│ Vendor Name <VENDOR                                         │
│ Vendor Address <VENDOR:ADD                                  │
│ Vendor City, State, Zip <VENDOR:CSZ                         │
└─────────────────────────────────────────────────────────────┘
```

Figure 10.4: *SED screen for ISCREEN1.FMT.*

```
* B:ISCREEN1.
@ 1,1 SAY "Cursor Control: ^E up :^X down :^D right :^S left :^G d"
@ 1,56 SAY "elete"
@ 3,1 SAY "------------------------------------------------------------"
@ 3,56 SAY "------"
@ 5,1 SAY "Part Number"
@ 5,14 GET PART:NO
@ 5,30 SAY "Date"
@ 5,36 GET DATE PICTURE "99/99/99"
@ 7,1 SAY "Title"
@ 7,14 GET TITLE
@ 9,1 SAY "Quantity in stock"
@ 9,20 GET QTY
@ 9,30 SAY "Unit Cost"
@ 9,41 GET COST
@ 11,1 SAY "Quantity on order"
@ 11,20 GET ON:ORDER
@ 11,30 SAY "Reorder point"
@ 11,45 GET REORDER
@ 13,1 SAY "Storage Location"
@ 13,19 GET LOCATION
@ 15,1 SAY "Vendor Name"
@ 15,14 GET VENDOR
@ 17,1 SAY "Vendor Address"
@ 17,17 GET VENDOR:ADD
@ 19,1 SAY "Vendor City, State, Zip"
@ 19,26 GET VENDOR:CSZ
```

Figure 10.5: ISCREEN1.FMT format file.

Next, we need to set up a loop so that the command file continues asking for part numbers (as long as the user does not wish to exit). To make it easy on the user, let's allow him to exit this program by pressing RETURN. However, to get the loop started, we'll store a random non-blank character to PART:NO, in this case, the letter X. Then we'll just use the standard @, SAY, GET, and READ commands to get the part number as below:

```
******************* Set up loop for part number.
STORE "X" TO PARTNUMB
DO WHILE PARTNUMB # " "
    ***************** Get proposed part number.
    ERASE
    STORE " " TO PARTNUMB
    @ 5,5 SAY "Enter part number " GET PARTNUMB
    READ
```

Next comes the task of checking to make sure that the part number that the user entered does not already exist. For consistency, we'll keep any alphabetic letters in the PART:NO field in uppercase. Since the MASTER file is indexed on the PART:NO field, we can just use the

The Master Inventory File   141

> Use master file and master file index
>
> Set up loop for adding new part numbers
>   Clear the screen
>   Ask user for new part number
>
>   Check to see if part number already exists
>
>   If user did not enter a part number,
>   clear the screen and return to menu
>
>   If part number exists, warn user of
>   the problem, and allow another try
>
>   If part number not already taken, let
>   user add it using ISCREEN1 format
>
> Continue loop for adding part numbers (while
>   user does not enter blank for part number)
>
> Release memory variables
> Return to master file menu

Figure 10.6: Pseudocode for the ADDNUMBS.CMD command file.

FIND command with a macro as below:

```
***************** Check to see if part number
***************** already exists.
STORE !(PARTNUMB) TO PARTNUMB
FIND &PARTNUMB
```

Now, the user's entry dictates what the command file will do next. If the user did not enter a part number, it should return control to the master file menu (MMENU.CMD). The first case statement in the DO CASE clause handles this situation:

```
***************** Decide what to do next.
DO CASE
****** If user did not enter a part number,
****** clear the screen and return to menu.
CASE PARTNUMB = " "
    ERASE
```

If the user entered a part number that already exists, the command file warns him and allows him to try again. The second CASE statement handles that situation:

```
****** If part number exists, warn user of
****** the problem.
CASE # > 0
   @ 10,10 SAY PARTNUMB+" already exits!"
   ? CHR(7)
   WAIT
```

The statement ? CHR(7) causes most computers to beep, thereby giving the user a little audible feedback with the warning.

Finally, if the user entered an acceptable part number, the command file should allow him to add the rest of the information about the part using the ISCREEN1 format. These lines handle that situation:

```
****** If part number not already taken, let
****** user add it.
CASE # = 0
   APPEND BLANK
   REPLACE PART:NO WITH PARTNUMB
   REPLACE DATE WITH T:DATE
   SET FORMAT TO ISCREEN1
   READ
   SET FORMAT TO SCREEN
ENDCASE
```

Let's examine the steps in the lines above. First, the CASE statement checks to make sure that the record number after the FIND command equals zero (CASE # = 0). This indicates that the user's new part number was not found, and therefore is unique. If this is the case, the program adds one new record to the database with all fields blank (APPEND BLANK). Since the user already typed in a part number (PARTNUMB), and since the date has previously been defined (T:DATE), these two fields are automatically filled in the so user need not retype them. Then the command file sets the format to the custom ISCREEN1 screen, reads in the data for the new record, and sets the format back to the regular dBASE II screen.

Next, the command file loops around again, assuming the user did not request to exit. If the user wishes to exit, the program releases a memory variable and returns to the MMENU command file, as shown in these lines:

```
ENDDO (partnum # " ")

RELEASE PARTNUMB
RETURN
```

The command file is shown in its entirety in Figure 10.7.

```
************************************* ADDNUMBS.CMD
*************** Add new items to the master file.
USE MASTER INDEX MASTER

******************** Set up loop for part number.
STORE "X" TO PARTNUMB
DO WHILE PARTNUMB # " "
   ****************** Get proposed part number.
   ERASE
   STORE "       " TO PARTNUMB
   @ 5,5 SAY "Enter part number " GET PARTNUMB
   READ
   ****************** Check to see if part number
   ****************** already exists.
   STORE !(PARTNUMB) TO PARTNUMB
   FIND &PARTNUMB

   ****************** Decide what to do next.
   DO CASE

      ****** If user did not enter a part number,
      ****** clear the screen and return to menu.
      CASE PARTNUMB = " "
           ERASE

      ****** If part number exists, warn user of
      ****** the problem.
      CASE # > 0
           @ 10,10 SAY PARTNUMB+" already exits!"
           ? CHR(7)
           WAIT

      ****** If part number not already taken, let
      ****** user add it.
      CASE # = 0
           APPEND BLANK
           REPLACE PART:NO WITH PARTNUMB
           REPLACE DATE WITH T:DATE
           SET FORMAT TO ISCREEN1
           READ
           SET FORMAT TO SCREEN

   ENDCASE

ENDDO (partnum # " ")

RELEASE PARTNUMB
RETURN
```

Figure 10.7: The ADDNUMBS.CMD command file.

Master File Reports

When the user selects option 2 to print reports from the master inventory, the MMENU.CMD command file branches to the

MREPORTS command file, which displays this menu of report options:

Master Inventory Report Options
1. Entire Inventory
2. Reorder Report
3. Items on Order
4. Place Orders
5. Return to Menu

Samples of the various reports, and the report formats for the first three reports are described below.

Current Stock Report

If the user selects option 1, a report displaying the entire inventory is presented as shown in Figure 10.8. The dBASE REPORT command is used to print the report. Create the report format by typing in these commands from the dot prompt:

```
USE MASTER
REPORT FORM ALLMAST
```

PAGE NO. 00001
10/30/84

Current Stock

Part #	Description	On Hand	Unit Cost	Reorder	Loc.	Last Update
A-111	Snowshoes	1	34.00	10	S-111	01/01/80
A-113	Tennis Rackets	6	44.00	30	T-11	01/01/80
B-232	Dog Biscuits	30	2.50	50	DB-99	01/01/80
B-232	Dog Bones	30	2.50	50	DB-99	01/01/80
B-232	Dog Blankets	30	2.50	50	DB-99	01/01/80
B-232	Collars	30	2.50	50	DB-99	01/01/80
Z-999	Bearskin Rugs	10	100.00	5	B-502	05/02/84

Figure 10.8: Entire inventory report for the inventory system.

Fill out the ensuing prompts as follows:

```
ENTER OPTIONS, M = LEFT MARGIN, L = LINES/PAGE, W = PAGE
WIDTH M=1,W=70
PAGE HEADING? (Y/N) Y
ENTER PAGE HEADING: Current Stock
DOUBLE SPACE REPORT? (Y/N) N
ARE TOTALS REQUIRED? (Y/N) N
COL    WIDTH,CONTENTS
001    05,PART:NO
ENTER HEADING: Part #
002    20,TITLE
ENTER HEADING: Description
003    5,QTY
ENTER HEADING: On-;Hand
004    9,COST
ENTER HEADING: Unit;Cost
005    7,REORDER
ENTER HEADING: Reorder
006    7,LOCATION
ENTER HEADING: Loc.
007    8,DATE
ENTER HEADING: Last;Update
```

Reorder Report

If the user selects option 2 from the REPORTS menu, the reorder report is displayed, as shown in Figure 10.9. Use the command REPORT FORM REORDER from the dot prompt to create the format for the reorder report, and fill in the prompts as below:

```
ENTER OPTIONS, M = LEFT MARGIN, L = LINES/PAGE, W = PAGE
WIDTH M=1,W=70
PAGE HEADING? (Y/N) Y
ENTER PAGE HEADING: Items to be Reordered
DOUBLE SPACE REPORT? (Y/N) N
ARE TOTALS REQUIRED? (Y/N) N
COL    WIDTH,CONTENTS
001    5,PART:NO
ENTER HEADING: Part;No.
002    20,TITLE
ENTER HEADING: Description
003    5,QTY
ENTER HEADING: On-;Hand
004    5,ON:ORDER
ENTER HEADING: On;Order
```

```
PAGE NO. 00001
01/01/80
                        Items to be Reordered
Part      Description      On      On      Re-      Vendor Name
No.                        Hand    Order   Order

A-111     Snowshoes         1       10      30      American Snowshoes, Inc.
A-113     Tennis Rackets    6       10      30      Zeppo's Radical Rackets
Z-999     Bearskin Rugs    10       10      30      Bearskins of La Jolla
```

Figure 10.9: *Inventory system reorder report.*

```
005     5,REORDER
ENTER HEADING: Re-;Order
006     20,VENDOR
ENTER HEADING: Vendor;Name
007
```

Items on Order Report

When the user selects option 3 from the REPORTS menu, a report displaying the goods currently on order is displayed, as shown in Figure 10.10.

```
PAGE NO. 00001
01/01/80
                        Items Currently on Order
Order     Part    Description     On      Unit     Total      Vendor Name
Date      No.                     Order   Cost     Cost

10/01/84  A-111   Snowshoes       10      34.00     340.00    American Snowsh
10/01/84  A-113   Tennis Rackets  10      44.00     440.00    Zeppo's Radical
10/15/84  B-232   Dog Biscuits    10       2.50      25.00    Zeppo's Custom
10/15/84  B-232   Dog Bones       10       2.50      25.00    Zeppo's Custom
10/15/84  B-232   Dog Blankets    10       2.50      25.00    Zeppo's Custom
10/15/84  B-232   Collars         10       2.50      25.00    Zeppo's Custom
10/01/84  Z-999   Bearskin Rugs   10     100.00    1000.00    Bearskins of La
** TOTAL          **                                1880.00
```

Figure 10.10: *Report of items currently on order.*

Use the command REPORT FORM ONORDER from the dot prompt to create this report. Fill in the prompts as below:

```
ENTER OPTIONS, M=LEFT MARGIN, L=LINES/PAGE, W=PAGE
WIDTH M=1,W=80
PAGE HEADING? (Y/N) Y
ENTER HEADING: Items Currently on Order
DOUBLE SPACE REPORT? N
ARE TOTALS REQUIRED? Y
SUBTOTALS IN REPORT? N
COL    WIDTH,CONTENTS
001    8,ORDER:DATE
ENTER HEADING: Order;Date
002    5,PART:NO
ENTER HEADING: Part;No.
003    20,TITLE
ENTER HEADING: Description
004    5,ON:ORDER
ENTER HEADING: On-;Order
ARE TOTALS REQUIRED? N
005    9,COST
ENTER HEADING: Unit;Cost
ARE TOTALS REQUIRED? N
006    9,COST*ON:ORDER
ENTER HEADING: Total;Cost
ARE TOTALS REQUIRED Y
007    15,$(VENDOR,1,15)
ENTER HEADING: Vendor Name
```

Placing Orders

The fourth option from the reports menu allows the user to place orders and print order slips automatically. When the user selects this option, the screen displays basic information about each item in stock that has fallen below the reorder point. Each item is displayed individually so the user can place an order immediately. Here is a sample:

```
Part number        : A-111
Name               : Snowshoes
On-hand            : 10
On order           : 10
Reorder            : 30
Unit Cost          : 12.11

Order how many? :_  :
```

The user can quickly see how many items are in stock, on order, and what the reorder point is. To order more, the user simply specifies the quantity to order in response to the last prompt. The next stock item below the reorder point will then appear on the screen, and the process continues until all items have been displayed. After the screen displays all items that need to be reordered, the command file prints the order forms. Figure 10.11 shows a sample order form created by the inventory system.

Presenting Report Options

The task of presenting the report options to the user, and then printing the appropriate report, is handled by the MREPORTS.CMD command file. Although MREPORTS.CMD is basically a simple menu program, it has a few unique features that deserve some discussion. To begin with, it starts with the usual comments, sets up the database to use, and begins a loop to display the menu repeatedly, as shown in the lines below:

```
*************************** MREPORTS.CMD
********* Present report options for master file.
USE MASTER INDEX MASTER
STORE " " TO REPCHOICE
DO WHILE REPCHOICE # "5"
   ERASE
   TEXT
```

Zeppo's Custom Dog Supplies
1234 Canine Way
San Juan Capistrano, CA 91234

Please send us the following items . . .

10 Dog Biscuits	2.50	25.00
10 Dog Bones	2.50	25.00
10 Dog Blankets	2.50	25.00

Total cost: 75.00

Mail to: My Company, Inc.
           123 A St.
           Anywhere, CA 91234

Figure 10.11: Sample order form created by the inventory system.

Master Inventory Report Options

1. Entire Inventory
2. Reorder Report
3. Items on Order
4. Place Orders
5. Return to Menu

```
ENDTEXT
@ 12,10 SAY "Enter choice (1-5) ";
   GET REPCHOICE PICTURE "9"
READ
```

The program first asks the user if he wishes a hardcopy of the report (unless the user is placing orders, in which case we can assume the printer will be used). The next few lines ask about the printer:

```
****** If not placing orders, ask about printer
ERASE
STORE " " TO YN,PRINTER
IF REPCHOICE < "4"
@ 5,5 SAY "Send report to printer? ";
   GET YN PICT "!"
READ
ERASE
```

If the user does request the printer, the command file stores the command TO PRINT to a memory variable called PRINTER. Later, the memory variable will be used as a macro with the REPORT FORM command.

```
************** Set up for printer.
IF YN = "Y"
   STORE "TO PRINT" TO PRINTER
ENDIF (yn=y)
ENDIF (rechoice < 4)
```

Next, the command file prints the appropriate report. If the Inventory, Reorder, or On-order report is chosen, the command file simply selects the appropriate report form file. The &PRINTER macro determines whether or not the report will be sent to the printer. The CASE statements below handle the first three report options:

```
DO CASE

   CASE REPCHOICE = "1"
      REPORT FORM ALLMAST &PRINTER

   CASE REPCHOICE = "2"
```

```
    REPORT FORM REORDERS FOR;
       (QTY+ON:ORDER) <= REORDER &PRINTER

CASE REPCHOICE = "3"
    REPORT FORM ONORDER FOR ON:ORDER > 0;
       &PRINTER
```

Notice that the first case prints all data from the master file. The second case prints only those records whose on-hand quantity (QTY) plus on-order quantity (ON:ORDER) is less than the reorder amount, using the REORDERS.FRM format. The third case, which displays items that are on order, only displays those items whose on-order amount (ON:ORDER) is greater than zero.

The fourth option, placing orders, is handled by a separate command file called ORDERS which we'll discuss in a moment. The fourth case statement calls the ORDERS command file. Add the case statement and close the DO CASE clause, as shown below:

```
CASE REPCHOICE = "4"
    DO ORDERS

ENDCASE
```

Then the command file simply pauses momentarily (if the report is not going to the printer, and the user is not exiting) to allow the user to view the report on the screen. Add these lines to handle that task:

```
******* If report not going to printer,
******* and not exiting program, pause.
IF YN # "Y" .AND. REPCHOICE # "5"
    ?
    ?
    ? "Press any key to return to menu . . ."
    WAIT
ENDIF (yn # y)
```

Then, add these lines to close the loop, release memory variables, and return to the MMENU command file when appropriate:

```
ENDDO (repchoice # "5")

RELEASE REPCHOICE,YN,PRINTER
RETURN
```

Figure 10.12 shows the entire MREPORTS.CMD command file.

So that the user can place and print orders, MREPORTS.CMD branches to the ORDERS.CMD command file. ORDERS.CMD must perform several tasks. First, it must step through each record on the master file and determine which items are due for reordering by

```
*************************************** MREPORTS.CMD
********* Present report options for master file.

USE MASTER INDEX MASTER
STORE " " TO REPCHOICE
DO WHILE REPCHOICE # "5"
   ERASE
   TEXT

      Master Inventory Report Options

         1. Entire Inventory
         2. Reorder Report
         3. Items on Order
         4. Place Orders

         5. Return to menu

   ENDTEXT
   @ 12,10 SAY "Enter choice (1-5) ";
      GET REPCHOICE PICTURE "9"
   READ

   ****** If not placing orders, ask about printer
   ERASE
   STORE " " TO YN,PRINTER
   IF REPCHOICE < "4"
      @ 5,5 SAY "Send report to printer? ";
         GET YN PICT "!"
      READ
      ERASE
      *************** Set up for printer.
      IF YN = "Y"
         STORE "TO PRINT" TO PRINTER
      ENDIF (yn=y)
   ENDIF (rechoice < 4)

   DO CASE

      CASE REPCHOICE = "1"
         REPORT FORM ALLMAST &PRINTER

      CASE REPCHOICE = "2"
         REPORT FORM REORDERS FOR;
            (QTY+ON:ORDER) <= REORDER &PRINTER

      CASE REPCHOICE = "3"
         REPORT FORM ONORDER FOR ON:ORDER > 0;
            &PRINTER

      CASE REPCHOICE = "4"
         DO ORDERS

   ENDCASE
   ******* If report not going to printer,
   ******* and not exiting program, pause.
   IF YN # "Y" .AND. REPCHOICE # "5"
```

Figure 10.12: The MREPORTS.CMD command file.

```
        ?
        ?
        ? "Press any key to return to menu..."
        WAIT
     ENDIF (yn # y)

  ENDDO (repchoice # "5")

  RELEASE REPCHOICE,YN,PRINTER
  RETURN
```

Figure 10.12: The MREPORTS.CMD command file (continued).

checking to see if the amount on hand plus the amount on order is below the reorder point. Each time it finds an item that needs reordering, it must ask the user how many to reorder. Once all the orders are placed, the program prints the orders, and also updates the "on-order" field in the master file. The pseudocode for ORDERS.CMD is shown in Figure 10.13.

We can build the ORDERS command file as follows. First, add the usual opening lines:

```
********************************* ORDERS.CMD
********* Create purchase orders for reordering.
ERASE
USE MASTER INDEX MASTER
```

Next, the program must loop through the master file and display data for those items whose total on-hand and on-order quantities are below the reorder point. For each of these items, the program must ask the user how many items to order. Add the DO WHILE loop below to have the program take the orders:

```
***** Loop through and display goods below
***** reorder point, and ask user how many
**** of each to order.
GO TOP
DO WHILE .NOT. EOF
   IF (QTY+ON:ORDER)<= REORDER
      ERASE
      @ 5,5 SAY "Part number "+PART:NO
      @ 5,30 SAY TITLE
      @ 6,5 SAY "On-hand "+STR(QTY,4)
      @ 7,5 SAY "On order "+STR(ON:ORDER,4)
      @ 8,5 SAY "Reorder "+STR(REORDER,3)
      @ 9,5 SAY "Unit Cost "+STR(COST,9,2)
      @ 12,5 SAY "Order how many? ";
         GET NEW:ORDER PICTURE "9999"
         REPLACE ORDER:DATE WITH T:DATE
```

```
    READ
ENDIF (qty+on:order<reorder)
SKIP
ENDDO (while not eof)
```

Notice that the amount to be ordered is stored in the NEW:ORDER field and that the order date is automatically set to today's date (T:DATE). Once all of the orders are placed, the program copies the items to be ordered to a separate temporary file called temp:

```
****** Next, make a temporary file of goods to be ordered.
ERASE
? "Preparing files . . . please wait"
? "(Prepare printer while waiting)"
COPY TO TEMP FOR NEW:ORDER > 0
```

Now that the items to be ordered are stored in a separate file, we need to make some changes to the master file. First, the ON:ORDER field needs to be incremented to show the quantity of items on order (the present quantity on order plus the quantity just ordered). Then, the NEW:ORDER field can be set back to zero. These lines handle that task:

```
****** Add new orders to on:order, then set all
****** new orders back to zero.
REPLACE NOUPDATE ALL ON:ORDER WITH;
   ON:ORDER + NEW:ORDER
REPLACE NOUPDATE ALL NEW:ORDER WITH 0
```

The NOUPDATE option here keeps dBASE from re-sorting the index, since neither ON:ORDER nor NEW:ORDER affect the index file.

To print the orders, the command file must use the temp file, and sort it into vendor order. These lines handle that job:

```
****** Use the temp file, sort it by vendor.
USE TEMP
INDEX ON !(VENDOR) TO TEMP
```

When the temp file is ready, the following lines make sure the command file informs the user to prepare the printer.

```
****** Files ready, inform user.
ERASE
? CHR(7)
? "Ready printer and press any key to print orders"
WAIT
```

Next, to produce orders for individual vendors, the program should loop through the entire temp file. For each common vendor, it will

> Clear the screen
> Use the master file with master index
>
> Start loop through master file
>   If on-hand + on-order quantity is less than reorder point . . .
>   Clear the screen
>   Show status of item to be reordered
>   Ask user how many to order
>   Update new:order and order-date fields
>   Skip to next record
> Continue loop through data file
>
> When all orders have been placed . . .
> Clear the screen
> Make temporary file of items to be ordered
> Update the on:order field on master file
> Set new:order field back to 0 on master file
>
> Use the temp file, (which contains orders)
> Index by vendor name
>
> Set printer on
> Loop through the temp file
>   For each vendor on the temp file
>   Print vendor name and address
>   For each item to order from this vendor
>   Print quantity, item, and cost to order
>
>   When done with this vendor
>   Print total cost of order
>
>   Print shipping name and address
>   Start on a new page
>
> Skip to next vendor
> Continue loop through temp file
>
> When all done, release memory variables, turn
> off printer, and return to MREPORTS

Figure 10.13: *Pseudocode for the ORDERS command file.*

print one order. This requires two nested loops. The first loop goes record-by-record through the temp file:

```
****** Loop through temp file, and through
****** individual vendors to print orders.
```

```
GO TOP
SET PRINT ON
DO WHILE .NOT. EOF
```

Within this loop, the command file stores the name of the current vendor to a memory variable called THIS:LOOP. For calculating the grand total of the order, it stores a zero to a memory variable called TOTAL. Then it prints the vendor name and address at the top of the invoice. The lines below are instructions to print the invoice heading:

```
*********************** Print 1 order.
STORE VENDOR TO THIS:LOOP
STORE 0 TO TOTAL
? VENDOR
? VENDOR:ADD
? VENDOR:CSZ
?
? "Please send us the following items . . . "
?
```

Now, as long as the vendor name does not change (VENDOR = THIS:LOOP), the program prints the quantity to be ordered (NEW:ORDER), title, and total cost (NEW:ORDER*COST). It also keeps a running total of the overall order. This loop handles that job:

```
DO WHILE VENDOR = THIS:LOOP .AND. .NOT. EOF
   ? NEW:ORDER,TITLE,COST,NEW:ORDER*COST
   STORE NEW:ORDER*COST + TOTAL TO TOTAL
   SKIP
ENDDO (while vendor = this:loop)
```

When the program is finished with this vendor, it prints the total cost of the order and the address to ship the order to. Then it skips to the next page in the printer, as shown in the routine below:

```
?
? "Total cost:                  ",TOTAL
?
? "Mail to: My Company, Inc."
? " 123 A St."
? " Anywhere, CA 91234"
EJECT
```

Next, the main loop through the entire file must continue, until orders for all vendors have been placed, by closing the DO WHILE loop with an ENDDO command, as below:

```
ENDDO (while not eof)
```

When all orders have been printed, the program releases the memory variables and returns to MREPORTS.CMD. Also, to keep the screen-pause from occuring at the bottom of the MREPORTS command file, store Y to the variable YN, which means that the report was printed on the printer. Then the MASTER file and index file are used, and the temp data base is deleted in the routine below:

```
********* Done. Release memory variables, turn
********* off printer, store yn to y, and return.
SET PRINT OFF
RELEASE THIS:LOOP,TOTAL
STORE "Y" TO YN
USE MASTER INDEX MASTER
IF FILE ("TEMP.DBF")
   DELETE FILE TEMP
ENDIF (temp file exists)

RETURN
```

The ORDERS command file is somewhat abstract so you should study it to understand it fully. Your time will be well spent because it presents a number of techniques that are useful to a variety of programming situations. Figure 10.14 shows the complete ORDERS.CMD command file.

Editing the Master File

Option 3 from the master file menu allows the user to edit the master file. The command file that performs this task is named MEDIT.CMD, and its pseudocode is presented in Figure 10.15.

Since we've already developed the ISCREEN1.FMT format file, we can use it for editing purposes also. This makes development of the MEDIT command file relatively easy. First, we set up the usual comments and use the master file and index:

```
****************************** MEDIT.CMD
****************** Edit the inventory master file.
USE MASTER INDEX MASTER
```

Then, we set up a loop that will allow the user to make several edits, or to exit by not entering a part number:

```
STORE "X" TO PARTNUMB
DO WHILE PARTNUMB # " "
```

```
*************************************** ORDERS.CMD
********* Create purchase orders for reordering.
ERASE

USE MASTER INDEX MASTER
***** Loop through and display goods below
***** reorder point, and ask user how many
**** to order of each.

GO TOP
DO WHILE .NOT. EOF
   IF (QTY+ON:ORDER)<= REORDER
      ERASE
      @ 5,5 SAY "Part number "+PART:NO
      @ 5,30 SAY TITLE
      @ 6,5 SAY "On-hand     "+STR(QTY,4)
      @ 7,5 SAY "On order    "+STR(ON:ORDER,4)
      @ 8,5 SAY "Reorder     "+STR(REORDER,3)
      @ 9,5 SAY "Unit Cost   "+STR(COST,9,2)
      @ 12,5 SAY "Order how many? ";
         GET NEW:ORDER PICTURE "9999"
         REPLACE ORDER:DATE WITH T:DATE
      READ
   ENDIF (qty+on:order<reorder)
   SKIP
ENDDO (while not eof)

****** Next, make a temporary file of goods to be ordered.
ERASE
? "Preparing files... please wait"
? "(Prepare printer while waiting)"
COPY TO TEMP FOR NEW:ORDER > 0

****** Add new orders to on:order, then set all
****** new orders back to zero.
REPLACE NOUPDATE ALL ON:ORDER WITH ON:ORDER+NEW:ORDER
REPLACE NOUPDATE ALL NEW:ORDER WITH 0

****** Use the temp file, sort it by vendor.
USE TEMP
INDEX ON !(VENDOR) TO TEMP

****** Files ready, inform user.
ERASE
? CHR(7)
? "Ready printer and press any key to print orders"
WAIT

****** Loop through TEMP file, and through
****** individual vendors to print orders.
GO TOP
SET PRINT ON
DO WHILE .NOT. EOF

   ********************** Print 1 order.

   STORE VENDOR TO THIS:LOOP
```

Figure 10.14: The ORDERS.CMD command file.

```
       STORE 0 TO TOTAL
       ? VENDOR
       ? VENDOR:ADD
       ? VENDOR:CSZ
       ?
       ? "Please send us the following items..."
       ?
       DO WHILE VENDOR = THIS:LOOP .AND. .NOT. EOF
          ? NEW:ORDER,TITLE,COST,NEW:ORDER*COST
          STORE NEW:ORDER*COST + TOTAL TO TOTAL
          SKIP
       ENDDO (while vendor = this:loop)
       ?
       ? "Total cost:                          ",TOTAL
       ?
       ? "Mail to:    My Company, Inc."
       ? "           123 A St."
       ? "           Anywhere, CA  91234"
       EJECT
ENDDO (while not eof)

********* Done. Release memory variables, turn
********* off printer, store yn to y, and return.
SET PRINT OFF
RELEASE THIS:LOOP,TOTAL
STORE "Y" TO YN
USE MASTER INDEX MASTER
IF FILE("TEMP.DBF")
   DELETE FILE TEMP
ENDIF (temp file exists)
RETURN
```

Figure 10.14: *The ORDERS.CMD command file (continued).*

Use the master file and master index
Start loop for performing edits

    Find out what part number to edit

    Try to find that part number

    If no part number entered, just return

    If part number found, edit using ISCREEN1 format

    Otherwise, warn user and allow another try

Continuing editing until user requests exit

When done editing, release variables and return

Figure 10.15: *Pseudocode for the MEDIT.CMD command file.*

Next, we need to add lines that will ask the user for the part number to edit:

```
********** Find out what part number to edit.
ERASE
STORE "          " TO PARTNUMB
@ 5,5 SAY "Edit for what part number? ";
   GET PARTNUMB
   READ
```

The next line instructs dBASE to find the requested part number:

```
*************** Try to find that part number.
STORE !(PARTNUMB) TO PARTNUMB
FIND &PARTNUMB
```

Now the command file must decide what to do next based on the user's response. If the user doesn't enter a part number, it just clears the screen and bypasses the other CASE statements. If a valid part number was entered, it allows an edit using the ISCREEN1 format file. If an invalid part number was entered, it warns the user. The DO CASE clause below handles the three possibilities:

```
*************** If found, edit using ISCREEN1
*************** format, otherwise warn user.
DO CASE

   **** If no part number entered, just return.
   CASE PARTNUMB = " "
      ERASE

   ***** If part number found, allow edit.
   CASE # > 0
      SET FORMAT TO ISCREEN1
      READ
      SET FORMAT TO SCREEN

   ****** If part number not found, warn user.
   CASE # = 0
      @ 10,5 SAY "There is no part " + PARTNUMB
      @ 12,5 SAY "Press any key to try again . . ."
      WAIT

ENDCASE
```

The DO WHILE loop is closed by an ENDDO command, which keeps asking the user for the next part number to edit:

```
ENDDO (while partnumb # " ")
```

Advanced Techniques in dBASE II

When the user is done editing, the program releases the memory variables and returns to MMENU.CMD:

```
****** Done editing, release variables and return.
RELEASE PARTNUMB
RETURN
```

Figure 10.16 displays the entire MEDIT.CMD command file.

```
***************************************** MEDIT.CMD
**************** Edit the inventory master file.
USE MASTER INDEX MASTER

STORE "X" TO PARTNUMB
DO WHILE PARTNUMB # " "
   *********** Find out what part number to edit.
   ERASE
   STORE "      " TO PARTNUMB
   @ 5,5 SAY "Edit for what part number? ";
     GET PARTNUMB
     READ

   *************** Try to find that part number.
   STORE !(PARTNUMB) TO PARTNUMB
   FIND &PARTNUMB

   *************** If found, edit using ISCREEN1
   *************** format, otherwise warn user.
   DO CASE

      **** If no part number entered, just return.
      CASE PARTNUMB = " "
         ERASE

      ***** If part number found, allow edit.
      CASE # > 0
         SET FORMAT TO ISCREEN1
         READ
         SET FORMAT TO SCREEN

      ****** If part number not found, warn user.
      CASE # = 0
         @ 10,5 SAY "There is no part "+PARTNUMB
         @ 12,5 SAY "Press any key to try again..."
         WAIT

   ENDCASE

ENDDO (while partnumb # " ")

****** Done editing, release variables and return.
RELEASE PARTNUMB
RETURN
```

Figure 10.16: The MEDIT.CMD command file.

The last option from the MMENU.CMD command file allows the user to update the master file from information held in the SALES and NEWSTOCK files. However, we can't test any updating programs until these files have some data in them. So we'll develop the updating programs after developing programs to handle the SALES and NEWSTOCK databases in the next two chapters.

Summary

We've explored several new programming techniques in this chapter and have used some techniques we used previously in the mailing system.

When adding new items to the MASTER inventory file, the ADDNUMBS.CMD command file automatically checks to make sure that the part number is unique. In any system using key fields to relate information among separate databases, it is important that the master database have unique data in the key field of each record. Having a program with a built-in check for uniqueness, such as ADDNUMBS.CMD, maintains the integrity of the master database.

We've also developed a number of reports for displaying the current inventory status, reorder report, and a report of items on order. We used the standard REPORT FORM report generator to create the reports, then made the MREPORTS.CMD command file to give the user a menu to select reports from.

The most advanced program in this chapter was the ORDERS.CMD command file for placing and printing orders automatically. The program loops through all records in the master file, and displays those records with on-hand quantities below the reorder point. The user can then place an order by typing in the amount to order. After all orders have been placed, the ORDERS command file prints the orders, which are ready for mailing. Perhaps the single most important technique in that command file is the ability to print a single order for each vendor, whether one item or dozens of items have been ordered from the vendor. This was accomplished by setting up a series of nested loops (DO WHILE .NOT. EOF and DO WHILE VENDOR = THIS:LOOP .AND. .NOT. EOF).

The MEDIT.PRG command file allows the user to edit data on the MASTER file, and uses techniques very similar to those used in the EDIT program of the mailing system.

CHAPTER 11
INVENTORY SALES SYSTEM

In this chapter, we'll create command files to add data to the sales file and print reports based upon invoice number or date. The data-entry program will be helpful to the user at the point of sale. The screen used to enter sales transactions will resemble a page from an invoice book, and the program will automatically fill in item names when the user enters part numbers. If the user enters a part number that does not exist, the screen will warn him of this and allow him to try again. The program will automatically calculate and display subtotals and totals as the user is entering data, and will also automatically create and store invoice numbers.

The sales portion of the inventory system will keep track of individual sales transactions. The data for individual sales transactions are stored on the SALES.DBF data file, which we created earlier with this structure:

STRUCTURE FOR FILE: B:SALES .DBF

FLD	NAME	TYPE	WIDTH	DEC
001	PART:NO	C	005	
002	INVOICE:NO	N	006	
003	CLERK	C	012	
004	CUSTOMER	C	012	
005	QTY	N	004	
006	PRICE	N	009	002
007	DATE	C	008	
008	POSTED	L	001	

Sales System Software Structure

The sales system command files are linked to the SMENU.CMD command file. There is one program for each of these tasks:

1. Adding new data.
2. Printing reports from the sales transaction file.
3. Editing the SALES file.

Figure 1.11 shows the structure of the command files.

In this chapter, we'll design and develop SMENU, POS, and SALREPS. We'll write the SALEDIT program in Chapter 13, since the editing procedures will be affected by updates.

Sales System Menu

When the user wishes to record sales transactions from the main menu, the sales system menu will appear as below:

Sales System Menu
1. Enter Point-of-Sale Routine
2. Print Sales Reports
3. Edit the Sales Data

After presenting this menu, the SMENU.CMD command file will

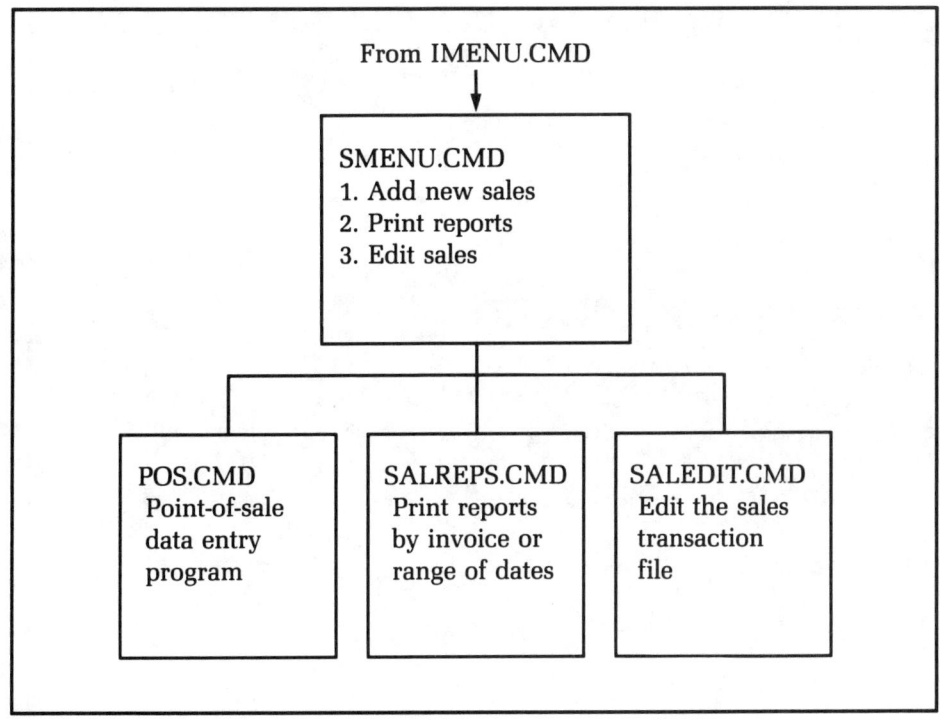

```
                    From IMENU.CMD
                           │
                           ▼
              ┌─────────────────────────┐
              │  SMENU.CMD              │
              │  1. Add new sales       │
              │  2. Print reports       │
              │  3. Edit sales          │
              └─────────────────────────┘
                           │
        ┌──────────────────┼──────────────────┐
        │                  │                  │
┌───────────────┐  ┌───────────────┐  ┌───────────────┐
│ POS.CMD       │  │ SALREPS.CMD   │  │ SALEDIT.CMD   │
│ Point-of-sale │  │ Print reports │  │ Edit the sales│
│ data entry    │  │ by invoice or │  │ transaction   │
│ program       │  │ range of dates│  │ file          │
└───────────────┘  └───────────────┘  └───────────────┘
```

Figure 11.1: Software structure for SALES system.

branch to a separate command file, based upon the user's menu selection. Since this is another simple menu program, we'll bypass the pseudocode and present the entire program in Figure 11.2.

Point-of-Sale Data Entry

The program to add new data to the SALES database will work as follows. First, when the user enters the point-of-sale system, the top portion of the invoice form will be displayed on the screen:

```
10/10/84                        Invoice Number: 23456
Clerk :_                        : Customer :                    :
─────────────────────────────────────────────────────────────────
Part #          Name            Qty      Price       Total
```

The program automatically fills in the date and invoice number, then the user types in his name and the customer's name. Next, he types in

```
*********************************** SMENU.CMD
** Menu for Sales portion of the Inventory system

***** Set up loop for presenting menu.
STORE " " TO SCHOICE
DO WHILE SCHOICE # "4"
   ERASE
   TEXT

                    Sales System Menu

              1. Enter Point-of-Sale Routine
              2. Print Sales Reports
              3. Edit the Sales Data

              4. Return to Main Menu
   ENDTEXT
   @ 10,15 SAY "Enter choice (1-4) " GET SCHOICE PICTURE "9"
   READ

   *************** Branch to appropriate program.
   DO CASE

      CASE SCHOICE = "1"
           DO POS

      CASE SCHOICE = "2"
           DO SALREPS

      CASE SCHOICE = "3"
           DO SALEDIT

   ENDCASE

ENDDO (while schoice # 4)

*************** When done, release memory variable
*************** and return to main menu.
RELEASE SCHOICE
RETURN
```

Figure 11.2: The SMENU.CMD command file.

sales transactions as follows. First, a prompt for the part number appears on the screen as below:

| 10/10/84 | | Invoice Number: 23456 | |
| Clerk :ACS | | : Customer : | Jane Doe : |

Part #	Name	Qty	Price	Total
:_ :				

The user then types in a part number. If the part number does not exist, the screen provides a warning, as shown below:

| 10/10/84 | Invoice Number: 23456 |
| Clerk :ACS | : Customer :   Jane Doe : |

Part #	Name	Qty	Price	Total
:300-Z: No such part number!!!				

At this point, the user can try again. If he types in a valid number, the name of the part and prompts for filling in the quantity and selling price will appear automatically:

| 10/10/84 | Invoice Number: 23456 |
| Clerk :ACS | : Customer :   Jane Doe : |

Part #	Name	Qty	Price	Total
:A-111:	Snowshoes	:_ :	:	. :

If the user types in 5 as the quantity sold, and $10.00 as the selling price, the screen fills in the subtotal and awaits the next part number:

| 10/10/84 | Invoice Number: 23456 |
| Clerk :ACS | : Customer :   Jane Doe : |

Part #	Name	Qty	Price	Total
:A-111:	Snowshoes	: 5:	: 10.00:	$50.00
:_ :				

If the user types in another valid transaction with the quantity sold and the selling price, the screen will again calculate and display the subtotal:

| 10/10/84 | Invoice Number: 23456 |
| Clerk :ACS | : Customer :   Jane Doe : |

Part #	Name	Qty	Price	Total
:A-111:	Snowshoes	: 5:	: 10.00:	$50.00
:Z-999:	Bearskin Rugs	: 1:	: 100.00:	$100.00
:_ :				

If there are no more items to include in this invoice, the user simply presses RETURN, rather than typing in a part number. The grand total of the invoice, as well as a prompt to pause the screen, will be displayed as follows:

```
10/10/84                       Invoice Number: 23456
Clerk :ACS                     : Customer :     Jane Doe :
```

Part #	Name	Qty	Price	Total
:A-111:	Snowshoes :	5:	: 10.00:	$50.00
:Z-999:	Bearskin Rugs:	1:	: 100.00:	$100.00
:	:			

Total $150.00

Do another? (Y/N) :_:

The user can create a new invoice with a new number by entering Y. When he is done entering invoices, the user merely answers N to the question "Do another? (Y/N)." The sales menu will reappear at this point.

The name of the point-of-sale command file is POS.CMD, and its pseudocode is presented in Figure 11.3.

The first task of the POS.CMD program is to determine the invoice number of the last transaction entered by the user. This is accomplished by simply storing the invoice number of the last transaction entered to a memory variable called MINVOICE in the the first routine of POS.CMD, as follows:

```
* * * * * * * * * * * * * * * * * * * * * * * * * * * * * * * * * * POS.CMD
* * * * * Point-of-sale data entry program for sales.

* * * * * Get next available invoice number from the
* * * * * SALES file.
SET DEFA TO B
USE SALES
GO BOTT
STORE INVOICE:NO TO MINVOICE
```

The POS program uses both the MASTER file, for checking the validity of part numbers and getting the titles, and the SALES data file, for storing sales transactions. The next lines set up the appropriate relationship:

```
* * * * Set up primary and secondary data files.
SELECT PRIMARY
USE MASTER INDEX MASTER
SELECT SECONDARY
USE SALES INDEX SALES
```

The next job of the command file is to set up a loop that will continue adding invoices. The variable AGAIN will control this loop.

Get next available invoice number from the SALES file

Set up primary (MASTER) and secondary (SALES) data files

Set up loop for displaying invoice forms
    Display top portion of invoice on the screen
    Increment invoice number by one
    Initialize memory variables
    Get top portion of invoice
    Start loop for each item on the invoice

        Set up loop for individual lines on the invoice

        Start loop to check validity of part number

            Ask for part number

            Make sure part number exists

            Decide what to do next based upon existence of part number

            Case 1: No part number was entered
                    End program

            Case 2: Part does not exist
                    Warn user, try again

            Case 3: Part does exist
                    Fill in title of part
                    Ask for quatity and selling price
                    Calculate and display subtotal
                    Calculate grand total
                    Add a blank record to SALES file,
                        then fill in the fields

        Continue loop (for valid part numbers)

    Continue loop (for individual invoice lines)

    Display grand total, and pause before next invoice

Continue loop for invoices while user does not request to exit

Release memory variables, close data files
Return to sales menu

Figure 11.3: Pseudocode for the POS.CMD program.

Each invoice should have a unique invoice number, so the variable MINVOICE will be incremented by one for each invoice. Also, the memory variables MCLERK and MCUST need to be initialized to store the salesman and customer names. The grand total of the invoice will be stored in the memory variable TOTAL, which must be initialized to zero for each invoice. Then, the top portion of the invoice will be displayed on the screen for the user to fill out. These lines handle those jobs:

```
***************** Start loop for filling in invoices.
STORE "Y" TO AGAIN
DO WHILE AGAIN = "Y"
   *************** Set up top portion of screen.
   ERASE
   STORE MINVOICE + 1 TO MINVOICE
   STORE "              " TO MCLERK,MCUST
   STORE 0 TO TOTAL
   @ 1,2 SAY T:DATE
   @ 1,30 SAY "Invoice number: " + STR(MINVOICE,5)
   @ 2,2 SAY "Clerk " GET MCLERK
   @ 2,35 SAY "Customer " GET MCUST
   @ 3,1 SAY     "----------------------------------"
   @ 4,1 SAY " Part #      Name        Qty   Price    Total"
   READ
```

Next, the command file must start a loop for each individual item on the invoice. The loop will begin accepting transactions at line six on the screen, and will continue accepting transactions until the screen is full (ROW = 20), or the user does not enter a part number (PARTNUMB = " "). These lines set up the variables and begin the loop:

```
************ Start loop for each item on ticket.
STORE 6 TO ROW
STORE "X" TO PARTNUMB

DO WHILE ROW < 20 .AND. PARTNUMB # " "
   STORE " " TO PARTNUMB
```

Next, we must create another loop to check the validity of part numbers. The variable OK will be true once a valid part number (or request to quit adding line items) is entered. To assure that the loop occurs at least once, the variable OK will be initialized as false. These lines set up that loop:

```
STORE F TO OK

******* Start loop to check part numbers.
DO WHILE .NOT. OK
```

The quantity and selling price of items sold will be stored in the memory variables QUANTITY and SEL:PRICE, so these must be initialized to zero in the lines below:

```
* * * * * * * * * * Set up ticket memory variables.
STORE 0 TO QUANTITY
STORE 0.00 TO SEL:PRICE
```

Now the command file can ask for the part number of the item sold, and store the answer to the memory variable PARTNUMB, as follows:

```
* * * * * * * * * * * Ask for part number.
STORE " " TO PARTNUMB
@ ROW,2 GET PARTNUMB
READ
```

Next, the program needs to check that the part number exists, as below:

```
* * * * * * * Make sure part number exists.
STORE !(TRIM(PARTNUMB)) TO PARTNUMB
SELE PRIM
FIND &PARTNUMB
```

We must set up a DO CASE clause to handle the next task, which is based upon whether the user requests to exit, enters an invalid part number, or enters a valid part number. If the user doesn't enter a part number, the variable OK is set to true because this is a valid entry, and the OK variable controls the DO WHILE .NOT. OK loop. The command file then skips the remaining CASE options, since the user is exiting, as shown below:

```
* * * * * * * * Decide what to do next based upon
* * * * * * * * existence of part number.
DO CASE

    * * Case 1: No part number was entered.
    CASE PARTNUMB = " "
        STORE T TO OK
```

If the user entered a nonexistent part number, the command file must display a warning and loop around to allow the user to try again. The program accomplishes this by making the OK variable false, as shown in the CASE statement below:

```
    * * * * * Case 2: Part does not exist.
    CASE # = 0
        @ ROW,10 SAY "No such part!!!"
        STORE F TO OK
```

If the user entered a valid part number, then the program should proceed and get the rest of the data for the transaction. First, it displays the name of the part (TITLE), then asks for the quantity (QUANTITY) and selling price (SEL:PRICE). These lines handle that task:

```
****** Case 3: Part does exist.
CASE # > 0
   @ ROW,10 SAY TITLE
   @ ROW,25 GET QUANTITY PICT "999"
   @ ROW,30 GET SEL:PRICE;
      PICT "999.99"
   READ
```

The program should then display the subtotal for the transaction, and add that amount to the grand total of the invoice (TOTAL). Also, the program should set the OK variable to true, since a valid part number was entered. The following lines accomplish those jobs.

```
****** Calculate and display subtotal.
@ ROW,40 SAY QUANTITY*SEL:PRICE;
   USING "$#,###.##"
STORE TOTAL + QUANTITY*SEL:PRICE TO;
   TOTAL
STORE T TO OK
```

Once the data are filled in for the transaction, they should be stored on the SALES (secondary) file. An APPEND BLANK command followed by a series of REPLACE commands will handle that job:

```
***** Then fill in one record.
SELECT SECONDARY
APPEND BLANK
REPLACE DATE WITH T:DATE
REPLACE CLERK WITH MCLERK
REPLACE INVOICE:NO WITH MINVOICE
REPLACE CUSTOMER WITH MCUST
REPLACE PART:NO WITH PARTNUMB
REPLACE QTY WITH QUANTITY
REPLACE PRICE WITH SEL:PRICE
REPLACE POSTED WITH F
```

That ends the DO CASE clause, and also the loop for checking the validity of the part number. These lines handle the job:

```
   ENDCASE
ENDDO (while part number not ok)
```

Now the user is ready to enter the next transaction. The variable ROW is incremented by one, since it determines which line on the screen is being used to enter the transaction:

```
    STORE ROW + 1 TO ROW
ENDDO (while still adding transactions)
```

Once the user enters all transactions for the invoice, the program displays the grand total, then asks whether or not to do another invoice, and then continues the loop (if the user wishes to add more invoices). The following lines accomplish these tasks:

```
* * * * * * * * * * * * * * Display grand total, and pause
* * * * * * * * * * * * * * before next invoice.
@ ROW,40 SAY TOTAL USING "$#,###.##"
@ ROW+2,2 SAY "Do another? (Y/N) ";
    GET AGAIN PICTURE "!"
    READ

ENDDO (while again = y)
```

When the user is done adding invoices, the command file can release all memory variables, close the primary and secondary data files, and return to the SMENU command file. These lines will do the trick:

```
* * * * * * * * * Release memory variables, close data
* * * * * * * * * files, and return to sales menu.
RELEASE MINVOICE,MCUST,QUANTITY,SEL:PRICE
RELEASE AGAIN,ROW,PARTNUMB,MCLERK,TOTAL,OK
SELE SECO
USE
SELE PRIM
USE
RETURN
```

Although the POS.CMD program is complex, it provides a great deal of convenience for the user. It also minimizes the likelihood of errors because it checks the validity of the part numbers typed in, and it performs all calculations. It is a very general point-of-sale program, and would probably need to be modified to suit the exact needs of a particular business. But the general procedures of looking up data on the master file, automatically calculating and filing in data, and storing the data on the sales transaction file will be the same for most point-of-sale programs. Figure 11.4 shows the entire POS.CMD command file.

Sales System Reports

Option 2 from the sales system menu allows the user to print reports from the sales database. Reports can be based on either a single

```
*************************************** POS.CMD
***** Point-of-sale data entry program for sales.

***** Get next available invoice number from the
***** SALES file.
SET DEFA TO B
USE SALES
GO BOTT
STORE INVOICE:NO TO MINVOICE

**** Set up primary and secondary data files.
SELECT PRIMARY
USE MASTER INDEX MASTER
SELECT SECONDARY
USE SALES INDEX SALES

*********** Set up loop for filling in invoices.
STORE "Y" TO AGAIN
DO WHILE AGAIN = "Y"
    *************** Set up top portion of screen.
    ERASE
    STORE MINVOICE + 1 TO MINVOICE
    STORE "             " TO MCLERK,MCUST
    STORE 0 TO TOTAL
    @ 1,2 SAY T:DATE
    @ 1,30 SAY "Invoice number: "+STR(MINVOICE,5)
    @ 2,2 SAY "Clerk " GET MCLERK
    @ 2,35 SAY "Customer " GET MCUST
    @ 3,1 SAY "--------------------------------------"
    @ 4,1 SAY "  Part #      Name       Qty  Price    Total"
    READ

    ************* Start loop for each item on ticket.
    STORE 6 TO ROW
    STORE "X" TO PARTNUMB

    DO WHILE ROW < 20 .AND. PARTNUMB # " "
        STORE "     " TO PARTNUMB
        STORE F TO OK

        ******* Start loop to check part numbers.
        DO WHILE .NOT. OK

            *********** Set up ticket memory variables.
            STORE 0 TO QUANTITY
            STORE 0.00 TO SEL:PRICE

            ************ Ask for part number.
            STORE "      " TO PARTNUMB
            @ ROW,2 GET PARTNUMB
            READ

        ******* Make sure part number exists.
        STORE !(TRIM(PARTNUMB)) TO PARTNUMB
        SELE PRIM
        FIND &PARTNUMB

            ******** Decide what to do next based upon
            ******** existence of part number.
            DO CASE
```

Figure 11.4: The POS.CMD command file.

```
            ** Case 1: No part number was entered.
            CASE PARTNUMB=" "
                STORE T TO Ok

            ***** Case 2: Part does not exist.
            CASE # = 0
                @ ROW,10 SAY "No such part!!!"
                STORE F TO OK

            ****** Case 3: Part does exist.
            CASE # > 0
                @ ROW,10 SAY TITLE
                @ ROW,25 GET QUANTITY PICT "999"
                @ ROW,30 GET SEL:PRICE;
                   PICT "999.99"
                READ

            ****** Calculate and display subtotal.
            @ ROW,40 SAY QUANTITY*SEL:PRICE;
                USING "$#,###.##"
            STORE TOTAL + QUANTITY*SEL:PRICE TO;
                TOTAL
            STORE T TO OK

            ***** Then fill in one record.
            SELECT SECONDARY
            APPEND BLANK
            REPLACE DATE WITH T:DATE
            REPLACE CLERK WITH MCLERK
            REPLACE INVOICE:NO WITH MINVOICE
            REPLACE CUSTOMER WITH MCUST
            REPLACE PART:NO WITH PARTNUMB
            REPLACE QTY WITH QUANTITY
            REPLACE PRICE WITH SEL:PRICE
            REPLACE POSTED WITH F
        ENDCASE
    ENDDO (while part number not ok)
    STORE ROW + 1 TO ROW
ENDDO (while still adding transactions)

*************** Display grand total, and pause
************* before next invoice.
@ ROW,40 SAY TOTAL USING "$#,###.##"
@ ROW+2,2 SAY "Do another? (Y/N) ";
    GET AGAIN PICTURE "!"
    READ

ENDDO (while again = y)

********* Release memory variables, close data
********* files, and return to sales menu.
RELEASE MINVOICE,MCUST,QUANTITY,SEL:PRICE
RELEASE AGAIN,ROW,PARTNUMB, MCLERK,TOTAL,OK
SELE SECO
USE
SELE PRIM
USE
RETURN
```

Figure 11.4: *The POS.CMD command file (continued).*

invoice number, or sales transactions for a range of dates (e.g. all sales transactions from 01/01/84 to 03/31/84). If the user opts to print a report of sales, the following menu appears on the screen:

Sales Report Options
1. By Invoice Number
2. By Dates
3. Return to Sales Menu

If the user selects option 1, the screen asks:

Look for what invoice number? :_

The user types in the invoice number, and the screen (or printer) displays data from the invoice, as shown below:

```
Invoice number : 12345        Date 05/04/84
Clerk: ACS                    Customer :D. Jones
Part #            Qty.  Price  Total
Z-999             2     12.00  24.00
A-113             3     15.00  45.00
A-111             1     90.00  90.00
```

If the user selects menu option 2 to display data for a range of dates, the screen will ask the user to:

Enter start date :   / / :
Enter end date :   / / :

The user can then type in the range of dates. At this point, the screen (or printer) will display a summary of all sales transactions for the period, as shown below:

PAGE NO. 00001   For Dates 05/05/84 to 05/06/84
05/06/84

Sales Transactions

Date	Invoice	Salesman	Customer	Part #	Qty.	Sale Price
05/05/84	123	SHS	D. Jones	A-111	2	20.00
05/05/84	123	SHS	D. Jones	A-113	2	14.00
05/05/84	123	SHS	D. Jones	Z-999	4	50.00
05/06/84	124	ACS	A. Smith	Z-999	3	25.00
05/06/84	124	ACS	A. Smith	A-111	5	10.00
05/06/84	125	CGG	Z. Zeppo	Z-999	3	30.00

You can create the summary report with dBASE's REPORT command.

From the dot prompt, type in the commands:

```
USE SALES
REPORT FORM SALES
```

and fill out the REPORT FORM questionnaire as follows:

```
ENTER OPTIONS, M=LEFT MARGIN, L=LINES/PAGE, W=PAGE
WIDTH M=1,W=65
PAGE HEADING? (Y/N) Y
ENTER PAGE HEADING: Sales Transactions
DOUBLE SPACE REPORT? (Y/N) N
ARE TOTALS REQUIRED? (Y/N) N
COL    WIDTH,CONTENTS
001    9,DATE
ENTER HEADING: Date
002    7,INVOICE:NO
ENTER HEADING: Invoice
003    14,CLERK
ENTER HEADING: Salesman
004    14,CUSTOMER
ENTER HEADING: Customer
005    6,PART:NO
ENTER HEADING: Part #
006    5,QTY
ENTER HEADING: Qty.
007    10,PRICE
ENTER HEADING: Sale Price
008
```

The command file that asks the user which report he wishes and that displays the reports is called SALREPS.CMD. Its pseudocode is presented in Figure 11.5.

The program starts by using the SALES file without an index. Recall that the index maintains an order by part number. For these reports, we want the sales transactions grouped by date and invoice number. Because the point-of-sale program automatically generates invoice numbers and fills in the dates, the records will be in the date order when no index file is used. The first line of the SALREPS command file opens the SALES database without an index file:

```
******************************* SALREPS.CMD
**************** Print reports from the sales file.
USE SALES
```

Next, we need to set up a loop for the menu. We also need to have the user's menu choice stored in the memory variable REPCHOICE, and the user's decision on printing the report stored to variable YN.

> Use the SALES data file
> Start a loop for the menu
> Present options
>
>   1. By Invoice Number
>   2. By Dates
>   3. Return to Sales Menu
> Get user's choice
>
> If not exiting, ask about the printer
>
> Print appropriate report based upon request
>
>   Case 1: Search by invoice number
>   Ask user for invoice number to print
>   Locate first transaction with that invoice number
>   If printer requested, set printer on
>   Print header information from first record
>   with that invoice number
>   Print data from remaining records with that
>   invoice number
>   Set the printer off
>
>   Case 2: Search by dates
>   Store blanks to search dates
>   Ask for starting date
>   Ask for ending date
>   Clear the screen
>   Set up macro for date search.
>   Set up macro for printer, if requested
>   Set up date heading for report
>   Print the report using SALES.FRM file
>
> If not going to printer, and not exiting, pause the screen
> Continue loop through menu (while user does not request exit)
> When done, release and return to SMENU

Figure 11.5: Pseudocode for SALREPS.PRG command file.

These lines set up the variables and the loop, then display the menu and wait for a response:

```
STORE " " TO REPCHOICE,YN
DO WHILE REPCHOICE # "3"
   ERASE
   TEXT
```

Sales Report Options
1. By Invoice number
2. By Dates
3. Return to Sales Menu
```
ENDTEXT
@ 8,12 SAY "Enter choice (1-3) ";
   GET REPCHOICE PICT "9"
READ
```

Next, add lines to ask the user if the report should be printed in hardcopy, as below:

```
************************* Ask about printer.
ERASE
STORE " " TO YN, PRINTER
IF REPCHOICE # "3"
   @ 5,5 SAY "Send to printer? ";
      GET YN PICT "!"
   READ
ENDIF (repchoice # 3)
```

Note that the command file only asks about the printer if the user did not pick option 3 (Return to main menu).

We must add a DO CASE clause so that the user can print the appropriate report. If the user wishes to print by invoice number, then the command file must ask for the invoice to print, find the first record with that invoice number, display the basic heading information (number, date, salesman, and customer), then list data from the various transactions associated with the invoice number. These lines handle that task:

```
****************** Print appropriate report.
ERASE
DO CASE
   ********* Case 1: Search by invoice number.
   CASE REPCHOICE = "1"
   INPUT "Look for what invoice number? ";
      TO ISEARCH
   ERASE
   LOCATE FOR INVOICE:NO = ISEARCH
   ********** If found, print invoice.
   IF .NOT. EOF
      IF YN = "Y"
         SET PRINT ON
      ENDIF (yn = y)
      ? "Invoice number ",INVOICE:NO
      ?? "Date ",DATE
```

```
        ? "Clerk",CLERK,"Customer",CUSTOMER
        ?
        ? "Part # Qty. Price Total"
        LIST OFF WHILE INVOICE:NO = ISEARCH;
           PART:NO,QTY,PRICE,(QTY*PRICE)
        EJECT
        SET PRINT OFF
    ENDIF (not eof)
```

If the user requests report option 2, the command file must ask for the starting and ending dates, and then use the SALES.FRM REPORT FORM file to print the report for all records that fall within the dates requested. The second CASE statement handles this:

```
        ******* Case 2: Search by dates.
    CASE REPCHOICE = "2"
        STORE "          " TO START,END
        @ 5,3 SAY "Enter start date ";
           GET START PICT "99/99/99"
        @ 7,3 SAY "Enter end date ";
           GET END PICT "99/99/99"
        READ
        ERASE

        ****** Set up macro for date search.
        STORE "FOR DATE >= START .AND. ;
           DATE <= END" TO MACRO
        ****** Set up macro for printer.
        IF YN="Y"
           STORE "TO PRINT" TO PRINTER
        ELSE
           STORE " " TO PRINTER
        ENDIF

        ******* Set up heading.
        SET HEAD TO For Dates &START to &END

        ******* Print the report.
        REPORT FORM SALES &MACRO &PRINTER

    ENDCASE
```

Notice the use of macros in the above lines of code. The user enters the starting and ending dates for which to print data, and the command file stores these in the memory variables START and END. Then the line:

    STORE "FOR DATE >= START .AND. DATE <= END" TO MACRO

creates a memory variable called MACRO. Also, if the user requested to use the printer, an IF clause stores the words "TO PRINT" to a variable called PRINTER.

Let's assume that the user entered 01/01/84 as the start date, and 03/31/84 as the end date, and answered yes (Y) to the printer question. The command file contains this line:

    REPORT FORM SALES &MACRO &PRINTER

When running the program, dBASE will substitute in the two macros, so the line that dBASE processes is:

    REPORT FORM SALES FOR DATE >= START .AND. DATE <= END;
       TO PRINT

This assures that only the records which fall within the requested range of dates will be sent to the report.

The next routine in SALREPS merely pauses the report on the screen if the user did not request to print the report or exit the program:

    ********* If not going to printer,
    ********* or exiting, pause the screen.
    IF YN # "Y" .AND. REPCHOICE # "3"
       ?
       ?
       WAIT
    ENDIF (yn # y)

The remaining lines close the DO WHILE loop, and release memory variables prior to returning to the SMENU command file.

    ENDDO (while choice # 3)

    **** When done, release and return to SMENU.
    RELE REPCHOICE,YN,PRINTER,START,END,MACRO,ISEARCH
    RETURN

Figure 11.6 shows the complete SALREPS command file.

A Note on Dates

The method we've used to search for sales transactions within a range of dates will only work reliably on a database that has dates that fall within a single year. If the dates spread across several years, some modifications will be necessary.

To understand the problem, try to think like a computer. Suppose a database contains dates from both 1984 and 1985. The user asks to see all records that fall between 01/01/85 and 01/31/85. The program, then,

```
******************************************* SALREPS.CMD
**************** Print reports from the sales file.
USE SALES
STORE " " TO REPCHOICE,YN
DO WHILE REPCHOICE # "3"
   ERASE
   TEXT
             Sales Report Options

             1. By Invoice number
             2. By Dates

             3. Return to Sales Menu
   ENDTEXT
   @ 8,12 SAY "Enter choice (1-3) ";
     GET REPCHOICE PICT "9"
   READ

   *********************** Ask about printer.
   ERASE
   STORE " " TO YN, PRINTER
   IF REPCHOICE # "3"
      @ 5,5 SAY "Send to printer? ";
        GET YN PICT "!"
      READ
   ENDIF (repchoice # 3)

   ****************** Print appropriate report.
   ERASE
   DO CASE

      ******** Case 1: Search by invoice number.
      CASE REPCHOICE = "1"
           INPUT "Look for what invoice number? ";
                 TO ISEARCH
           ERASE
           LOCATE FOR INVOICE:NO=ISEARCH
           ********* If found, print invoice.
           IF .NOT. EOF
              IF YN = "Y"
                 SET PRINT ON
              ENDIF (yn=y)
              ? "Invoice number ",INVOICE:NO
              ?? "Date ",DATE
              ? "Clerk",CLERK,"Customer",CUSTOMER
              ?
              ? "Part #   Qty.     Price     Total"
              LIST OFF WHILE INVOICE:NO = ISEARCH;
                   PART:NO,QTY,PRICE,(QTY*PRICE)
              EJECT
              SET PRINT OFF
           ENDIF (not eof)

      ******* Case 2: Search by dates.
      CASE REPCHOICE = "2"
           STORE "        " TO START,END
           @ 5,3 SAY "Enter start date ";
                GET START PICT "99/99/99"
```

Figure 11.6: The SALREPS.CMD command file.

```
                @ 7,3 SAY "Enter end date ";
                    GET END PICT "99/99/99"
            READ
            ERASE

            ****** Set up macro for date search.
            STORE "FOR DATE >= START .AND. ;
                DATE <= END" TO MACRO
            ****** Set up macro for printer.
            IF YN="Y"
                STORE "TO PRINT" TO PRINTER
            ELSE
                STORE " " TO PRINTER
            ENDIF

            ******* Set up heading.
            SET HEAD TO For Dates &START to &END

            ******* Print the report.
            REPORT FORM SALES &MACRO &PRINTER
   ENDCASE
   ********* If not going to printer,
   ********* pause the screen.
   IF YN # "Y" .AND. REPCHOICE # "3"
       ?
       ?
       WAIT
   ENDIF (yn # y)

ENDDO (while choice # 3)

**** When done, release and return to SMENU.
RELE REPCHOICE,YN,PRINTER,START,END,MACRO,ISEARCH
RETURN
```

Figure 11.6: *The SALREPS.CMD command file (continued).*

uses the following search command to weed out records within the appropriate range of dates:

FOR DATE >= "01/01/85" .AND. DATE <= "01/31/85"

Unfortunately, lots of dates from 1984 will be included in the list, including 01/15/84. For example, the date 01/15/84 would be displayed. If you remove the slashes from the dates, you'll see why: 011584 is greater than 010185, and is less than 013185. Hence, dBASE considers 01/15/84 to be between 01/01/85 and 01/31/84. What can we do about this?

The problem lies in the MM/DD/YY format we usually use for storing dates. Proper comparisons only work if the most significant digit, the year, is considered first. For example, suppose dBASE were to list dates that fall between 85/01/01 and 85/01/31, then 84/01/15 would not be listed, because it is less than 85/01/01 (that is, 840115 is not within the range 850101 to 850131).

So we need to modify the search routine so that it looks at the year first when comparing dates. In the SALREPS command file, dates to search for were stored to the memory variables START and END in MM/DD/YY format. The following lines of code would change these to the necessary YY/MM/DD format:

```
STORE $(START,7,2) + $(START,1,6) TO START
STORE $(END,7,2) + $(END,1,6) TO END
```

Next, the data in the DATE field must be switched to the YY/MM/DD format to make the comparison also, as in the FOR statement below:

```
FOR $(DATE,7,2)+$(DATE,1,6) >= START .AND.;
   $(DATE,7,2)+$(DATE,1,6) <= END
```

Let's examine the routines. The two STORE commands flip the year to the front of the dates stored in the variables START and END. Then the FOR command compares the database dates (modified in the same fashion to YY/MM/DD) to the modified START and END dates.

Dates should be converted to YY/MM/DD when sorting a database also. For example, if you wanted to sort the SALES database by the DATE field, it would be best to use the command:

```
INDEX ON $(DATE,7,2)+$(DATE,1,6) TO SALDATES
```

To find a particular date, or list all records with a particular date, you would have to use a routine as below:

```
******** Get date to search for (MM/DD/YY format).
STORE " " TO LOOKFOR
@ 5,5 SAY "Enter date to look up ";
   GET LOOKFOR PICT "99/99/99"
READ

******** Convert date to YY/MM/DD format.
STORE $(LOOKFOR,7,2)+$(LOOKFOR,1,6) TO LOOKFOR

******** Find first record with that date.
FIND &LOOKFOR

******** List all records with that date.
LIST WHILE $(DATE,7,2)+$(DATE,1,6) <= LOOKFOR
```

There is an alternative procedure: The user could simply enter all the dates in YY/MM/DD format. This would eliminate the need to move the year to the front, as in the routine above. However, people are accustomed to filling in dates in a MM/DD/YY format, so it is easier for the user if we add a special routine. Just remember, in any search for data that fall within a given range of dates, the year must be placed first.

Summary

In this chapter we've developed the portion of the inventory system for recording and managing individual sales transactions. The SALES.DBF database stores the sales transaction data. The SMENU.CMD command file presents a menu of options for managing the sales transactions.

The POS.CMD allows the user to enter sales data. A number of programming techniques were discussed in this program to:

- Check the validity of a part number, and fill in the part name automatically.
- Permit several individual transactions to be stored on a single invoice.
- Subtotal and total invoice transactions automatically.

During the development of the SALREPS.CMD command file, we discussed techniques for displaying data within a range of dates. We also discussed techniques for handling dates stored in MM/DD/YY format.

The third option in the SMENU is to edit the SALES file. This will be discussed in Chapter 13 under updating. In the next chapter, we'll develop the portion of the inventory system used to record new incoming stock.

CHAPTER 12
INVENTORY NEW STOCK SYSTEM

The new stock portion of the inventory allows the user to record new items that come into the store. These data are stored on the NEWSTOCK.DBF data file, which we created previously with the following structure:

STRUCTURE FOR FILE: B:NEWSTOCK.DBF

FLD	NAME	TYPE	WIDTH	DEC
001	PART:NO	C	005	
002	QTY	N	004	
003	COST	N	009	002
004	DATE	C	008	
005	VENDOR	C	025	
006	POSTED	L	001	

We created the index file NEWSTOCK.NDX by typing in the command INDEX ON PART:NO TO NEWSTOCK.

At this point, the user is able to select option 3 from the inventory system main menu. He will then be presented the following new stock menu:

New Stock System Menu
1. Record New Items
2. Print New Stock Reports
3. Edit the New Stock Data
4. Return to Main Menu

Notice that this menu is very similar to the sales system menu. Both of these menus will allow the user to do the following: add transactions, print reports, edit data, or return to the inventory system main menu.

New Stock System Software Structure

Let's examine the new stock system software structure. The new stock system consists of the four command files listed below:

1. NMENU, which presents the menu.
2. NEWSTOCK, which allows the user to add new data.
3. NEWREPS, which prints reports.
4. NEWEDIT, which allows for editing.

Figure 12.1 shows the software structure for this portion of the inventory system. In this figure, you will see how each of the four command files work together.

New Stock System Menu

The menu for the new stock portion of the inventory system is handled by the NMENU.CMD command file. Since it is a simple menu program, it is presented in Figure 12.2. We'll develop the NEWSTOCK.CMD and NEWREPS.CMD command files in this chapter, then create NEWEDIT.CMD in the next.

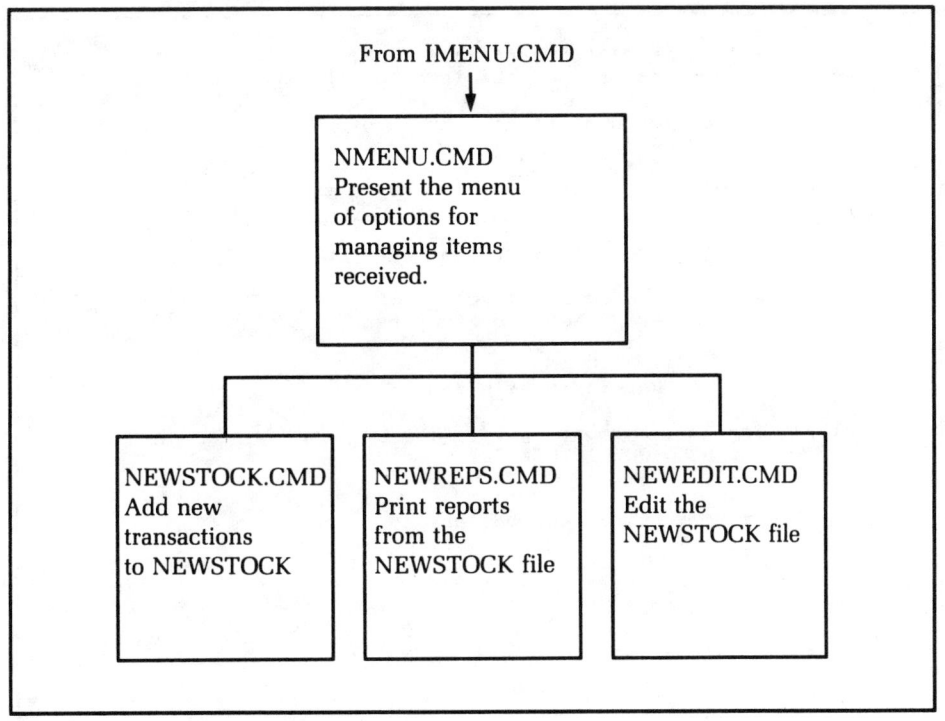

```
                    From IMENU.CMD
                           │
                           ▼
              ┌──────────────────────┐
              │ NMENU.CMD            │
              │ Present the menu     │
              │ of options for       │
              │ managing items       │
              │ received.            │
              └──────────────────────┘
                           │
          ┌────────────────┼────────────────┐
          │                │                │
┌───────────────────┐ ┌───────────────┐ ┌───────────────┐
│ NEWSTOCK.CMD      │ │ NEWREPS.CMD   │ │ NEWEDIT.CMD   │
│ Add new           │ │ Print reports │ │ Edit the      │
│ transactions      │ │ from the      │ │ NEWSTOCK file │
│ to NEWSTOCK       │ │ NEWSTOCK file │ │               │
└───────────────────┘ └───────────────┘ └───────────────┘
```

Figure 12.1: Software structure for new stock system.

New Stock Data-Entry Program

When the user selects option 1 from the NEWSTOCK system menu, the screen will clear, then the following prompt will appear:

    Enter data for goods received
    Part number :_   :

If the user types in an invalid part number, an audible beep sounds, and this screen message appears:

    Enter data for goods received
    Part number :X-999: No such part!!!

At this point, the user will be given an opportunity to try again. If he enters a valid part number this time, the screen will display the name of the part, the date of the transaction, and the vendor (which may be changed, if necessary), and prompts for filling in the quantity received

```
*************************************** NMENU.CMD
** Menu for new stock part of the inventory system

***** Set up loop for presenting menu.
STORE " " TO NCHOICE
DO WHILE NCHOICE # "4"
    ERASE
    TEXT

                    New Stock System Menu

                    1. Record New Items
                    2. Print New Stock Reports
                    3. Edit the New Stock Data

                    4. Return to Main Menu
    ENDTEXT
    @ 10,15 SAY "Enter choice (1-4) ";
            GET NCHOICE PICTURE "9"
    READ

    ************** Branch to appropriate program.
    DO CASE

        CASE NCHOICE = "1"
             DO NEWSTOCK

        CASE NCHOICE = "2"
             DO NEWREPS

        CASE NCHOICE = "3"
             DO NEWEDIT

    ENDCASE

ENDDO (while schoice # 4)

************** When done, release memory variable
************** and return to main menu.
RELEASE NCHOICE
RETURN
```

Figure 12.2: The NMENU.CMD command file.

and the purchase price, as shown below:

    Enter data for goods received
    Part number :A-111:   Snowshoes
    Quantity :_   :   Price :   .:
    Date :10/10/84:   Vendor :American Snowshoe Co. :

Then the user fills in the quantity received and the purchase price, and a new screen asks for the next transaction. When the user is done adding transactions, he presses RETURN rather than typing in a part number. This brings back the NEWSTOCK system menu.

The pseudocode for the NEWSTOCK command file is presented in Figure 12.3.

The NEWSTOCK command file must use the master file for checking the validity of part numbers, and the newstock data file for recording individual transactions. The first few lines set up the two data files as primary and secondary databases:

```
*********************************** NEWSTOCK.CMD
************************* Record goods received.
SELECT PRIMARY
USE MASTER INDEX MASTER
SELECT SECONDARY
USE NEWSTOCK INDEX NEWSTOCK
SELECT PRIMARY
```

Define primary (MASTER) and secondary (NEWSTOCK) data files

Set up loop for recording goods received
    Clear the screen
    Get part number for next transaction

    If a part number was entered
        Find the part number on the master file

        If part cannot be found, warn user,
            and allow another try

        If part number exists
           Display title of part
           Add a blank record to NEWSTOCK.DBF
           Fill in the part number
           Fill in the date received
           Fill in the vendor name
           Get the quantity and cost of items received

Continue loop (while user does not quit)

Release memory variable
Return to the new stock system menu

Figure 12.3: *Pseudocode for the NEWSTOCK.CMD command file.*

Next, the program must begin a loop for adding new transactions. The following lines handle that task:

```
******* Set up loop for recording goods received.
STORE "X" TO PARTNUMB
DO WHILE PARTNUMB # " "
   ERASE
   STORE " " TO PARTNUMB
   @ 2,2 SAY " Enter data for goods received"
   @ 4,4 SAY " Part number " GET PARTNUMB PICT "!!!!!"
   READ
```

If the user does not wish to exit, the program tries to find the part number on the master file using the FIND command as below:

```
IF PARTNUMB # " "
   FIND &PARTNUMB
```

Next, the command file must respond to the user's input: if the user enters an invalid part number, he must be informed; if he enters a valid part number, he should be able to continue. The first CASE statement in the DO CASE clause below handles invalid part numbers:

```
DO CASE
   CASE # = 0
      ****** If part not found, warn user.
      @ 4,25 SAY "No such part!!!"
      ? CHR(7)
```

If the user enters a valid part number, the part title should be presented on the screen, a blank record should be added to the NEW-STOCK.DBF (secondary) file, and data for the transaction should be filled in. The PART:NO, DATE, and VENDOR fields are filled in automatically by data already available to the program, so the user only needs to type in the quantity (QTY) and cost (COST). These lines handle all these tasks:

```
CASE # > 0
   ******* If found, get rest of data.
   @ 4,25 SAY TITLE

   SELECT SECONDARY
   APPEND BLANK
   REPLACE PART:NO WITH PARTNUMB
   REPLACE S.DATE WITH T:DATE
   REPLACE S.VENDOR WITH P.VENDOR
   @ 6,2 SAY "Quantity " GET S.QTY
   @ 6,22 SAY "Price " GET S.COST;
```

```
    PICT "99999.99"
@ 8,2 SAY "Date " GET DATE;
    PICT "99/99/99"
@ 8,22 SAY "Vendor" GET S.VENDOR
READ
SELECT PRIMARY
```

Notice the the field names that are common to both the master (primary) and newstock (secondary) files, QTY, COST, VENDOR, are further specified with either P. for primary (i.e. P.VENDOR), or S. for secondary (S.QTY, S.COST). This ensures that the program uses fields from the correct database.

The remainder of the program simply closes the DO CASE, IF, and DO WHILE statements already in the program. If the user elects to exit, then the PARTNUMB memory variable is released, the secondary and primary files are closed, and the program returns to the NMENU command file:

```
    ENDCASE

  ENDIF (partnumb # " ")

ENDDO (while partnumb # " ")

RELEASE PARTNUMB
SELECT SECONDARY
USE
SELECT PRIMARY
USE
RETURN
```

Figure 12.4 shows the complete NEWSTOCK command file.

NEWSTOCK System Reports

The NEWSTOCK system allows the user to review stock by part number or stock received within a range of dates. These reports can help resolve discrepencies with vendors, or discrepencies between a computer's report and actual availability of stock. Also, these data can allow a store manager to review the sales of a particular item over a period of time, which can help determine reorder points.

When the user opts to print reports, the menu of options appears as below:

New Stock Report Options

1. By Part number
2. By Dates
3. Return to New Stock Menu

```
*********************************** NEWSTOCK.CMD
************************ Record goods received.
SELECT PRIMARY
USE MASTER INDEX MASTER
SELECT SECONDARY
USE NEWSTOCK INDEX NEWSTOCK
SELECT PRIMARY

******* Set up loop for recording goods received.
STORE "X" TO PARTNUMB
DO WHILE PARTNUMB # " "
   ERASE
   STORE "     " TO PARTNUMB
   @ 2,2 SAY " Enter data for goods received"
   @ 4,4 SAY " Part number " GET PARTNUMB PICT "!!!!!"
   READ
   IF PARTNUMB # " "
      FIND &PARTNUMB

         DO CASE

            CASE # = 0
               ****** If part not found, warn user.
               @ 4,25 SAY "No such part!!!"
               ? CHR(7)

            CASE # > 0
               ******* If found, get rest of data.
               @ 4,25 SAY TITLE

               SELECT SECONDARY
               APPEND BLANK
               REPLACE PART:NO WITH PARTNUMB
               REPLACE S.DATE WITH T:DATE
               REPLACE S.VENDOR WITH P.VENDOR
               @ 6,2 SAY "Quantity " GET S.QTY
               @ 6,22 SAY "Price " GET S.COST;
                  PICT "99999.99"
               @ 8,2 SAY "Date " GET DATE;
                  PICT "99/99/99"
               @ 8,22 SAY "Vendor" GET S.VENDOR
               READ
               SELECT PRIMARY

         ENDCASE

   ENDIF (partnumb # " ")

ENDDO ( while partnumb # " ")

RELEASE PARTNUMB
SELECT SECONDARY
USE
SELECT PRIMARY
USE
RETURN
```

Figure 12.4: The NEWSTOCK.CMD command file.

If the user selects option 1, the screen asks if the report should be sent to the printer, then displays the prompt:

Look for what part number? :_   :

The user enters a part number, and all transactions for goods received for that part number are displayed on a report similar to the one below:

PAGE NO. 00001
01/01/80

                    Inventory Items Received

Part Numb.	Qty.	Purchase Price	Date	Vendor name
A-111	15	10.00	02/28/84	American Snowshoes, Inc.
A-111	12	10.00	04/15/84	American Snowshoes, Inc.
A-111	12	10.00	05/10/84	American Snowshoes, Inc.
A-111	12	10.00	06/10/84	American Snowshoes, Inc.
A-111	15	12.00	09/10/84	American Snowshoes, Inc.
A-111	15	12.00	10/10/84	American Snowshoes, Inc.

The user may also view all transactions which occured between two specified dates. When the user selects option 2 from the reports menu, the screen asks:

Enter starting date :_ /   /   :
Enter ending date :   /   /   :

When the user types in the starting and ending dates, the program displays all transactions that transpired between and including those dates in a report similar to the one below:

PAGE NO. 00001   For Dates 10/01/84 to 10/30/84
01/01/80

                    Inventory Items Received

Part Numb.	Qty.	Purchase Price	Date	Vendor name
A-111	15	10.00	10/01/84	American Snowshoes, Inc.
Z-999	10	10.00	10/15/84	Bearskins of La Jolla
A-112	12	24.00	10/20/84	Zeppo's Custom Dog Supply
B-123	23	11.55	10/10/84	Mentor Book Co.

Both report options use a REPORT FORM file called NEWSTOCK-.FRM. It was created by typing in the commands:

USE NEWSTOCK
REPORT FORM NEWSTOCK

from the dBASE dot prompt, and filling out the questionnaire as follows:

```
ENTER OPTIONS, M = LEFT MARGIN, L = LINES/PAGE, W = PAGE
WIDTH m = 1,w = 55
PAGE HEADING? (Y/N) y
ENTER PAGE HEADING: Inventory Items Received
DOUBLE SPACE REPORT? (Y/N) n
ARE TOTALS REQUIRED? (Y/N) n
COL     WIDTH,CONTENTS
001     5,PART:NO
ENTER HEADING: Part Numb.
002     4,QTY
ENTER HEADING: Qty.
003     9,COST
ENTER HEADING: Purchase Price
004     8,DATE
ENTER HEADING: Date
005     25,VENDOR
ENTER HEADING: <Vendor name
006
```

The logic for the NEWREPS.CMD command file is virtually identical to that of the SALREPS.CMD command file in the last chapter.

Like most programs with menus, this one begins by setting up a loop, presenting a menu, and waiting for a response from the user. The user's selection is stored in a memory variable named REPCHOICE. The lines below display the menu and ask for the user's choice:

```
* * * * * * * * * * * * * * * * * * * * * * * * * * * NEWREPS.CMD
* * * * * * * * * * * * * Print reports from the newstock file.
STORE " " TO REPCHOICE,YN
DO WHILE REPCHOICE # "3"
   ERASE
   TEXT

      New Stock Report Options
   1. By Part number
   2. By Dates
   3. Return to New Stock Menu
   ENDTEXT
   @ 8,12 SAY "Enter choice (1-3) ";
      GET REPCHOICE PICT "9"
   READ
```

If the user does not exit the program, the command file should ask about the printer. It does so in the following lines:

```
* * * * * * * * * * * * * * * * * * * * * * * * Ask about printer.
ERASE
STORE " " TO YN, PRINTER
IF REPCHOICE # "3"
    @ 5,5 SAY "Send to printer? ";
       GET YN PICT "!"
    READ
ENDIF (repchoice # 3)
```

If the user answers Y to the "Send to the printer?" prompt, the command file stores the words "TO PRINT" to a memory variable named PRINTER. If the user does not answer Y, the PRINTER variable is left blank. The lines below set up the PRINTER variable, which will later be used as a macro with the REPORT FORM command to determine whether the report is displayed on the screen or printer:

```
* * * * * * Set up macro for printer.
IF YN = "Y"
    STORE "TO PRINT" TO PRINTER
ELSE
    STORE " " TO PRINTER
ENDIF (yn = y)
```

Next, the command file must display the report. If the user requested to display the report by part number, the command file asks him which part number to seek out. To speed processing, the program assigns the NEWSTOCK.NDX (index of part numbers) to the NEWSTOCK.NDX database, and uses the FIND and WHILE commands. The first CASE statement in the DO CASE clause below handles the job of displaying the report by part number:

```
* * * * * * * * * * * * * * * * * Print appropriate report.
ERASE
DO CASE
    * * * * * * * * Case 1: Search by part number.
    CASE REPCHOICE = "1"
    USE NEWSTOCK INDEX NEWSTOCK
    STORE " " TO NSEARCH
       @ 5,5 SAY "Look for what part number? ";
          GET NSEARCH PICT "!!!!!"
       READ
       ERASE
       FIND &NSEARCH
       REPORT FORM NEWSTOCK WHILE;
          PART:NO = NSEARCH &PRINTER
```

If the user wants to display transactions that occurred within a range of dates, the command file first asks for the range of dates to include in the report. Then, as in the SALREPS.CMD command file we created earlier, the START and END dates are used in a macro with the REPORT FORM command to display the report. The CASE clause below handles displaying the report by date:

```
******* Case 2: Search by dates.
CASE REPCHOICE = "2"
   USE NEWSTOCK
   STORE "             " TO START,END
   @ 5,3 SAY "Enter start date ";
      GET START PICT "99/99/99"
   @ 7,3 SAY "Enter end date ";
      GET END PICT "99/99/99"
   READ
   ERASE

   ****** Set up macro for date search.
   STORE "FOR DATE >= START .AND. ;
      DATE <= END" TO MACRO

   ******* Set up heading.
   SET HEAD TO For Dates &START to &END

   ******* Print the report.
   REPORT FORM NEWSTOCK &MACRO &PRINTER
   SET HEADING TO

ENDCASE
```

Finally, if the user selected N at runtime, the program will pause on the screen, then either repeat the loop for the menu, or release memory variables and return to NMENU.CMD. These lines handle those tasks:

```
********* If not going to printer,
********* pause the screen.
IF YN # "Y" .AND. REPCHOICE # "3"
   ?
   ?
   WAIT
ENDIF (yn # y)

ENDDO (while choice # 3)

**** When done, release and return to NMENU.
USE
RELE REPCHOICE,YN,PRINTER,START,END,MACRO,NSEARCH
RETURN
```

Figure 12.5 presents the entire NEWREPS.CMD command file.

```
*********************************** NEWREPS.CMD
************ Print reports from the newstock file.
STORE " " TO REPCHOICE,YN
DO WHILE REPCHOICE # "3"
   ERASE
   TEXT
             New Stock Report Options

             1. By Part number
             2. By Dates

             3. Return to New Stock Menu
   ENDTEXT
   @ 8,12 SAY "Enter choice (1-3) ";
      GET REPCHOICE PICT "9"
   READ

   *********************** Ask about printer.
   ERASE
   STORE " " TO YN, PRINTER
   IF REPCHOICE # "3"
      @ 5,5 SAY "Send to printer? ";
         GET YN PICT "!"
      READ
   ENDIF (repchoice # 3)

     ****** Set up macro for printer.
     IF YN="Y"
        STORE "TO PRINT" TO PRINTER
     ELSE
        STORE " " TO PRINTER
     ENDIF (yn=y)


     ***************** Print appropriate report.
     ERASE
     DO CASE

        ******* Case 1: Search by part number.
        CASE REPCHOICE = "1"
        USE NEWSTOCK INDEX NEWSTOCK
        STORE "      " TO NSEARCH
           @ 5,5 SAY "Look for what part number? ";
                GET NSEARCH PICT "!!!!!"
           READ
           ERASE
           FIND &NSEARCH
           REPORT FORM NEWSTOCK WHILE;
                PART:NO=NSEARCH &PRINTER


        ******* Case 2: Search by dates.
        CASE REPCHOICE = "2"
           USE NEWSTOCK
           STORE "         " TO START,END
           @ 5,3 SAY "Enter start date ";
                GET START PICT "99/99/99"
```

Figure 12.5: The NEWREPS.PRG command file.

```
                @ 7,3 SAY "Enter end date ";
                    GET END PICT "99/99/99"
                READ
                ERASE

                ****** Set up macro for date search.
                STORE "FOR DATE >= START .AND. ;
                   DATE <= END" TO MACRO


                ******* Set up heading.
                SET HEAD TO For Dates &START to &END

                ******* Print the report.
                REPORT FORM NEWSTOCK &MACRO &PRINTER
                SET HEADING TO

           ENDCASE
           ********* If not going to printer,
           ********* pause the screen.
           IF YN # "Y" .AND. REPCHOICE # "3"
              ?
              ?
              WAIT
           ENDIF (yn # y)

      ENDDO (while choice # 3)

      **** When done, release and return to NMENU.
      USE
      RELE REPCHOICE,YN,PRINTER,START,END,MACRO,NSEARCH
      RETURN
```

Figure 12.5: The NEWREPS.PRG command file (continued).

Summary

Now we've created all three major portions of the inventory system. However, we still must perform the crucial final step. We need to develop a command file that can read data from both the sales and newstock files, and update the status of the master file based upon those data. We also need to develop programs to allow the user to edit the sales and newstock files after an update has already taken place. We'll develop these in the next chapter.

CHAPTER 13
INVENTORY SYSTEM UPDATING

Now that we've developed the command files to handle the master inventory file and the sales and new stock transaction files, we need to write the program to handle master file updates. The program must subtract the quantities that are in the sales file from the master file, since these items have been sold. Then, it must add the quantities from the new stock file to the master file quantities, since these are now in stock.

Also, the command file must subtract the quantities in the new stock file from the on-order quantities in the master file, since these have been received. Finally, the command file will replace the purchase price of items in the master file with the purchase price in the new stock file, since this is the most recent price. Furthermore, the command file will replace the dates in the master file with the dates in the transaction files as a means of keeping track of when the last update occurred.

Updating the Master File

The user updates the master file by simply selecting option 4 from the master file system menu, which we placed in the command file MMENU.CMD. The command file to perform the update is called UPDATER.CMD. Its pseudocode is presented in Figure 13.1.

The UPDATER command file will clear the screen, then present the message "Updating the master file from the sales file . . ." during what may be a fairly long process. Next, the command file will use the sales file and index, and copy all records that have not already been updated to a temporary (temp) data file, as shown in the lines below:

```
********************************* UPDATER.CMD
** Update the master file from sales and newstock.
ERASE
? "Updating the master file from the sales file . . ."

**** Use the sales file indexed by part number.
USE SALES INDEX SALES
**** Copy all nonupdated records to temp file.
COPY TO TEMP FOR .NOT. POSTED
```

At this point, the temp file has all the records that need to be used to update the master file, except that the quantities are all positive numbers. Since these are sales transactions, they need to be subtracted. The dBASE UPDATE command does not have a subtract option, so we'll need to make all the QTY fields in the temp file negative numbers, then perform the update. Before doing anything, however, the command file should check that there are data in the temp file. The lines below check to make sure there are records in temp, and if so, makes all the QTY fields negative:

```
******** Make sure there are records in temp.
USE TEMP
GO BOTT
IF # > 0
    **** Make all quantities negative numbers.
    REPLACE ALL QTY WITH -1 * QTY
```

Next, the master file with the master index is used, since it is the file being updated:

```
**** Use the master file for updating.
USE MASTER INDEX MASTER
```

Clear the screen
Display a message so user knows computer is working
Use the sales file indexed by part number

Copy all nonupdated records to temp file

Make sure there are records in temp
If there are . . .
   Use the temp file
   Make all quantities negative numbers to subtract

   Use the master file and index for updating

   Update from the temporary sales file, adding the
      quantities and replacing the dates from temp

   Use the original sales file
   And make all POSTED fields "True"

Update master from the newstock file

Copy nonupdated records to temp file

Make sure there are records in temp
   If there are . . .
      Use the master file and index for updates.

      Update from the temporary newstock file, adding the
         quantities and replacing the cost and date

      Make all the POSTED fields True in newstock

      Next, update the master file on-order field
         with the negative equivalent of the
         newstock quantity (QTY) field.
      Make temp primary
      Make master and index secondary
      Set up a loop through the temp file
         For each record in the temp file
            Find identical part number in master
               Subtract new stock quantity from master on-order
               field

Release memory variable
Close data files
Return to MMENU.CMD

Figure 13.1: Pseudocode for UPDATER.CMD.

Then the update is performed, adding the quantities (which are negative numbers in temp), and replacing the dates:

```
**** Update from the temporary sales file.
UPDATE ON PART:NO FROM TEMP ADD QTY REPLACE DATE
```

Next, the records in the sales file must be marked so that they are not accidentally posted again in the future. The POSTED field acts as a flag, and is set to true (T) to indicate that the record has been posted (updated to the master file):

```
**** Go back to the original sales file . . .
USE SALES INDEX SALES
```

```
***** and make all POSTED fields true.
REPLACE NOUPDATE ALL POSTED WITH T
```

Now we can close the IF clause that was used to determine if the temp file had data in it:

```
ENDIF (# > 0)
```

The command file needs to perform a similar update from the newstock file. The newstock file and index are used, and the records that have not been posted yet are copied to a temporary file:

```
******* Now update master from the newstock file.
? "Updating from the new stock file . . . ."
USE NEWSTOCK INDEX NEWSTOCK
```

```
******* Copy nonupdated records to temp file.
COPY TO TEMP FOR .NOT. POSTED
```

Again, to save time and errors, the command file makes sure that there are records in temp before proceeding with the update:

```
******* Check number of records in temp file.
USE TEMP
GO BOTT
IF # > 0
```

Next, the master file and index are put in use again:

```
******* Use the MASTER file for updates.
USE MASTER INDEX MASTER
```

The command file then updates from the temp file, adding the quantities, and replacing the COST and DATE fields:

```
******* Update from the temporary newstock file.
UPDATE ON PART:NO FROM TEMP ADD QTY REPLACE DATE,COST
```

Then, all the POSTED fields in the newstock file must be set to true so that they are not accidentally updated again in the future:

```
******** Make all the POSTED fields true in the newstock file.
USE NEWSTOCK INDEX NEWSTOCK
REPLACE NOUPDATE ALL POSTED WITH T
```

Next, the master file ON:ORDER field must be updated, by subtracting the quantities recently received from the on:order amount. Since the field names (ON:ORDER and QTY) do not match here, we can't use the UPDATE command. Both the temp and master files need to be open at the same time, so we set them up as primary and secondary databases:

```
******* Next, update the master file on-order field
******* with the negative equivalent of the newstock
******* QTY field.
SELECT PRIMARY
USE TEMP
SELECT SECONDARY
USE MASTER INDEX MASTER
```

Now we need to begin a loop through each record of the temp data file:

```
SELECT PRIMARY
DO WHILE .NOT. EOF
```

For each record in the temp file, the command file needs to find the equivalent part number in the master file, then subtract the quantity in the temp file (P.QTY) from the ON:ORDER field in the master file. These lines handle that job:

```
STORE P.PART:NO TO SEARCH
SELECT SECONDARY
FIND &SEARCH
REPLACE ON:ORDER WITH ON:ORDER - P.QTY
```

Then the loop must continue, skipping to the next record in the temp (primary) data file.

```
    SELECT PRIMARY
    SKIP
ENDDO (while .not. eof)
```

To complete the update procedure, we can close the IF clause that determined whether or not there were records in the temp file:

```
ENDIF (# > 0)
```

Our only remaining job is to release a memory variable, close the data files, and return to the MMENU.CMD menu. Here are the correct lines for this procedure:

```
******** Return to MMENU.CMD
RELEASE SEARCH
SELE SECO
USE
SELE PRIM
USE
RETURN
```

Figure 13.2 shows the entire UPDATER.CMD command file.

Editing the Sales File

Now we have a small dilemma. Suppose the user edits a record on the sales file data *after* the update has occurred? For example, suppose the user accidentally records 100 sales of part number A-111, and later discovers the correct number was 10. The user can simply edit the sales file, but the master file would be 90 items off. Or, suppose the user records a sales of 10 part numbers A-111, but later discovers that they were supposed to be part number A-112. Again, when the user makes the correction to the sales file, the master file will be incorrect.

There is a simple solution: write a routine that allows the user to make any changes he wishes to the sales file. Then, that same command file simply makes the appropriate correction to the master file. The logic for doing so is as follows:

1. Allow the user to change data for a record in the sales file.
2. If the user changed a part number, add the quantity to the old part number, and subtract it from the new part number.
3. If the user changed a quantity in the sales file, find the difference between the old quantity and the new quantity, and subtract that difference from the quantity in the master file.

If the user changes the date, we could also change that on the master file, but it is not necessary to do so. The date will still reflect the date of the last update, rather than the date of the edit.

When the user opts to edit the sales file, the screen clears and displays the prompt:

Enter invoice number to edit (0 if none) :_

Inventory System Updating

```
*************************************** UPDATER.CMD
** Update the master file from sales and newstock.
ERASE
? "Updating from the sales file....."

**** Use the sales file indexed by part number.
USE SALES INDEX SALES

**** Copy all nonupdated records to temp file.
COPY TO TEMP FOR .NOT. POSTED

******* Make sure there are records in temp.
USE TEMP
GO BOTT
IF # > 0

   **** Make all quantities negative numbers.
   REPLACE ALL QTY WITH -1 * QTY

   **** Use the master file for updating.
   USE MASTER INDEX MASTER

   **** Update from the temporary sales file.
   UPDATE ON PART:NO FROM TEMP ADD QTY REPLACE DATE

   **** Go back to the original sales file.
   USE SALES INDEX SALES

   ***** And make all POSTED fields "True"
   REPLACE NOUPDATE ALL POSTED WITH T

ENDIF (# > 0)

******* Now update master from the newstock file.
? "Updating from the new stock file....."
USE NEWSTOCK INDEX NEWSTOCK

******* Copy nonupdated records to TEMP file.
COPY TO TEMP FOR .NOT. POSTED

******* Check number of records in temp.
USE TEMP
GO BOTT
IF # > 0

   ******* Use the master file for updates.
   USE MASTER INDEX MASTER

   ******* Update from the temporary newstock file.
   UPDATE ON PART:NO FROM TEMP ADD QTY REPLACE DATE,COST

   ******** Make all the POSTED fields True in newstock.
   USE NEWSTOCK INDEX NEWSTOCK
   REPLACE NOUPDATE ALL POSTED WITH T

   ******* Next, update the master file on-order field
```

Figure 13.2: The UPDATER.CMD command file.

```
      ****** with the negative equivalent of the newstock
      ****** QTY field.
   SELECT PRIMARY
   USE TEMP
   SELECT SECONDARY
   USE MASTER INDEX MASTER
   SELECT PRIMARY
   DO WHILE .NOT. EOF
      STORE P.PART:NO TO SEARCH
      SELECT SECONDARY
      FIND &SEARCH
      REPLACE NOUPDATE ON:ORDER WITH ON:ORDER-P.QTY
      SELECT PRIMARY
      SKIP
   ENDDO (while .not. eof)
ENDIF (# > 0)

******** Return to MMENU.CMD.
RELEASE SEARCH
SELE SECO
USE
SELE PRIM
USE
RETURN
```

Figure 13.2: *The UPDATER.CMD command file (continued).*

The user types in the invoice number, and if there are several part numbers on the invoice, it displays the individual transactions as follows:

```
00099   A-111    10    10.50    ACS    J. Smith    12/12/84
00100   Z-999     3    12.99    ACS    J. Smith    12/12/84
00100   B-232    14    11.99    ACS    J. Smith    12/12/84
         Which line? (left-column number) :_
```

Once the user selects the transaction he wishes to edit or delete, its data are displayed on the screen as shown below:

Edit Sales Transaction . . .

Invoice number :   123:   Part Number :A-111:

Salesman :ACS   :   Customer :J.Smth   :

Quantity :   10:   Selling price :   10.50:   Date :12/12/84:

Delete this record? (Y/N) :   :

On this screen, the user can move the cursor to edit data. Or, he can type Y into the field labeled "Delete the record? (Y/N)" in order to delete the record. The command file will then handle all aspects of adjusting the master file, if necessary, and allow the user to edit more sales transactions.

The command file to allow the user to edit the sales file is called SALEDIT.CMD, and its pseudocode is presented in Figure 13.3.

Now we can develop the SALEDIT command file. Let's begin by setting up a variable to count how many records the user has deleted (NO:DELS), and initializing the variable used to search for invoice numbers (SEARCH) in the first lines:

```
* * * * * * * * * * * * * * * * * * * * * * * * * * * * * SALEDIT.CMD
* * * * * * * * * Edit the sales file, and update the master file.

* * * * * * * * Set up memory variables.
STORE 0 TO NO:DELS
STORE 1 TO SEARCH
```

Next, we must instruct the command file to use the sales file with the sales index, and ask the user for the invoice number that needs editing:

```
* * * * * * * * Get part number for data to edit.
DO WHILE SEARCH < > 0
   USE SALES INDEX SALES
   ERASE
   INPUT "Enter invoice number to edit (0 if none) ";
      TO SEARCH
```

If the user does not request to exit, the command file should count how many records on the data file have the requested invoice number, then store that number to the memory variable HOWMANY:

```
* * If user did not request exit, continue with edit.
IF SEARCH > 0
   * * * Count the records with that invoice number.
   COUNT FOR INVOICE:NO = SEARCH TO HOWMANY
```

If there are no transactions with that invoice number, the screen should warn the user. These lines take care of the task:

```
DO CASE
   * * * If invoice not found, warn user.
   CASE HOWMANY = 0
      ? "          No such invoice number!!"
      ? CHR(7)
```

If several records have that invoice number, the screen should display each transaction and ask for a record number. Then the program can go to that record number. Here are the correct lines for that job:

```
   * * * * If invoice number found, proceed.
   CASE HOWMANY > 0
```

Set up memory variables
Set up loop for invoice numbers

    Use the sales file with the sales index
    Get invoice number for data to edit
    If user does not request exit . . .

    Count the records with that invoice number

        If invoice not found, warn user, and allow another try

        If several records with that invoice found . . .
            Display all transactions with invoice number
            Get record number from user

        Locate record, and store the original values to
            memory variables

        Display data on edit screen and allow edit

        After edit complete, adjust master file
        if record has already been posted, and
        part number or quantity have been changed

            If record posted, but now deleted
                Mark record for deletion
                Locate part number on master file
                Increment inventory quantity by the
                    quantity in sales file

            If record posted, and user changed the part number . . .
                Locate old part number on master file
                Add old quantity back into master quantity
                Find the new part number on master file
                Subtract quantity from master file

            If record posted, and quantity was changed
                Calculate difference between old and new
                    quantities
                Find part number on master file
                Subtract difference from master quantity

Continue loop to allow user more edits

If records have been deleted, pack the sales data file

Release memory variables
Return to SMENU.CMD

Figure 13.3: *The SALEDIT.CMD command file.*

```
***** If several sales transaction have that
***** invoice number, get more information . . .
IF HOWMANY > 1
   ERASE
   LIST FOR INVOICE:NO = SEARCH PART:NO,QTY,;
      PRICE,CLERK,CUSTOMER,DATE
   ?
   INPUT "Which line (left-column number) ";
      TO RECNO
   GOTO RECNO
```

If only one record has the requested invoice number, the program can go directly to that record:

```
***** otherwise, go to the record.
ELSE
   LOCATE FOR INVOICE:NO = SEARCH
   STORE # TO RECNO
ENDIF (howmany > 1)
```

Next, the program stores the original part number and quantity to memory variables OLD:PART and OLD:QTY, so that later it can detect whether or not these fields have been changed:

```
***** Store the original field values to
***** memory variables.
STORE PART:NO TO OLD:PART
STORE QTY TO OLD:QTY
```

Now, the program sets up a screen so the user can edit the data in the record:

```
***** Display edit screen and allow edit.
ERASE
STORE " " TO DELETED
@ 1,1 SAY " Edit Sales Transaction . . . ."
@ 3,1 SAY "Invoice Number " GET INVOICE:NO
@ 3,33 SAY "Part Number " GET PART:NO;
   PICT "!!!!!"
@ 5,1 SAY "Salesman " GET CLERK
@ 5,40 SAY "Customer " GET CUSTOMER
@ 7,1 SAY "Quantity " GET QTY
@ 7,20 SAY "Selling price " GET PRICE
@ 7,45 SAY "Date ";
GET DATE PICT "99/99/99"
@ 9,2 SAY "Delete this record? (Y/N) ";
   GET DELETED PICT "!"

READ
```

If the user edited a record, the program checks to see if the master file needs updating. If the user deleted a record, the program re-adds the quantity from the sales transaction back into the master file, and increments the variable that counts how many records have been marked for deletion:

```
****** After edit complete, adjust master file
****** if necessary.
DO CASE

   **** If sales transaction deleted, re-add its
   **** quantity back to the master file.
   CASE POSTED .AND. DELETED = "Y"
      DELETE
      STORE NO:DELS+1 TO NO:DELS
      USE MASTER INDEX MASTER
      FIND &OLD:PART
      REPL QTY WITH QTY+OLD:QTY
```

If the user changed the part number, the program adds the quantity from the sales file back into the old part number on the master file (since it originally subtracted it). Then, it subtracts the quantity of the sale from the new part number on the master file:

```
***** If part number changed, add quantity
***** to old part number, and subtract from
***** the new part number.
CASE POSTED .AND. PART:NO # OLD:PART
   STORE QTY TO NEW:QTY
   STORE PART:NO TO NEW:PART
   USE MASTER INDEX MASTER
   FIND &OLD:PART
   REPLACE QTY WITH QTY+OLD:QTY
   FIND &NEW:PART
   REPLACE QTY WITH QTY-NEW:QTY
```

If the user changed only the quantity of the sale, the program adjusts the quantity on the master file accordingly:

```
          ***** If user changed only the quantity,
          ***** adjust the master file quantity.
          CASE POSTED .AND. QTY # OLD:QTY
             STORE QTY-OLD:QTY TO DIFF
             USE MASTER INDEX MASTER
             FIND &OLD:PART
             REPLACE QTY WITH QTY-DIFF

       ENDCASE
     ENDCASE
   ENDIF (search > 0)

ENDDO (while search > 0)
```

Finally, the program packs the deleted records from the sales file if necessary:

```
******************* If records have been deleted,
******************* pack the sales data file.
IF NO:DELS > 0
   ERASE
   ? "Packing deleted records from the sales file . . ."
   USE SALES INDEX SALES
   PACK
ENDIF (no.dels > 0)
```

Then it releases the memory variables, and returns to the SMENU.CMD command file:

```
***** Release memory variables.
RELEASE OLD:QTY,OLD:PART,NEW:PART,NO:DELS
RELEASE SEARCH,HOWMANY,DIFF,DELETED
USE
RETURN
```

Figure 13.4 shows the complete SALEDIT.CMD command file.

Editing the New Stock File

The procedure for editing the newstock file and updating the master file accordingly is very similar to the procedure used in the SALEDIT.CMD program. However, the edit program for the newstock file has to take into consideration changes to the master file COST and ON:ORDER fields since the master file gets this information directly from the newstock database. Another difference is that when the user wants to edit records, he'll have to do so based on the PART:NO field in the newstock file, because there is no invoice number field as in the sales data file.

The NEWEDIT.CMD command file handles edits to the NEWSTOCK.DBF database. At the outset, it looks very similar to the SALEDIT program, except that it asks the user for the part number, rather than the invoice number, of the transaction to edit, as shown in the opening lines to the program below:

```
******************************** NEWEDIT.CMD
********* Edit the newstock file, and update the master file.

******** Set up memory variables.
STORE 0 TO NO:DELS
```

```
*********************************** SALEDIT.CMD
********* Edit the sales file, and update master.

******** Set up memory variables.
STORE 0 TO NO:DELS
STORE 1 TO SEARCH

******** Get part number for data to edit.
DO WHILE SEARCH <> 0
   USE SALES INDEX SALES
   ERASE
   INPUT "Enter invoice number to edit (0 if none) ";
         TO SEARCH

   ** If user did not request exit, continue with edit.
   IF SEARCH > 0
      *** Count the records with that invoice number.
      COUNT FOR INVOICE:NO = SEARCH TO HOWMANY

      DO CASE

         *** If invoice not found, warn user.
         CASE HOWMANY = 0
            ? "          No such invoice number!!"
            ? CHR(7)

         **** If invoice number found, proceed.
         CASE HOWMANY > 0

         ***** If several sales transaction have that
         ***** invoice number, get more information...
         IF HOWMANY > 1
            ERASE
            LIST FOR INVOICE:NO = SEARCH PART:NO,QTY,;
                 PRICE,CLERK,CUSTOMER,DATE
            ?
            INPUT "Which line (left-column number) ";
                  TO RECNO
            GOTO RECNO
         ***** otherwise, go to the record.
         ELSE
            LOCATE FOR INVOICE:NO = SEARCH
            STORE # TO RECNO
         ENDIF (howmany > 1)

         ***** Store the original field values to
         ***** memory variables.
         STORE PART:NO TO OLD:PART
         STORE QTY TO OLD:QTY

         ***** Display edit screen and allow edit.
         ERASE
         STORE " " TO DELETED
         @ 1,1 SAY " Edit Sales Transaction...."
         @ 3,1 SAY "Invoice Number " GET INVOICE:NO
         @ 3,33 SAY "Part Number " GET PART:NO;
           PICT "!!!!!"
```

Figure 13.4: The SALEDIT.CMD command file.

```
            @ 5,1 SAY "Salesman " GET CLERK
            @ 5,40 SAY "Customer " GET CUSTOMER
            @ 7,1 SAY "Quantity " GET QTY
            @ 7,20 SAY "Selling price " GET PRICE
            @ 7,45 SAY "Date ";
               GET DATE PICT "99/99/99"
            @ 9,2 SAY "Delete this record? (Y/N) ";
               GET DELETED PICT "!"

            READ


            ****** After edit complete, adjust master file
            ****** if necessary.
            DO CASE

               **** If sales transaction deleted, re-add its
               **** quantity back to the master file.
               CASE POSTED .AND. DELETED = "Y"
                    DELETE
                    STORE NO:DELS+1 TO NO:DELS
                    USE MASTER INDEX MASTER
                    FIND &OLD:PART
                    REPL QTY WITH QTY+OLD:QTY

               ***** If part number changed, add quantity
               ***** to old part number, and subtract from
               ***** the new part number.
               CASE POSTED .AND. PART:NO # OLD:PART
                    STORE QTY TO NEW:QTY
                    STORE PART:NO TO NEW:PART
                    USE MASTER INDEX MASTER
                    FIND &OLD:PART
                    REPLACE QTY WITH QTY+OLD:QTY
                    FIND &NEW:PART
                    REPLACE QTY WITH QTY-NEW:QTY

               ***** If user just changed the quantity,
               ***** adjust the master file quantity.
               CASE POSTED .AND. QTY # OLD:QTY
                    STORE QTY-OLD:QTY TO DIFF
                    USE MASTER INDEX MASTER
                    FIND &OLD:PART
                    REPLACE QTY WITH QTY-DIFF
               ENDCASE
         ENDCASE
      ENDIF (search > 0)

ENDDO (while search > 0)
****************** If records have been deleted,
****************** pack the sales data file.
IF NO:DELS > 0
   ERASE
   ? "Packing deleted records from the sales file..."
   USE SALES INDEX SALES
   PACK
ENDIF (no.dels > 0)
```

Figure 13.4: *The SALEDIT.CMD command file (continued).*

```
***** Release memory variables.
RELEASE OLD:QTY,OLD:PART,NEW:PART,NO:DELS
RELEASE SEARCH,HOWMANY,DIFF,DELETED,NEW:QTY
USE
RETURN
```

Figure 13.4: *The SALEDIT.CMD command file (continued).*

```
STORE "1" TO SEARCH

******** Get part number for data to edit.
DO WHILE SEARCH # "0"
   USE NEWSTOCK INDEX NEWSTOCK
   ERASE
   ACCEPT "Enter part number to edit (0 if none) ";
      TO SEARCH
   STORE !(SEARCH) TO SEARCH
```

Then, the program counts how many records in the newstock file have the requested part number:

```
** If user did not request exit, continue with edit.
IF SEARCH # "0"
   *** Count the records with that part number.
   FIND &SEARCH
   COUNT WHILE PART:NO = !(SEARCH) TO HOWMANY
```

If the requested part number does not exist, the program gives the user a warning:

```
DO CASE
   *** If part not found, warn user.
   CASE HOWMANY = 0
      ? "        No such part number!!"
      ? CHR(7)
```

If several records on the newstock file have the requested part number, then they are displayed and the user is requested to pick one by number:

```
   **** If part number found, proceed.
   CASE HOWMANY > 0

   ***** If several new stock transaction have that
   ***** part number, get more information.
   IF HOWMANY > 1
      ERASE
      FIND &SEARCH
```

```
        LIST WHILE PART:NO = !(SEARCH) PART:NO,QTY,;
           COST,DATE,VENDOR
        ?
        INPUT "Which line (left-column number) ";
           TO RECNO
     GOTO RECNO
```

If only one record on the newstock file has the requested part number, then that record is located and its record number is stored to a variable called RECNO:

```
        ***** otherwise, go to the record.
     ELSE
        FIND &SEARCH
        STORE # TO RECNO
     ENDIF (howmany > 1)
```

Next, the program stores some of the original field data for the record to be edited to memory variables. Once again, this allows the command file to make decisions about updating the master file after the edit takes place:

```
        ***** Store the original field values to
        ***** memory variables.
        STORE PART:NO TO OLD:PART
        STORE QTY TO OLD:QTY
        STORE COST TO OLD:COST
```

Next, the command file displays the record on the newstock file to allow the user to edit or delete it:

```
        ***** Display edit screen and allow edit.
        ERASE
        STORE " " TO DELETED
        @ 1,1 SAY " Edit New Stock Transaction . . . ."
        @ 3,1 SAY "Part Number " GET PART:NO;
           PICT "!!!!!"
        @ 5,1 SAY "Quantity " GET QTY
        @ 5,20 SAY "Purchase price ";
           GET COST
        @ 7,1 SAY "Date ";
           GET DATE PICT "99/99/99"
        @ 7,15 SAY "Vendor " GET VENDOR
        @ 9,2 SAY "Delete this record? (Y/N) ";
           GET DELETED PICT "!"
        READ
```

Now the command file must decide what adjustments to make to the master file. First, if the cost has been changed on the newstock file, then it should be changed on the master file:

```
****** After edit complete, adjust master file
****** if necessary.

****** First, handle change in cost, if necessary.
IF COST # OLD:COST
   STORE PART:NO TO NEW:PART
   STORE COST TO NEW:COST
   USE MASTER INDEX MASTER
   FIND &NEW:PART
   REPLACE COST WITH NEW:COST
   USE NEWSTOCK INDEX NEWSTOCK
   GOTO RECNO
   ENDIF (cost # old:cost)
```

If the record is deleted from the newstock file after the update has taken place, then the corresponding record on the master file has too many items in its quantity field (QTY), and too few items on order (ON:ORDER). The first case statement takes care of this adjustment:

```
DO CASE
   **** If new stock transaction deleted, subtract
   **** its quantity from the master file,
   **** re-add it to the on-order field.
   CASE POSTED .AND. DELETED = "Y"
      DELETE
      STORE NO:DELS+1 TO NO:DELS
      USE MASTER INDEX MASTER
      FIND &OLD:PART
      REPL QTY WITH QTY-OLD:QTY
      REPL ON:ORDER WITH ON:ORDER+OLD:QTY
```

If the user changed the part number on a newstock file record that was already updated, then the corresponding part on the master file would have too many items in the quantity field for the old part number, and too few items for the new part number. Also, it would have too few items on order for the old part number, and too many for the new one. The second case statement adjusts the master file for this situation:

```
***** If part number changed, subtract quantity
***** from old part number, and add to new. Do
***** the opposite for on-order field.
CASE POSTED .AND. PART:NO # OLD:PART
   STORE QTY TO NEW:QTY
   STORE PART:NO TO NEW:PART
   USE MASTER INDEX MASTER
   FIND &OLD:PART
   REPLACE QTY WITH QTY-OLD:QTY
```

```
        REPLACE ON:ORDER WITH ON:ORDER + OLD:QTY
        FIND &NEW:PART
        REPLACE QTY WITH QTY + NEW:QTY
        REPLACE ON:ORDER WITH ON:ORDER - NEW:QTY
```

If the user changed the quantity only, then the master file QTY and ON:ORDER fields would have to be adjusted for the difference between the quantity that was originally used in the update, and the new corrected quantity. The third case statement handles this situation:

```
            * * * * * If user changed only the quantity,
            * * * * * adjust the master file quantity.
            CASE POSTED .AND. QTY # OLD:QTY
                STORE QTY - OLD:QTY TO DIFF
                USE MASTER INDEX MASTER
                FIND &OLD:PART
                REPLACE QTY WITH QTY + DIFF
                REPLACE ON:ORDER WITH ON:ORDER - DIFF
            ENDCASE
        ENDCASE
    ENDIF (search # 0)

ENDDO (while search # 0)
```

The lines above also close the DO CASE, IF, and DO WHILE clauses.

When the user is ready to exit, the program will first pack any records that have been marked for deletion:

```
        * * * * * * * * * * * * * * * * * If records have been deleted,
        * * * * * * * * * * * * * * * * * pack the newstock data file.
IF NO:DELS > 0
    ERASE
    ? "Packing deleted records from the new stock file . . ."
    USE SALES INDEX SALES
    PACK
ENDIF (no.dels > 0)
```

Then, the program can release the memory variables and return to the NMENU.CMD command file from which it was called:

```
    * * * * * Release memory variables.
    RELEASE OLD:QTY,OLD:PART,NEW:PART,NO:DELS,OLD:COST
    RELEASE SEARCH,HOWMANY,DIFF,DELETED,NEW:COST,NEW:QTY
    USE
    RETURN
```

The entire NEWEDIT.CMD command file is displayed in Figure 13.5.

```
************************************* NEWEDIT.CMD
******* Edit the newstock file, and update master.

******** Set up memory variables.
STORE 0 TO NO:DELS
STORE "1" TO SEARCH

******** Get part number for data to edit.
DO WHILE SEARCH # "0"
   USE NEWSTOCK INDEX NEWSTOCK
   ERASE
   ACCEPT "Enter part number to edit (0 if none) ";
         TO SEARCH
   STORE !(SEARCH) TO SEARCH

   ** If user did not request exit, continue with edit.
   IF SEARCH # "0"
      *** Count the records with that part number.
      FIND &SEARCH
      COUNT WHILE PART:NO = !(SEARCH) TO HOWMANY

      DO CASE

         *** If part not found, warn user.
         CASE HOWMANY = 0
            ? "        No such part number!!"
            ? CHR(7)

         **** If part number found, proceed.
         CASE HOWMANY > 0

         ***** If several new stock transaction have that
         ***** part number, get more information.
         IF HOWMANY > 1
            ERASE
            FIND &SEARCH
            LIST WHILE PART:NO=!(SEARCH) PART:NO,QTY,;
                 COST,DATE,VENDOR
            ?
            INPUT "Which line (left-column number) ";
                  TO RECNO
            GOTO RECNO
         ***** otherwise, go to the record.
         ELSE
            FIND &SEARCH
            STORE # TO RECNO
         ENDIF (howmany > 1)

         ***** Store the original field values to
         ***** memory variables.
         STORE PART:NO TO OLD:PART
         STORE QTY TO OLD:QTY
         STORE COST TO OLD:COST
         ***** Display edit screen and allow edit.
         ERASE
         STORE " " TO DELETED
         @ 1,1 SAY " Edit New Stock Transaction...."
```

Figure 13.5: The NEWEDIT.CMD command file.

```
@ 3,1 SAY "Part Number " GET PART:NO;
  PICT "!!!!!"
@ 5,1 SAY "Quantity " GET QTY
@ 5,20 SAY "Purchase price ";
  GET COST
@ 7,1 SAY "Date ";
  GET DATE PICT "99/99/99"
@ 7,15 SAY "Vendor " GET VENDOR
@ 9,2 SAY "Delete this record? (Y/N) ";
  GET DELETED PICT "!"
  READ


****** After edit complete, adjust master file
****** if necessary.

****** First, handle change in cost, if necessary.
IF COST # OLD:COST
   STORE PART:NO TO NEW:PART
   STORE COST TO NEW:COST
   USE MASTER INDEX MASTER
   FIND &NEW:PART
   REPLACE COST WITH NEW:COST
   USE NEWSTOCK INDEX NEWSTOCK
   GOTO RECNO
ENDIF (cost # old:cost)

DO CASE

   **** If new stock transaction deleted, subtract
   **** its quantity from the master file,
   **** re-add it to the on-order field.
   CASE POSTED .AND. DELETED = "Y"
        DELETE
        STORE NO:DELS+1 TO NO:DELS
        USE MASTER INDEX MASTER
        FIND &OLD:PART
        REPL QTY WITH QTY-OLD:QTY
        REPL ON:ORDER WITH ON:ORDER+OLD:QTY


   ***** If part number changed, subtract the
   ***** quantity from the old part number,
   ***** and add to the new.  Do the opposite
   ***** for the ON:ORDER field.
   CASE POSTED .AND. PART:NO # OLD:PART
        STORE QTY TO NEW:QTY
        STORE PART:NO TO NEW:PART
        USE MASTER INDEX MASTER
        FIND &OLD:PART
        REPLACE QTY WITH QTY-OLD:QTY
        REPLACE ON:ORDER WITH ON:ORDER+OLD:QTY
        FIND &NEW:PART
        REPLACE QTY WITH QTY+NEW:QTY
        REPLACE ON:ORDER WITH ON:ORDER-NEW:QTY
```

Figure 13.5: *The NEWEDIT.CMD command file (continued).*

```
                ***** If user just changed the quantity,
                ***** adjust the master file quantity.
                CASE POSTED .AND. QTY # OLD:QTY
                     STORE QTY-OLD:QTY TO DIFF
                     USE MASTER INDEX MASTER
                     FIND &OLD:PART
                     REPLACE QTY WITH QTY+DIFF
                     REPLACE ON:ORDER WITH ON:ORDER-DIFF
                ENDCASE
        ENDCASE
   ENDIF (search # 0)

ENDDO (while search # 0)

******************* If records have been deleted,
******************* pack the newstock data file.
IF NO:DELS > 0
   ERASE
   ? "Packing deleted records from the new stock file..."
   USE SALES INDEX SALES
   PACK
ENDIF (no.dels > 0)

***** Release memory variables.
RELEASE OLD:QTY,OLD:PART,NEW:PART,NO:DELS,OLD:COST
RELEASE SEARCH,HOWMANY,DIFF,DELETED,NEW:COST,NEW:QTY
USE
RETURN
```

Figure 13.5: The NEWEDIT.CMD command file (continued).

Summary

The inventory system we've developed is complex for a programmer to write, but easy for a novice to use. The system provides a great deal of power for storing data about sales and incoming stock transactions and printing useful reports. It also allows the store manager to update the master file from these transaction files by simply choosing an option from the menu. If a user discovers an error in either the sales or new stock file, he can simply edit the transaction. The system automatically takes care of making all the proper corrections to the master file.

In the next chapters, we'll deal with program design and techniques to use with bookkeeping systems. In many ways, bookkeeping is similar to inventory management: there are files to keep track of individual transactions and a master file which keeps track of the status of various accounts. Many of the techniques you learned in previous chapters will also apply to the bookkeeping system.

CHAPTER 14
A BOOKKEEPING SYSTEM

Our next project will be a custom bookkeeping system. Like the previous systems, the bookkeeping package will be menu-driven and easy to use for a nonsophisticated end user. Here are some new techniques we'll develop along the way:

1. Allowing the user custom installation procedures
2. Maintaining an audit trail
3. Calculating balances
4. Translating numbers to English for check-writing
5. Updating multiple-fields

The bookkeeping system will also require many of the techniques that we used in the mailing and inventory systems.

Bookkeeping System Goals

The bookkeeping system will allow the user to set up a custom chart of accounts to suit his bookkeeping needs. The system will require that each account have a unique number and title. Then, the user can track income and expenses throughout the year by simply typing in transactions. The system will only accept transactions with valid account numbers, thereby maintaining the accuracy of the data. The system will also allow the user to make adjustments in transactions in order to correct errors, thereby providing an audit trail during the course of a year.

At any time during the year, the user may review the transactions, either for the current month or for any range of dates. He may also print a copy of the chart of accounts with month-to-date, quarter-to-date, and year-to-date balances of all the accounts, as well as totals. The system will also print checks automatically, maintain a check register, and allow the user to view the checking account balance quickly.

As an added feature, the bookkeeping system will allow for *subaccounts*, accounts which only keep track of funds spent or earned. For example, suppose the user writes a loan payment check for $100. Although he only writes one check, he might wish to record how much of the payment was interest, and how much was principal. In this case, the user can set up three accounts, as shown below:

Account Number	Description
500.00	Business Loan
500.10	Principal on Business Loan
500.20	Interest on Business Loan

If the user enters $100 into account 500.00, $80.00 into account 500.10, and $20.00 into account 500.20, a check will be printed for the amount in account 500.00 only, and the amount in line 500 will be considered as the only expense when the user calculates balances. The amounts in the two subaccounts will also be recorded, but for informational purposes only. The subaccount information is useful for tax purposes, since the interest on the loan may be tax-deductible.

Bookkeeping System Database Design

The bookkeeping system will consist of four data files:

1. GENINFO.DBF   General information file. Contains information of general use to the system, including company name, date of last chart of accounts update, and the last check number used.

2. COA.DBF Chart of accounts. Contains the account number, title, and month-to-date, quarter-to-date, and year-to-date balance of each account.
3. TRANS.DBF Transaction file. Contains each individual income and expense transaction that the user enters. For each transaction, it maintains the account number, reason for the expense or source of the income, the amount, and date. If a check is involved, it records the check number and to whom the check was (or is to be) paid. Also contains various fields for keeping track of updates.
4. REGISTER.DBF Check register file. Keeps a running history of all deposits to, and checks written from, the checking account. Includes check number, description, to whom paid, amount, and date.

The relationships among the data files are displayed in Figure 14.1. The GENINFO file is independent. The COA file updates its balances from data in the trans file. The register file gets information from the trans file, but in an appending rather than updating fashion, as we shall see while developing the software.

The geninfo file, which contains only one record, has this structure:

STRUCTURE FOR FILE: B:GENINFO .DBF
NUMBER OF RECORDS: 00001

FLD	NAME	TYPE	WIDTH	DEC	CONTENTS
001	COMPANY	C	025		Company name
002	LAST:UPDAT	C	008		Date of last update
003	LAST:CHECK	N	004		Last check no. written

Note: We have placed a description next to each field, but when you create the data file, just key in the field names, types, widths, and decimal places.

The trans file keeps track of individual income and expense transactions. Its structure is displayed below:

STRUCTURE FOR FILE: B:TRANS .DBF

FLD	NAME	TYPE	WIDTH	DEC	CONTENTS
001	ACCT	N	006	002	Account number (key field)
002	REASON	C	020		Reason or source
003	AMOUNT	N	012	002	Amount of transaction
004	TYPE	N	001		Type: 1 = check, 2 = other
005	CHECK:NO	N	004		Check number
006	TO:WHOM	C	020		To whom check was paid
007	DATE	C	008		Date of transaction

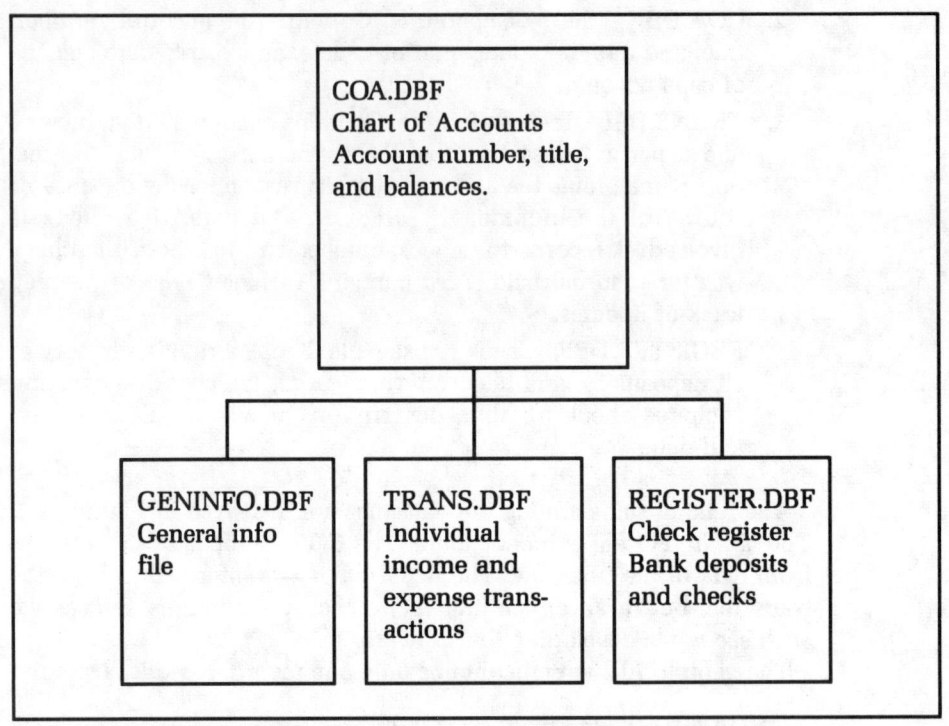

```
                       ┌─────────────────────┐
                       │   COA.DBF           │
                       │   Chart of Accounts │
                       │   Account number,   │
                       │   title,            │
                       │   and balances.     │
                       └─────────┬───────────┘
                                 │
         ┌───────────────────────┼───────────────────────┐
         │                       │                       │
┌────────────────┐   ┌────────────────┐   ┌────────────────┐
│ GENINFO.DBF    │   │ TRANS.DBF      │   │ REGISTER.DBF   │
│ General info   │   │ Individual     │   │ Check register │
│ file           │   │ income and     │   │ Bank deposits  │
│                │   │ expense trans- │   │ and checks     │
│                │   │ actions        │   │                │
└────────────────┘   └────────────────┘   └────────────────┘
```

Figure 14.1: Data file structure for the bookkeeping system.

```
008   POSTED       L   001   Posted to COA yet?
009   WRITTEN      L   001   Check written yet?
010   REGISTERED   L   001   Sent to check register yet?
011   MARKER       C   001   Marks subaccounts
```

Notice that the trans file has a number of *logical* fields. These are used as markers for keeping track of which records have already been posted to the chart of accounts (POSTED), which have had checks written already (WRITTEN), and which have been sent to the checks register (REGISTERED). The MARKER field marks records which are subaccounts.

Since the system allows the user to display transactions in either account number or date order, trans is indexed on the ACCT field to one index file, and the DATE field to another. After creating the trans file, use these commands to create the index files:

```
USE TRANS
INDEX ON ACCT TO ACCT
INDEX ON $(DATE,7,2)+$(DATE,1,6) TO DATES
```

Since the user's fiscal year may extend through two years (e.g. June 1 to May 31), the year is made primary in the dates index file. The ACCT (account number) field is common to both the COA (chart of accounts) and trans (transactions) file, and is used as the key field in performing updates.

The chart of accounts will be stored on a data file named COA.DBF. It includes account numbers, titles, and month-to-date, quarter-to-date, and year-to-date balances.

STRUCTURE FOR FILE: B:COA .DBF

FLD	NAME	TYPE	WIDTH	DEC	CONTENTS
001	ACCT	N	006	002	Account number
002	TITLE	C	020		Account description
003	AMOUNT	N	012	002	Month-to-date balance
004	QTD	N	012	002	Quarter-to-date balance
005	YTD	N	012	002	Year-to-date balance
006	MARKER	C	001		Marks subaccounts

Notice that the ACCT field, which stores account numbers, is identical in name, type, width, and decimal places to the ACCT field on the trans file. This is because the account number will be the key field for updating the COA data file from the trans data file. The AMOUNT field is the current (month-to-date) balance of the account. The COA data file also has a MARKER field, which is used to mark subaccounts.

The chart of accounts will always be displayed in account number order. Furthermore, in order to check the validity of account numbers added to the trans file, we'll need to look up account numbers in the COA file. Therefore, the COA file will be indexed on the ACCT field. After you create the COA data file as displayed above, you should create an index file named COA.NDX using these commands:

USE COA
INDEX ON ACCT TO COA

The register file maintains the check register, including checks written (which are pulled directly from the trans file), and deposits to the checking account (which the user types in individually, since a deposit to the checking account is neither an income nor an expense). The file structure, as well as brief descriptions for the contents of the fields, are displayed below:

STRUCTURE FOR FILE: B:REGISTER.DBF

FLD	NAME	TYPE	WIDTH	DEC	CONTENTS
001	CHECK:NO	N	004		Check number
002	TO:WHOM	C	020		To whom paid

003	REASON	C	020		Reason for check
004	AMOUNT	N	012	002	Check amount
005	DATE	C	008		Check date
006	DEPOSIT	L	001		Is this a deposit?

The REGISTER.DBF contains one logical (true-or-false) field called DEPOSIT. This field is set to true for those records which are deposits, and false for checks. This makes it easy for a user to calculate balances easily, since a command file can easily sum the amounts for deposits (DEPOSIT is true), and sum the amounts for the checks (DEPOSIT is false), then simply subtract the sum of the checks from the sum of the deposits to arrive at the checking account balance.

The register file has a number of field names in common with the trans file (CHECK:NO, TO:WHOM, REASON, AMOUNT, DATE), because it gets all of its information about checks directly from the trans file. The common field names simplify the process of transferring trans data directly to the register file.

Bookkeeping System Software Structure

Like our previous software systems, the bookkeeping system will have a main menu command file, and various command files to edit, add data to, and print data from the various data files. Also, it will have a command file to update the chart of accounts from the transaction file of individual income and expenses. A unique *installation* program will allow the user to set up a chart of accounts prior to using the bookkeeping system. The installation program will provide many on-screen instructions to help the user develop his chart of accounts.

The software structure for the bookkeeping system is shown in Figure 14.2. The BINSTALL.CMD command file is the installation program. It is a separate command file, not directly linked to any others, because it is only used once to set up the initial chart of acounts, as well as some general information; the chart of accounts and the starting number of the first check to be written. BOOKS.CMD is the bookkeeping system main menu, and the remaining command files are called from DO commands within the main menu program.

The BREPORTS and BEDIT command files in Figure 14.2 branch down further to other command files. We'll design and develop those programs in due time.

In the next chapter, we'll begin designing and writing the code for the bookkeeping system, beginning with the installation (BINSTALL.CMD) and main menu (BOOKS.CMD) command files.

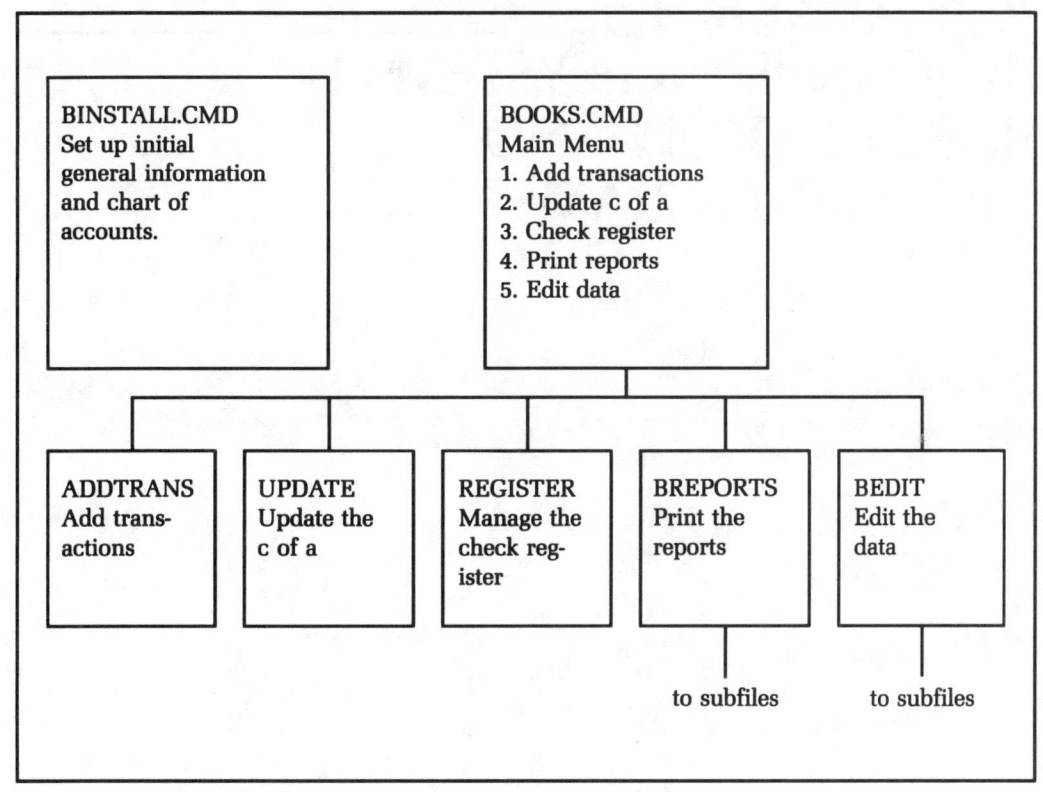

```
┌─────────────────────────────────────────────────────────────────────┐
│                                                                     │
│   ┌──────────────────────┐      ┌──────────────────────┐            │
│   │ BINSTALL.CMD         │      │ BOOKS.CMD            │            │
│   │ Set up initial       │      │ Main Menu            │            │
│   │ general information  │      │ 1. Add transactions  │            │
│   │ and chart of         │      │ 2. Update c of a     │            │
│   │ accounts.            │      │ 3. Check register    │            │
│   │                      │      │ 4. Print reports     │            │
│   │                      │      │ 5. Edit data         │            │
│   └──────────────────────┘      └──────────┬───────────┘            │
│                                            │                        │
│         ┌────────────┬────────────┬────────┼────────┬────────────┐  │
│   ┌─────┴────┐ ┌─────┴────┐ ┌─────┴────┐ ┌─┴──────┐ ┌─┴────────┐    │
│   │ ADDTRANS │ │ UPDATE   │ │ REGISTER │ │BREPORTS│ │ BEDIT    │    │
│   │ Add trans│ │ Update   │ │ Manage   │ │Print   │ │ Edit the │    │
│   │ actions  │ │ the c of │ │ the check│ │the     │ │ data     │    │
│   │          │ │ a        │ │ register │ │reports │ │          │    │
│   └──────────┘ └──────────┘ └──────────┘ └───┬────┘ └────┬─────┘    │
│                                              │           │          │
│                                         to subfiles  to subfiles    │
└─────────────────────────────────────────────────────────────────────┘
```

Figure 14.2: *Partial software structure for the bookkeeping system.*

Summary

In this chapter we've designed a menu-driven bookkeeping system that is easy to use. We've incorporated several features that are used in many bookkeeping systems, such as audit trails, monthly, quarterly, and yearly balances in various accounts, check writing, and check register maintenance.

The system will consist of four main database files:

GENINFO.DBF: Contains general information.
COA.DBF: Maintains the chart of accounts as well as monthly, quarterly, and yearly balance of each account.
TRANS.DBF: Records individual income and expense transactions.

Numerous command files will be used to manage all these data. We'll start developing them in the next chapter.

CHAPTER 15
BOOKKEEPING SYSTEM INSTALLATION AND MENU PROGRAMS

To use the bookkeeping system, the user should first design a custom chart of accounts, then key it into the computer, along with a company name (to be used on report headings), and the number of the first check to be printed. The user only performs this procedure once. If he decides to add, change, or delete an account at some future point, he can use a simple edit option from the main menu to do so.

When designing a bookkeeping system, we must first consider what numbering scheme for the accounts would identify income accounts and expense accounts. A more sophisticated numbering system would also integrate assets, liabilities, cost of goods sold, and other types of accounts. For our present system, we'll simply divide accounts into income and expense categories.

Account numbers will be stored in the format XXX.XX, which accepts account numbers ranging from 100.00 to 999.99. Since there are likely to be more expense accounts than income accounts, we'll divide the range of numbers such that account numbers 100.00 through 299.99 are for income, and 300.00 through 999.99 are for expenses:

Account Numbers	Type of Account
100.00–299.99	Income accounts
300.00–999.99	Expense accounts

Recall that in our design, we also stated that the user may create subaccounts, used for storing additional information about transactions, but are not for calculating balances or for writing checks. We need to come up with a rule for identifying subaccounts so the software we develop can handle them properly. Since our account numbers allow two decimal places, we can simply make the rule that any account with a nonzero decimal place is a subaccount. For example, suppose the user wishes to create one account for utilities, and print only one check for utilities. But he also wishes to record how much payment went to gas, and how much to electricity. He could set up three accounts as follows:

400.00	Utilities
400.10	Gas
400.20	Electricity

Utilities is a regular expense account because it is greater than 299.99, and has zeroes in both decimal places. Gas and electricity are subaccounts, because both have nonzero decimal places. This is an important to rule to remember when designing and developing the program.

Now that we've developed a set of rules for identifying account types, let's begin developing the bookkeeping system:

Bookkeeping System Installation Program

The installation program will be named BINSTALL.CMD. The user can call it up from the dBASE dot prompt with the command DO BINSTALL (or DO B:BINSTALL), and it will display the following instructions on the screen:

Start the Bookkeeping System

This program allows you to set up general information and a chart of accounts for the bookkeeping system. You need to use this

program only once. The edit option under the
BOOKS main menu allows you to make changes later.

Enter the name of the company or user :   :

Enter starting check number for writing checks :   :

Once the user fills in the company name and starting check number, the next screen appears as below:

Next, you need to set up the chart of accounts.
Account numbers use the format XXX.XX (e.g. 100.00).
Account numbers in the range of 100.00 to 299.99
are for INCOME only. Account numbers in the range
300.00 to 999.99 are for EXPENSES only.

Press any key to continue . . .

The user presses any key to bring up the next set of instructions, which appear on the screen as follows:

Accounts that have a nonzero decimal portion
are subaccounts, and are not included in totals.
Hence, you may want to break transactions that
involve a single check into subaccounts. For
example, you write only one check for utilities.
You may, however, wish to record the amount of
this single check that went toward gas, and the
amount that went toward electricity. To do so,
set up three accounts as follows:

Account Number	Title
400.00	Utilities
400.10	Gas
400.20	Electricity

In this example, only one check will be written,
for account 400. Accounts 400.10 and 400.20 will
be recorded, but checks will not be written.

Press RETURN to continue, ESC to quit . . . .

Next, the program allows the user to key in his chart of accounts, one account at a time. The screen for typing in account numbers, titles, and initial balances is displayed below:

Type in account number, title, and current balance.
Enter Ctrl-W to quit

Account Number :_   .   :
Title   :   :

Month-to-date   :   . :
Quarter-to-date   :   . :
Year-to-date   :   . :

The user can continue adding transactions, then type in CTRL-W to quit. At that point, the following instructions appear on the screen, as well as the dBASE dot prompt.

Returning to dot prompt. To use the bookkeeping system, type DO BOOKS when dot appears.

The pseudocode for the BINSTALL.CMD command file is displayed in Figure 15.1.

Set dBASE parameters

Clear the screen
Use the general information data file
Delete any existing data from it
Then add one blank record to it

Display first page of instructions for the install program

Get company name from user
Get starting check number
Store both on the general information file

Display instructions for account numbers

Prepare the chart of accounts file by deleting
    any existing accounts

Set up a loop for typing in account numbers
    Display instructions
    Get account number, title, and initial balances
        for each account

Continue loop (while user does not exit)

Display closing instructions

Make sure no accounts with account
number equal to zero stay on chart

Release memory variables
Return to the dot prompt

Figure 15.1: *Pseudocode for the BINSTALL.CMD command file.*

The BINSTALL program is a fairly simple one. First, it sets up the appropriate dBASE parameters:

```
* * * * * * * * * * * * * * * * * * * * * * * * * * * * * * * * BINSTALL.CMD
* * * * * * * * * * * * * * * Start the chart of accounts.
SET TALK OFF
SET DEFA TO B
```

Next, it uses the geninfo file, deletes any existing records from it, then appends a blank record for storing the user's input:

```
* * * * * * * * * * * * * * * * * * * * * * Get general information.
ERASE
USE GENINFO
DELE ALL
PACK
APPEND BLANK
```

Next, it displays the first set of instructions on the screen, and waits for the user to enter the company name and starting check number:

```
TEXT

        Start the Bookkeeping System

    This program allows you to set up general
    information and a chart of accounts for the
    bookkeeping system. You need to use this
    program only once. The edit option under the
    BOOKS main menu allows you to make changes later.

ENDTEXT
11,1 SAY "Enter the name of the Company or User"
11,41 GET COMPANY
13,1 SAY "Enter starting check number for writing checks"
13,50 GET LAST:CHECK
READ
```

After the user keys in this initial information, the program displays instructions for assigning accounts to income and expense categories, and waits for the user to press a key prior to proceeding:

```
* * * * * * * * * * * * * * * * * Next, display instructions for
* * * * * * * * * * * * * * * * * account numbers.
ERASE

TEXT
    Next, you need to set up the chart of accounts.
    Account numbers use the format XXX.XX (e.g. 100.00).
    Account numbers in the range of 100.00 to 299.99
    are for INCOME only. Account numbers in the range
    300.00 to 999.99 are for EXPENSES only.
```

Press any key to continue . . .
ENDTEXT
WAIT

Next, the program displays instructions for identifying subaccounts, and again waits for a response from the user:

```
***************** Then display instructions for
***************** identifying subaccounts.
ERASE

TEXT
     Accounts that have a nonzero decimal portion
     are subaccounts, and are not included in totals.
     Hence, you may want to break transactions that
     involve a single check into subaccounts. For
     example, you only write one check for utilities.
     However, you may wish to record the amount of
     this single check that went toward gas, and the
     amount that went toward electricity. To do so,
     set up three accounts as follows:

         Account
         Number    Title

         400.00    Utilities
         400.10    Gas
         400.20    Electricity

     In this example, only one check will be written,
     for account 400. Accounts 400.10 and 400.20 will
     be recorded, but checks will not be written.

     Press RETURN to continue, ESC to quit . . . .
ENDTEXT
WAIT
```

Then the command file uses the chart of accounts file (COA.DBF) with the account number index (COA.NDX), and deletes any existing records from it:

```
********* Prepare the COA file for setting up the
********* chart of accounts.
ERASE
USE COA INDEX COA
DELE ALL
PACK
```

The command file sets up a loop that provides some basic instructions, and allows the user to key in account numbers, titles, and initial balances:

```
***************** Allow the user to type in a
***************** chart of accounts.
STORE T TO ADDING
DO WHILE ADDING
   APPEND BLANK
   ERASE
   @ 1, 0 SAY "Type in Account Number, Title,"
   @ 1,32 SAY "and Current Balance."
   @ 2, 0 SAY "Enter Ctrl-W to Quit"
   @ 4, 0 SAY "Account Number"
   @ 4,16 GET ACCT
   @ 5, 0 SAY "Title"
   @ 5,16 GET TITLE
   @ 6, 0 SAY "Month-to-Date"
   @ 6,16 GET AMOUNT
   @ 7, 0 SAY "Quarter-to-Date"
   @ 7,16 GET QTD
   @ 8, 0 SAY "Year-to-Date"
   @ 8,16 GET YTD
   READ
   ************ Check for 0 as account.
   IF ACCT = 0
      STORE F TO ADDING
   ENDIF
ENDDO (while adding)
```

When the user is done typing in account numbers, the program displays closing instructions on the screen:

```
************* Done adding.
ERASE
TEXT
   Returning to dot prompt. To use the bookkeeping
   system, type DO BOOKS when dot appears.
ENDTEXT
```

Then the program deletes any accounts that were assigned zero as an account number from the data file:

```
************* Make sure no accounts with account
************* number equal to zero stay on chart.
DELE ALL FOR ACCT = 0
PACK
```

When finished, the command file simply releases all memory variables, closes the COA database file, and returns to the dBASE dot prompt.

```
************* End the BINSTALL program.
RELEASE ALL
USE
```

The complete BINSTALL.CMD command file is shown in Figure 15.2.

```
*********************************** BINSTALL.CMD
****************** Start the chart of accounts.
SET TALK OFF
SET DEFA TO B

********************* Get general information.
ERASE
USE GENINFO
DELE ALL
PACK
APPEND BLANK

TEXT

          Start the Bookkeeping System

   This program allows you to set up general
   information and a chart of accounts for the
   bookkeeping system.  You need to use this
   program only once.  The edit option under the
   BOOKS main menu allows you to make changes later.

ENDTEXT
@ 11,1 SAY "Enter the name of the Company or User"
@ 11,41 GET COMPANY
@ 13,1 SAY "Enter starting check number for writing checks"
@ 13,50 GET LAST:CHECK
READ

***************** Next, display instructions for
***************** account numbers.
ERASE

TEXT
   Next, you need to set up the chart of accounts
   Account numbers use the format XXX.XX (e.g. 100.00)
   Account numbers in the range of 100.00 to 299.99
   Are for INCOME only.  Account numbers in the range
   300.00 to 999.99 are for EXPENSES only.

   Press any key to continue...

ENDTEXT
WAIT

***************** Then display instructions for
***************** identifying subaccounts.
ERASE

TEXT
   Accounts that have a nonzero decimal portion
   are subaccounts, and are not included in totals.
   Hence, you may want to break transactions that
   involve a single check into subaccounts.  For
   example, you only write one check for utilities.
   You may, however, wish to record the amount of
   this single check that went toward gas, and the
```

Figure 15.2: The BINSTALL.CMD command file.

```
        amount that went toward electricity.  To do so,
        Set up three accounts as follows:

            Account
            Number       Title

            400.00       Utilities
            400.10       Gas
            400.20       Electricity

        In this example, only one check will be written,
        for account 400.  Accounts 400.10 and 400.20 will
        be recorded, but checks will not be written.

        Press RETURN to continue, ESC to QUIT....

ENDTEXT
WAIT

********* Prepare the COA file for setting up the
********* chart of accounts.
ERASE
USE COA INDEX COA
DELE ALL
PACK

****************** Allow the user to type in a
****************** chart of accounts.
STORE T TO ADDING
DO WHILE ADDING
   APPEND BLANK
   ERASE
   @  1, 0 SAY "Type in Account Number, Title,"
   @  1,32 SAY "and Current Balance."
   @  2, 0 SAY "Enter Ctrl-W to Quit"
   @  4, 0 SAY "Account Number"
   @  4,16 GET ACCT
   @  5, 0 SAY "Title"
   @  5,16 GET TITLE
   @  6, 0 SAY "Month-to-Date"
   @  6,16 GET AMOUNT
   @  7, 0 SAY "Quarter-to-Date"
   @  7,16 GET QTD
   @  8, 0 SAY "Year-to-Date"
   @  8,16 GET YTD

   READ
   ************ Check for 0 as account.
   IF ACCT = 0
      STORE F TO ADDING
   ENDIF
ENDDO (while adding)

************* Done adding.
ERASE
TEXT
   Returning to dot prompt.  To use the bookkeeping
   System, type DO BOOKS when dot appears.
```

Figure 15.2: The BINSTALL.CMD command file (continued).

```
ENDTEXT

************** Make sure no accounts with account
************** number equal to zero stay on chart.
DELE ALL FOR ACCT = 0
PACK

************* End the BINSTALL program.
RELEASE ALL
USE
```

Figure 15.2: The BINSTALL.CMD command file (continued).

Prior to developing any additional programs, you should do the BINSTALL program, and add some accounts so that there will be data to test the programs with. You can set up a small personal chart of accounts as shown below:

Account Number	Title	Month	Quarter	Year
100.00	Regular Income	0.00	0.00	0.00
110.00	Royalty Income	0.00	0.00	0.00
120.00	Interest Income	0.00	0.00	0.00
300.00	Federal Witholding	0.00	0.00	0.00
310.00	State Witholding	0.00	0.00	0.00
400.00	House Payment	0.00	0.00	0.00
400.10	House Interest	0.00	0.00	0.00
400.20	House Principal	0.00	0.00	0.00
500.00	Car Payment	0.00	0.00	0.00
510.00	Car Insurance	0.00	0.00	0.00
520.00	Gasoline	0.00	0.00	0.00
530.00	Car Repairs	0.00	0.00	0.00
600.00	Medical Expense	0.00	0.00	0.00
610.00	Pharmacy Expense	0.00	0.00	0.00
620.00	Dental Expense	0.00	0.00	0.00
630.00	Medical Insurance	0.00	0.00	0.00
700.00	Entertainment (Per.)	0.00	0.00	0.00
710.00	Entertainment (Bus.)	0.00	0.00	0.00

Bookkeeping System Main Menu

The main menu for the bookkeeping system is stored under the filename BOOKS.CMD. It first displays the computer's system date

[DATE( )], and allows the user to change it. The variable T:DATE is then used as "today's date" throughout the system. The program then displays the main menu, as displayed below:

Bookkeeping System Main Menu
1. Add New Transactions
2. Update Chart of Accounts
3. Manage Check Register
4. Print Reports
5. Edit Data
6. Exit

Since the BOOKS command file is similar to the other menu programs we've developed so far, we'll display it entirely in Figure 15.3.

```
**************************************** BOOKS.CMD
****************** Bookkeeping system main menu.
SET TALK OFF
SET DEFA TO B
SET BELL OFF
STORE 0 TO CHOICE

*************** First, get today's date.
ERASE
STORE DATE() TO T:DATE
@ 5,1 SAY "Enter today's date";
   GET T:DATE PICT "99/99/99"
READ
**************** Display main menu.
DO WHILE CHOICE <> 6
   ERASE
   TEXT
            Bookkeeping System Main Menu

               1. Add New Transactions
               2. Update Chart of Accounts
               3. Manage Check Register
               4. Print Reports
               5. Edit Data
               6. Exit

   ENDTEXT

   @ 12,10 SAY "Enter your choice (1-6) from above"
   @ 12,45 GET CHOICE PICT "9"
   READ

   ************** Branch accordingly.
   DO CASE
```

Figure 15.3: The BOOKS.CMD command file.

```
            CASE CHOICE = 1
                DO ADDTRANS

            CASE CHOICE = 2
                DO UPDATE

            CASE CHOICE = 3
                DO REGISTER

            CASE CHOICE = 4
                DO BREPORTS

            CASE CHOICE = 5
                DO BEDIT
        ENDCASE
ENDDO (while choice <> 6)
QUIT
```

Figure 15.3: *The BOOKS.CMD command file (continued).*

Summary

In this chapter, we've developed the first two command files in the bookkeeping system. These are:

1. BINSTALL.CMD, which describes the rules for assigning account numbers to the user, and allows him to enter an initial chart of accounts. Also, it allows the user to enter the name of his company, which will appear in report headings, and the starting check number for printing checks.
2. BOOKS.CMD, which is the main menu program for the bookkeeping system.

In the next chapter, we'll develop the ADDTRANS.CMD command file for adding transactions to the trans data file.

CHAPTER 16
ADDING AND UPDATING TRANSACTIONS

In this chapter, we'll develop the command files for adding new transactions to the TRANS.DBF data file, and for updating the chart of accounts (COA.DBF data file) from the transaction file.

Recording Bookkeeping Transactions

The command file to add transactions to the bookkeeping system will be designed both for the convenience and safety of the user. If the user types in an account number that does not exist, the screen will display a warning message, and allow the user to try again. If the user types in a valid account number, its title will be displayed on the screen, and the user can proceed with the transaction.

To record bookkeeping transactions, the user selects option 1 from the main menu. This causes the following screen to be displayed:

    --- Enter new transactions (0 when done) ---
    Account Number :_   . :

If the user types in an invalid account number, the computer beeps, displays a warning, and asks for another account number as shown below:

```
--- Enter new transactions (0 when done) ---
Account Number :999.99:   No such account!
```

If the user types in a valid account number, the screen asks for additional information:

```
--- Enter new transactions (0 when done) ---
Account Number :100.00:   Regular Income

Description :_            :
Amount :        . :
Date :10/10/84:
```

The user can either type in a description or just press the RETURN key, and the account title will be filled in as the description. For example, if the user had keyed in account number 710, the screen would have displayed the account title [Entertainment (Bus.)], and waited for a description. The description here might be "Lunch with Terri Nichols," which the user could just type in. However, when the user types in an account such as 100, the account title, "Regular Income" is sufficient as a description, so he can just press the RETURN key, and the title automatically fills in the description prompt, as below:

```
--- Enter new transactions (0 when done) ---

Account Number :100.00:   Regular Income
Description :Regular Income    :
Amount :_   . :
Date :10/10/84:
```

The user can then type in the amount of the transaction, and then either use the date that was automatically filled in (today's date), or type in another date.

Since the above transaction is for an income account, the screen will not ask for any additional information. Instead, it will ask for the account number of the next transaction. Suppose the user keys in account number 300 for federal witholding tax. Again, the user can press the RETURN key to fill in the account title as the description, and then type in the amount and use the existing date. Since this is an expense transaction, the program will require additional information from the user, as below:

```
--- Enter new transactions (0 when done) ---
Account Number :300.00:    Federal Witholding
Description :Federal Witholding   :
Amount :    398.76:
Date :10/10/84:
Type (1 = Check, 2 = Other) :_:
```

The program wants to know what type of expense this was. If a check is involved, the user should type in 1. However, since this is a withheld expense, the user should enter 2. At that point, the screen asks for the next transaction.

In the next transaction, the user enters account number 710, and fills in the description field rather then pressing RETURN. He then fills in the amount and date, then types in 1 to indicate that a check is involved. The screen then asks for additional information about the check, as shown below:

```
--- Enter new transactions (0 when done) ---
Account Number :710.00:    Entertainment (Bus.)
Description :Lunch with Terri   :
Amount :    12.99:
Date :10/10/84:
Type (1 = Check, 2 = Other) :1:
Check number :_234:
To whom paid? :                      :
Print a check? (Y/N) :   :
```

The system automatically tracks check numbers, so the user can just use the check number suggested or type in another. Then he needs to fill in the prompt about who the check was (or is to be) written to, and then answer Y or N to "Print a check?" Obviously, if the user already wrote the check, there is no need to print another. However, if the user wishes the system to print the check, he can answer Y to this question, and a check will be printed when the user requests that option from the menu.

The command file to perform these feats is called ADDTRANS.CMD. Its pseudocode is displayed in Figure 16.1.

OK, here we go. First, we'll start out with the usual comments and get the last check number used from the general information file. Note that the memory variable CNO stores the check number:

```
* * * * * * * * * * * * * * * * * * * * * * * * * ADDTRANS.CMD
* * * * * * * * * * * * * * * * * * * * * * * * * Add new transactions.

* * * * * * * * * * * * * * * * * First, get last check number.
```

Get last check number from general information file

Define primary and secondary files

Set up a loop for adding transactions
    Add a blank record to the transactions file
    Fill in the date field with today's date
    Display instructions

    Set up a loop for rejecting invalid numbers
        Ask for account number
        If the user enters a number (not zero)
            Make sure account exists on COA
            If number exists, get account title
            If number does not exist, display warning,
                beep, and loop to account number prompt

        If no account number entered, exit

    Get rest of transaction if user not exiting
        Get reason for transaction
        If no reason typed in, use account title
        Get amount and date

        If expense transaction, ask about type
        (check or not?)

        If check to be written, ask for check information
            Display and ask for check number
            Ask to whom paid
            Print a check?

        If check not to be printed, flag as already written

        Increment check number counter by one

Continue loop for adding transactions (unless exiting)

When done adding transactions, close files, get rid of blank record, and update the general information file

Release memory variables
Return to main menu

Figure 16.1: Pseudocode for the ADDTRANS command file.

Adding and Updating Transactions

```
USE GENINFO
STORE LAST:CHECK TO CNO
```

Next the command file needs to open both the trans data file, for adding the new transactions to, and the COA file, for verifying account numbers and looking up titles:

```
SELE PRIM
USE COA INDEX COA
SELE SECO
USE TRANS INDEX ACCT,DATES
```

Now we need to set up loop for adding transactions:

```
* * * * * * * * * * * * * * * * * * * Start loop for adding transactions.
STORE T TO ADDING
DO WHILE ADDING
```

Once the loop is started, the program needs to add a blank record to the trans file, and fill in the DATE field with today's date. Then it clears the screen and displays brief instructions:

```
APPEND BLANK
REPLACE DATE WITH T:DATE
ERASE
@ 1, 0 SAY "-- Enter new transactions (0 when done)"
```

Now we need a loop for checking account numbers. If the user types in an invalid account number, the program needs to loop and ask for the account number again. The variable OK controls this loop. Then the command file asks for the account number:

```
* * * * * * * * * * * * * Ask for account number of
* * * * * * * * * * * * * transaction, and set up loop
* * * * * * * * * * * * * for rejecting invalid numbers.
STORE N TO OK
DO WHILE .NOT. OK
   @ 3, 0 SAY "Account Number"
   @ 3,15 GET ACCT
   READ
```

If the user entered an account number (greater than zero), the command file needs to look up the account number on the chart of accounts (primary) file:

```
IF ACCT > 0
   * * * * * * * * * * * * * Make sure account exists on COA.
   STORE STR(ACCT,6,2) TO LOOKUP
   SELE PRIM
   FIND &LOOKUP
```

If the account number exists, the program displays the account title on the screen, and stores it to the memory variable MTITLE. If the account number does not exist, the program beeps and warns the user:

```
IF # > 0
    * * * * * If found, get account title.
    STORE T TO OK
    @ 3,26 SAY TITLE
    STORE TITLE TO MTITLE
ELSE
    * * * * * If not found, warn user.
    @ 3,26 SAY "No such account!"
    ? CHR(7)
ENDIF (account number exists)
```

If the user did not enter an account number at all, the program modifies the looping variables (ADDING and OK), and then drops to the ENDDO commands (LOOP). The current values of ADDING and OK are such that both loops will terminate, and the program will begin terminating:

```
    ELSE
        STORE F TO ADDING
        STORE T TO OK
        LOOP
    ENDIF (acct > 0)
    SELE SECO
ENDDO (while .NOT. ok)
```

If the user did not request to exit, the program asks for a description of the transaction:

```
* * Get rest of transaction if user not exiting.
IF ADDING
    * * * * * * * * * * * * * Get reason for transaction.
    @ 5, 0 SAY "Description"
    @ 5,12 GET REASON
    READ
```

If the user did not type in a description, the program automatically fills in and displays the account title:

```
    * * * * * * * * * * * * * * If no reason typed in,
    * * * * * * * * * * * * * * use account title.
    IF REASON = " "
        REPLACE REASON WITH MTITLE
        @ 5,13 SAY REASON
    ENDIF (reason = " ")
```

Next, it asks for the amount and date of the transaction:

```
* * * * * * * * * * * * * * Get amount and date.
@ 7, 0 SAY "Amount"
@ 7, 7 GET AMOUNT
@ 9, 0 SAY "Date"
@ 9, 5 GET DATE
READ
```

Now, if the transaction being typed in is an expense transaction, (and is not a subaccount), the program asks for the transaction type (1 = check, 2 = other). Since we made the rule that all subaccounts have nonzero decimal places, we can easily determine if an account is a regular or subaccount by seeing if the integer value of the account is identical to the account number. That is, if the account number is 100.00, then its integer equivalent (100) is identical to its full amount (100.00). However, the integer equivalent of subaccount 123.45 (123) is not identical to the full number (123.45). This routine makes that decision, and asks for additional data if appropriate:

```
* * * * * * * * * * * Ask about type if expense
* * * * * * * * * * * account and not a subaccount.
IF ACCT > 299.99 .AND. INT(ACCT) = ACCT
   @ 11, 0 SAY "Type (1 = Check, 2 = Other)"
   @ 11,24 GET TYPE
   READ
```

Now, if a check is involved (TYPE = 1), the program displays the check number (modifiable), asks for payee, and asks if a check should be printed. These data are stored on the trans file in the fields CHECK:NO, TO:WHOM, and WRITTEN:

```
* * * * * * * * * * * * If check is involved,
* * * * * * * * * * * ask for check information.
IF TYPE = 1
   REPL CHECK:NO WITH CNO
   STORE " " TO YN
   @ 13, 0 SAY "Check Number"
   @ 13,13 GET CHECK:NO
   @ 15, 0 SAY "To Whom Paid"
   @ 15,13 GET TO:WHOM
   @ 17,0 SAY "Print a check? (Y/N)"
   @ 17,22 GET YN PICT "!"
   READ
```

If there is no need to print a check, the program flags the WRITTEN field for this transaction as T (true), meaning the check has already been written:

```
********* If check not to be printed,
********* flag as already written.
IF YN = "N"
   REPLACE WRITTEN WITH T
ENDIF (yn=y)
```

Then it increments the check number counter (CNO) by one, and closes the IF and DO WHILE clauses:

```
            ********* Increment check number.
            STORE CHECK:NO TO CNO
            STORE CNO +1 TO CNO
         ENDIF (type = 1
      ENDIF (acct > 299.99)

   ENDIF(if adding)

ENDDO (while adding)
```

When done adding transactions, the program deletes the last appended blank record, closes all data files, releases memory variables, updates the geninfo file with the new last check number, and returns to the main menu:

```
************* When done adding transactions,
************* close files, get rid of blank
************* record, and update the
************* general information file.
SELE SECO
DELE ALL FOR ACCT=0
PACK
SELE PRIM
USE
USE GENINFO
REPLACE LAST:CHECK WITH CNO
USE
RELEASE CNO,ADDING,OK,LOOKUP,MTITLE
RETURN
```

The complete ADDTRANS.CMD command file is displayed in Figure 16.2.

Updating the Chart of Accounts

Main menu option 2 allows the user to update the chart of accounts from the transactions. The user can update at any time, but must tell

Adding and Updating Transactions

```
********************************* ADDTRANS.CMD
************************* Add new transactions.

****************** First, get last check number.
USE GENINFO
STORE LAST:CHECK TO CNO

SET BELL OFF
SELE PRIM
USE TRANS INDEX ACCT,DATES
SELE SECO
USE COA INDEX COA

SELE PRIM

******************** Get data for transactions.
STORE T TO ADDING
DO WHILE ADDING
   APPEND BLANK
   REPLACE DATE WITH T:DATE

   ERASE
   @  1, 0 SAY "--- Enter new transactions (0 when done)"

   ************** Ask for account number of
   ************** transaction, and set up loop
   ************** for rejecting invalid numbers.
   STORE N TO OK
   DO WHILE .NOT. OK
      @  3, 0 SAY "Account Number"
      @  3,15 GET ACCT
      READ

      IF ACCT > 0
         ************** Make sure account exists on COA.
         STORE STR(ACCT,6,2) TO LOOKUP
         SELE SECO
         FIND &LOOKUP
         IF # > 0
            ***** If found, get account title.
            STORE T TO OK
            @ 3,26 SAY TITLE
            STORE TITLE TO MTITLE
         ELSE
            ***** If not found, warn user.
            @ 3,26 SAY "No such account!"
            ? CHR(7)
         ENDIF (account number exists)
      ELSE
         STORE F TO ADDING
         STORE T TO OK
         LOOP
      ENDIF (acct > 0)
   SELE PRIM
ENDDO (while .NOT. ok)
```

Figure 16.2: The ADDTRANS.CMD command file.

```
** Get rest of transaction if user not exiting.
IF ADDING
   ************** Get reason for transaction.
   @  5, 0 SAY "Description"
   @  5,12 GET REASON
   READ

   *************** If no reason typed in,
   *************** use account title.
   IF REASON = " "
      REPLACE REASON WITH TITLE
      @ 5,13 SAY REASON
   ENDIF

   *************** Get amount and date.
   @  7, 0 SAY "Amount"
   @  7, 7 GET AMOUNT
   @  9, 0 SAY "Date"
   @  9, 5 GET DATE
   READ

   *********** Ask about type if expense
   *********** account and not a subaccount.
   IF ACCT > 299.99 .AND. INT(ACCT)=ACCT
      @ 11, 0 SAY "Type (1=Check, 2=Other)"
      @ 11,24 GET TYPE
      READ
      ************ If a check is involved,
      ************ ask for check information.
      IF TYPE = 1
         REPL CHECK:NO WITH CNO
         STORE " " TO YN
         @ 13, 0 SAY "Check Number"
         @ 13,13 GET CHECK:NO
         @ 15, 0 SAY "To Whom Paid"
         @ 15,13 GET TO:WHOM
         @ 17,0 SAY "Print a check? (Y/N)"
         @ 17,22 GET YN PICT "!"
         READ

         ********* If check not to be printed,
         ********* flag as already written.
         IF YN = "N"
            REPLACE WRITTEN WITH T
         ENDIF

         ********* Increment check number.
         STORE CHECK:NO TO CNO
         STORE CNO +1 TO CNO
      ENDIF (type = 1
      ENDIF (acct > 299.99)

   ENDIF(if adding)

ENDDO (while adding)
```

Figure 16.2: *The ADDTRANS.CMD command file (continued).*

```
************** When done adding transactions,
************** close files, get rid of blank
************** record, and update the
************** general information file.
SELE SECO
USE
SELE PRIM
DELE ALL FOR ACCT=0
PACK
USE
USE GENINFO
REPLACE LAST:CHECK WITH CNO
USE
RELEASE CNO,ADDING,OK,LOOKUP,MTITLE,YN
RETURN
```

Figure 16.2: *The ADDTRANS.CMD command file (continued).*

the program if the update marks the beginning of a new month, quarter, and year. If the user updates in the middle of a month, then the transaction file amounts are simply added to the month-to-date, quarter-to-date, and year-to-date amounts. If an update represents the beginning of a new month, then the existing month-to-date totals must be set to zero prior to incrementing by the amounts in the transaction file. This is accomplished similarly for the quarter-to-date and year-to-date values.

If the user selects option 2 from the main menu, the update procedure begins. First, the command file displays the message:

> This program should be performed to bring the
> chart of accounts balances up-to-date
>
> Is this the program you want? :   :

Assuming the user did not accidentally select this option, he can answer Y, and continue with the update. The screen then displays:

> Chart of accounts was last updated on 10/10/84
>   Is this the start of a new month? :_:

If the user answers Y, the command file then also displays prompts for the quarter-to-date and year-to-date fields, as shown below:

> Chart of accounts was last updated on 10/10/84
>   Is this the start of a new month? :Y:
>   Is this the start of a new quarter? :_:
>   Is this the start of a new year? :   :
>   OK? (Y/N) :   :

The user then answers the remaining questions, and the "OK?" prompt holds the answers on the screen so the user has a chance to think twice. An accident here can be costly, but the only protection we can offer the user at this point is a chance to double-check and think twice. If the user notices an error in the answers above the "OK?" prompt, he can type in N, and the prompts will be redisplayed.

Once the user answers yes to the "OK?" prompt, the command file performs the update, and returns to the main menu. It also records the date of this update on the general information file.

Bookkeeping system updates are handled by the UPDATE.CMD command file. The pseudocode is presented in Figure 16.3.

We'll now develop the UPDATE command file. First, the opening remarks and the option to immediately return to the main menu:

```
************************************* UPDATE.CMD
************ Update the chart of accounts (COA)
************ file from transactions (trans).
ERASE
? "This program should be performed to bring the "
? "Chart of Accounts balances up-to-date"
?
STORE " " TO YN
5,2 SAY "Is this the program you want? " GET YN
READ
************** Return to main menu, if requested.
IF !(YN) <> "Y"
    RETURN
ENDIF (yn <> y)
```

Next, the command file needs to get the date of the last update from the general information file to display on the screen as a convenience and reminder to the user:

```
****** Get date of last update from the general
****** information file.
USE GENINFO
STORE LAST:UPDAT TO LAST:DATE
```

Now the command file needs to display the date of the last update, and ask the user if this is the start of a new month. If it is a new month the command file also asks if it is a new quarter and year too. The prompts are placed in a loop so that if the user makes a mistake, he can try again. These lines handle that task:

```
**** Ask about how to perform the update, and
**** double-check for safety.
STORE F TO OK
```

Display opening message

If user does not want this option, return to main menu

Get date of last update from the general information file

Clear the screen
Display date of the last update

Start loop for asking how to perform update
    Ask if this is the start of a new month
    If the start of a new month . . .
        Ask if start of new quarter
        Ask if start of new year
        Ask if OK to continue
    If not OK, loop and redisplay update options

Begin update
Copy all nonposted records from the trans file to a temp file, then flag all trans records as posted

Open the chart of accounts file
If starting a new month, set all month-to-date
    values to zero

If starting a new quarter, set all quarter-to-date
    values to zero

If starting a new year, set all year-to-date
    values to zero

Set up primary (COA) and secondary (temp) files for update

Loop through each record of the temp file
    Find temp acct number on COA file
    Increment COA MTD amount by temp file amount
    Increment COA QTD amount by temp file amount
    Increment COA YTD amount by temp file amount
    Skip to next record in the temp file
Continue update loop (until end of temp file)

Update the general information file with new date of last update

Close data files
Release memory variables
Return to main menu

Figure 16.3: *Pseudocode for the UPDATE.CMD command file.*

```
        DO WHILE .NOT. OK
           ERASE
           STORE " " TO NEW:QTR,NEW:MONTH,NEW:YEAR
           @ 5,2 SAY "Chart of accounts was last updated"
           @ 5,36 SAY "on " + LAST:DATE
           @ 8,2 SAY "Is this the start of a new month? "
           @ 8,38 GET NEW:MONTH PICT "!"
           READ
           IF NEW:MONTH = "Y"
              @ 10,2 SAY "Is this the start of a new quarter? "
              @ 10,38 GET NEW:QTR PICT "!"
              @ 12,2 SAY "Is this the start of a new year? "
              @ 12,38 GET NEW:YEAR PICT "!"
              READ
           ENDIF (new:month = y)
           @ 14,20 SAY "OK? (Y/N) " GET OK PICT "!"
           READ
        ENDDO (while not ok)
```

Once the user is ready to proceed, the program takes all the nonupdated transactions from the trans file, and places them on a temporary file (temp). Then it flags all the records in the trans file as having been posted (POSTED = T):

```
        * * * * * * * * * * * * Copy all nonposted records from
        * * * * * * * * * * * * the trans file to a temp file,
        * * * * * * * * * * * * then flag all records as posted.
        ERASE
        ? "Performing the update. . . ."
        USE TRANS INDEX ACCT
        COPY TO TEMP FOR .NOT. POSTED
        REPLACE NOUPDATE ALL POSTED WITH T
```

Now, if this update marks the beginning of a new month, all the month-to-date values in the chart of accounts must be set to zero prior to updating. These lines handle that:

```
        * * * * * * * * * * * * * Set month-to-date field (AMOUNT)
        * * * * * * * * * * * * * to zero if starting a new month.
        USE COA INDEX COA
        IF NEW:MONTH = "Y"
           REPLACE NOUPDATE ALL AMOUNT WITH 0
        ENDIF (new:month = y)
```

Similarly, if this update begins a new quarter or year, the chart of accounts quarter-to-date (QTD) and year-to-date (YTD) fields must also be set back to zero, as below:

```
        * * * * * * * * * * * * * If start of new quarter, replace all
        * * * * * * * * * * * * * quarterly balances with zeroes too.
```

```
IF NEW:QTR = "Y"
   REPLACE NOUPDATE ALL QTD WITH 0
ENDIF (new:qtr = y)
* * * * * * * * * * * * * If start of new year, replace all
* * * * * * * * * * * * * yearly balances with zeroes too.
IF NEW:YEAR = "Y"
   REPLACE NOUPDATE ALL YTD WITH 0
ENDIF (new:year = y)
```

To perform the update, the program will loop through the temporary file, individually read each record, and update the appropriate record in the chart of accounts file. The UPDATE command will not do the trick for us here, because we need to have control over how the QTD and YTD fields in the chart of accounts get incremented. The UPDATE command could update the AMOUNT field on the COA file from the AMOUNT field on the temp file, but then incrementing only the appropriate QTD and YTD fields would be impossible.

We'll need to have both files open to perform this update, so the lines below set up the primary and secondary relationships:

```
* * * * * * * * * * * * * Set up data files for the update.
SELE PRIM
USE COA INDEX COA
SELE SECO
USE TEMP
```

Now the update is performed by reading each record in the temp file, finding the record in the COA file with the same account number, and incrementing the COA AMOUNT, QTD, and YTD fields by the amount in the temp file. The loop below handles the update:

```
* * * * * * * * * * * * * * * * * * * * * * * * * * * * Do the update.
DO WHILE .NOT. EOF
   STORE STR(ACCT,6,2) TO LOOKUP
   SELE PRIM
   FIND &LOOKUP
   REPLACE NOUPDATE P.AMOUNT WITH P.AMOUNT + S.AMOUNT
   REPLACE NOUPDATE QTD WITH QTD + S.AMOUNT
   REPLACE NOUPDATE YTD WITH YTD + S.AMOUNT
   SELE SECO
   SKIP
ENDDO (while not end of secondary file)
```

When the loop is done, the update is complete. We merely need to close the primary and secondary data files:

```
* * * * * * * * * * * * * When done with update, close the
* * * * * * * * * * * * * data files.
```

```
SELE SECO
USE
SELE PRIM
USE
```

Then, the program needs to store the date of this update in the general information file in the next lines:

```
************* Update general information file
************* with new date of last update.
USE GENINFO
REPLACE LAST:UPDAT WITH T:DATE
```

Now we can close the geninfo file, release the memory variables, and return to the main menu:

```
USE
RELEASE LAST:DATE,NEW:MONTH,NEW:QTR,NEW:YEAR
RELEASE LOOKUP,YN,OK
RETURN
```

Figure 16.4 displays the complete UPDATE command file.

```
*********************************** UPDATE.CMD
************ Update the chart of accounts (COA)
************ file from transactions (trans).
ERASE
? "This program should be performed to bring the "
? "Chart of Accounts balances up-to-date"
?
STORE " " TO YN
@ 5,2 SAY "Is this the program you want? " GET YN
READ
************** Return to main menu, if requested.
IF !(YN) <> "Y"
   RETURN
ENDIF (yn <> y)

****** Get date of last update from the general
****** information file.
USE GENINFO
STORE LAST:UPDAT TO LAST:DATE

**** Ask about how to perform the update, and
**** double-check for safety.
STORE F TO OK
DO WHILE .NOT. OK
   ERASE
   STORE " " TO NEW:QTR,NEW:MONTH,NEW:YEAR
```

Figure 16.4: The UPDATE.CMD command file.

```
    @ 5,2 SAY "Chart of accounts was last updated "
    @ 5,36 SAY "on "+LAST:DATE
    @ 8,2 SAY "Is this the start of a new month? "
    @ 8,38 GET NEW:MONTH PICT "!"
    READ
    IF NEW:MONTH="Y"
       @ 10,2 SAY "Is this the start of a new quarter? "
       @ 10,38 GET NEW:QTR PICT "!"
       @ 12,2 SAY "Is this the start of a new year? "
       @ 12,38 GET NEW:YEAR PICT "!"
       READ
    ENDIF (new:month = y)
    @ 14,20 SAY "OK? (Y/N) " GET OK PICT "!"
    READ
ENDDO (while not ok)

************* Copy all non-posted records from
************* the trans file to a temp file,
************* then flag all records as posted.
ERASE
? "Performing the update...."
USE TRANS INDEX ACCT
COPY TO TEMP FOR .NOT. POSTED
REPLACE ALL POSTED WITH T NOUPDATE
************* Set month-to-date field (AMOUNT)
************* to zero if starting a new month.
USE COA INDEX COA
IF NEW:MONTH = "Y"
   REPLACE ALL AMOUNT WITH 0 NOUPDATE
ENDIF (:new:month = y)

************* If start of new quarter, replace all
************* quarterly balances with zeroes too.
IF NEW:QTR="Y"
   REPLACE ALL QTD WITH 0 NOUPDATE
ENDIF (new:qtr=y)

************* If start of new year, replace all
************* yearly balances with zeroes too.
IF NEW:YEAR="Y"
   REPLACE ALL YTD WITH 0 NOUPDATE
ENDIF (new:year=y)

************* Set up data files for update.
SELE PRIM
USE COA INDEX COA
SELE SECO
USE TEMP

***************************** Do the update.
DO WHILE .NOT. EOF
   STORE STR(ACCT,6,2) TO LOOKUP
   SELE PRIM
   FIND &LOOKUP
   REPLACE P.AMOUNT WITH P.AMOUNT+S.AMOUNT
   REPLACE QTD WITH QTD + S.AMOUNT
   REPLACE YTD WITH YTD + S.AMOUNT
```

Figure 16.4: The UPDATE.CMD command file (continued).

```
        SELE SECO
        SKIP
ENDDO (while not end of secondary file)

************** When done with update, close the
************** data files.
SELE SECO
USE
SELE PRIM
USE

************** Update general information file
************** with new date of last update.
USE GENINFO
REPLACE LAST:UPDAT WITH T:DATE
USE

RELEASE LAST:DATE,NEW:MONTH,NEW:QTR,NEW:YEAR
RELEASE LOOKUP,YN,OK
```

Figure 16.4: The UPDATE.CMD command file (continued).

Summary

In this chapter, we've developed two more command files for the bookkeeping system. These are:

1. ADDTRANS.CMD, which allows the user to add new transactions to the bookkeeping system. This program demonstrates several techniques that are useful in all bookkeeping systems, including:

    - Check for valid account numbers
    - Automatic display of account names
    - Optional check printing
    - Automatic check numbering

2. UPDATE.CMD, which automatically updates all balances on all accounts based on new transactions. The program also asks the user if the update represents the beginning of a new month, quarter, or year, and adjusts the account balances accordingly.

In the next chapter, we'll develop programs to manage the check register.

CHAPTER 17
MANAGING THE CHECK REGISTER

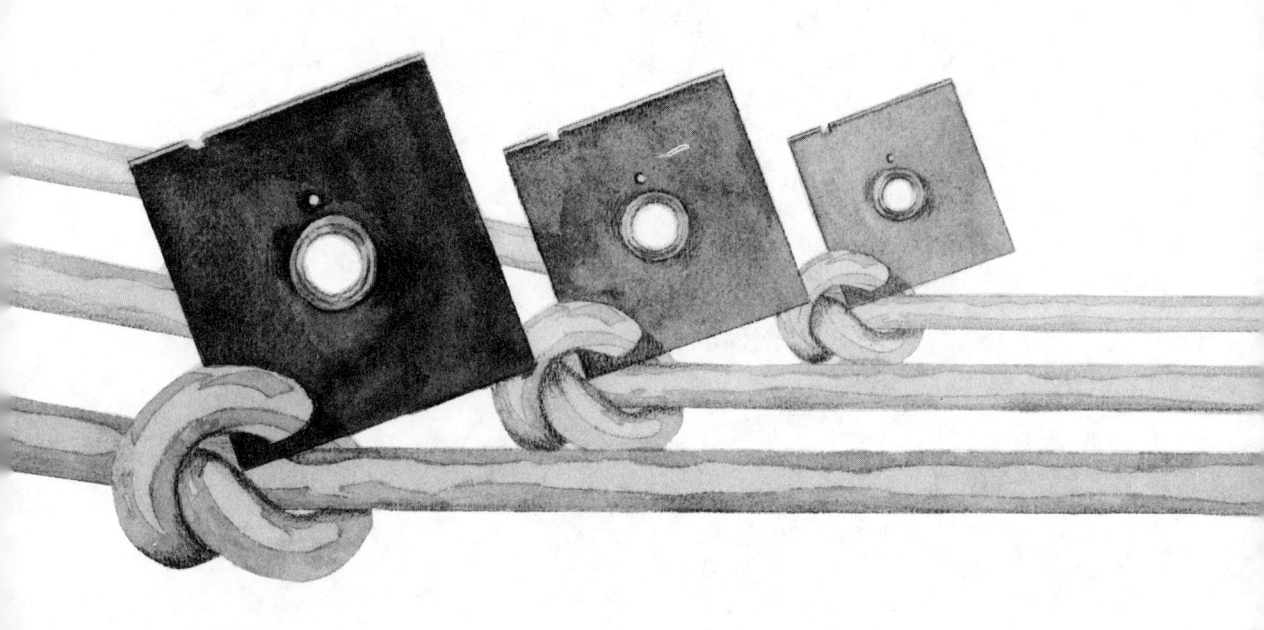

The bookkeeping system allows the user to specify if a check was used to pay an expense when he is entering transaction data. In addition, the user can ask that the system print the checks. Furthermore, the system maintains an electronic check register, and allows the user to record deposits, print the current balance, and print the register for any range of dates. In this chapter, we'll develop the programs to perform these three check register functions.

The first command file that we will develop, REGISTER.CMD, records deposits and displays the balance. Data for the check register are stored on the register database file, which we created previously with the structure:

STRUCTURE FOR FILE: B:REGISTER.DBF

FLD	NAME	TYPE	WIDTH	DEC	CONTENTS
001	CHECK:NO	N	004		Check number
002	TO:WHOM	C	020		To whom paid
003	REASON	C	020		Reason for check
004	AMOUNT	N	012	002	Amount
005	DATE	C	008		Check date
006	DEPOSIT	L	001		Is this a deposit?

To manage the check register, the user selects option 3 from the bookkeeping system main menu. He will then see the following submenu:

Check Register Options
1. Make Deposit
2. Check Balance
3. Return to Main Menu

If the user selects option 1, the screen clears and displays a summary of past deposits similar to the one below:

Existing deposits . . .

01/01/84   2500.00
02/01/84   5000.00
03/01/84   2500.55
04/05/84   2450.55

Add another deposit? (Y/N)

This helps the user to see if he has already recorded the deposit he's planning to enter. If the user wishes to add a deposit, he just types Y, the screen clears, and displays prompts for filling in information, as shown below:

Enter Date :   /   /   :
Enter Amount :   . :
Source of check? :   :

The user then types in the information requested, and the deposit is stored on the check register file.

If the user selects option 2, "Check Balance" from the submenu, the screen clears and briefly displays the message:

Calculating . . . .

and then displays the checking account balance:

Current balance is : 1234.67

The user can then select option 3 from the submenu to return to the main menu.

Recording Deposits, Calculating Balances

The pseudocode for the REGISTER.CMD command file is displayed in Figure 17.1. The REGISTER command file begins by setting up a loop for the menu, displaying the menu, and waiting for a response:

```
*********************************** REGISTER.CMD
***** Add deposits, get balance from check register.
STORE " " TO RCHOICE
DO WHILE RCHOICE # "3"
   ERASE
   TEXT

      Check Register Options

   1. Make a Deposit
   2. Check Balance
   3. Return to Main Menu

ENDTEXT
@ 8,15 SAY "Enter choice (1-3) ";
   GET RCHOICE
READ
```

When the user makes his request, a DO CASE clause performs the appropriate task. If the user selects option 1, the first CASE statement opens the REGISTER.DBF data file, and lists all existing deposits (those records with T stored in the logical DEPOSIT field):

```
********* Perform requested task.
DO CASE
   CASE RCHOICE = "1"
      ************* Make deposits.
   ERASE
USE REGISTER
   ************* Display existing deposits.
? " Existing deposits . . ."
?
```

> Set up loop for displaying menu
>   Clear the screen
>   Display the menu
>   Wait for response
>
>   Perform requested task
>
>   If the user requests to make a deposit . . .
>   Clear the screen
>   Use the register data file
>   Display existing deposits
>   Set up loop for adding deposits
>   Get data for deposit from user
>   Ask user if he wants to make more deposits
>   Continue loop while user adds deposits
>
>   If the user requests to see balance
>   Sum deposit amounts
>   Sum check amounts
>   Display balance (deposits – checks)
>   Pause screen
>
> Continue menu loop (until exit requested)
>
> Release memory variables
> Return to main menu

Figure 17.1: Pseudocode for the REGISTER.CMD command file.

```
LIST OFF FOR DEPOSIT DATE,AMOUNT
?
```

Next, it sets up a loop for adding deposits. It repeatedly asks the user for deposit information until the user wishes to stop adding. These lines will handle the job:

```
STORE Y TO ADDING
DO WHILE ADDING
? " Add another deposit? (Y/N) "
WAIT TO YN
```

When the user asks to add a deposit, the program adds a blank record to the REGISTER.DBF data file, places a T in the DEPOSIT field, puts the word "Deposit" in the TO:WHOM field, and asks for the remaining information. The additional lines below close the IF and DO

WHILE clauses in this CASE statement:

```
IF !(YN) = "Y"
   APPEND BLANK
   REPLACE DEPOSIT WITH T
   REPL TO:WHOM WITH "Deposit"
   ERASE
   @ 5,2 SAY "Enter Date " GET DATE PICT "99/99/99"
   @ 7,2 SAY "Enter Amount " GET AMOUNT
   @ 9,2 SAY "Source of check? " GET REASON
   READ
ELSE
   STORE F TO ADDING
ENDIF (while adding)
ENDDO (while adding)
```

If the user asks to check the account balance, the command file sums all the amount fields for the deposits to a variable called DEPS. Then, it sums all the check amount (.NOT. DEPOSIT) to a variable called CHEX, and displays the difference on the screen. It then waits for the user to press any key prior to returning to the submenu:

```
CASE RCHOICE = "2"
******** Calculate and display balance.
ERASE
? "Calculating . . . . ."
USE REGISTER
SUM AMOUNT FOR DEPOSIT TO DEPS
SUM AMOUNT FOR .NOT. DEPOSIT TO CHEX
@ 10,10 SAY "Current balance is " +;
STR(DEPS-CHEX,9,2)
?
?
? "Press any key to continue . . . . ."
WAIT

ENDCASE
```

When the user asks to return to the main menu, the menu loop is terminated, memory variables are released, and the program returns control to the main menu:

```
ENDDO (while rchoice # 3)
RELE RCHOICE,ADDING,YN,DEPS,CHEX
RETURN
```

The REGISTER.CMD command file is displayed in Figure 17.2.

Advanced Techniques in dBASE II

```
************************************ REGISTER.CMD
** Add deposits, get balance from check register.
STORE " " TO RCHOICE
DO WHILE RCHOICE # "3"
    ERASE
    TEXT
                Check Register Options

                1. Make a Deposit
                2. Check Balance

                3. Return to Main Menu

    ENDTEXT
    @ 8,15 SAY "Enter choice (1-3) ";
        GET RCHOICE
    READ

    ********* Perform requested task.
    DO CASE

        CASE RCHOICE = "1"
        ************* Make deposits.
        ERASE
        USE REGISTER
        ************* Display existing deposits.
        ? " Existing deposits... "
        ?
        LIST OFF FOR DEPOSIT DATE,AMOUNT
        ?
        STORE Y TO ADDING
        DO WHILE ADDING

            ? " Add another deposit? (Y/N) "
            WAIT TO YN

            IF !(YN)="Y"
                APPEND BLANK
                REPLACE DEPOSIT WITH T
                REPL TO:WHOM WITH "Deposit"
                ERASE
                @ 5,2 SAY "Enter Date ";
                    GET DATE PICT "99/99/99"
                @ 7,2 SAY "Enter Amount " GET AMOUNT
                @ 9,2 SAY "Source of check? ";
                    GET REASON
                READ
            ELSE
                STORE F TO ADDING
            ENDIF (while adding)
        ENDDO (while adding)
        CASE RCHOICE = "2"
            ******** Calculate and display balance.
            ERASE
            USE REGISTER
            ? "Calculating....."
```

Figure 17.2: *The REGISTER.CMD command file.*

```
              SUM AMOUNT FOR DEPOSIT TO DEPS
              SUM AMOUNT FOR .NOT. DEPOSIT TO CHEX
              @ 10,10 SAY "Current balance is "+;
                 STR(DEPS-CHEX,9,2)
              ?
              ?
              ? "Press any key to continue....."
              WAIT

         ENDCASE

    ENDDO (while rchoice # 3)

    RELE RCHOICE,ADDING,YN,DEPS,CHEX
    RETURN
```

Figure 17.2: The REGISTER.CMD command file (continued).

Printing the Check Register

Option 4 from the bookkeeping system allows the user to print reports. This calls up another submenu:

Bookkeeping Report Options
1. Current Transactions
2. Chart of Accounts
3. Write Checks
4. Check Register
5. Return to Main Menu

If the user selects option 4, the screen briefly displays the message:

Updating register file . . . .

then asks for a range of dates for printing the register, and asks if the report should be printed, using a screen as below:

Enter starting date :   /   /   :
Enter ending date :   /   /   :
Send to printer? (Y/N) :   :

The user can fill in a range of dates and opt to display the register on the printer. The program then prints the register and balance for the deposits and checks within the range of dates, as below:

PAGE NO. 00001
03/31/84

		Check Register		
Chck No.	To Whom paid	Purpose	Amount	Date
100	Bank of America	Payment on rental	999.99	01/15/84
101	Allstate Finance	Car Payment	223.13	01/15/84
102	Allstate Insurance	Insurance	222.22	01/15/84
103	Bob's Auto Finance	Porsche Payment	6543.21	02/01/84
0	Deposit	Interest Income	123.00	02/15/84
0	Deposit	Salary	5000.00	02/15/84
0	Deposit	Loan repayment	234.56	03/01/84
104	Bank of America	House Payment	600.00	03/01/84
0	Deposit	Salary	5555.55	03/05/84
	Balance		2324.56	

The report is printed from a REPORT FORM format file called REGISTER.FRM, that was created by typing in the commands:

```
USE REGISTER
REPORT FORM REGISTER
```

from the dot prompt, and answering the prompts as follows:

```
ENTER OPTIONS, M=LEFT MARGIN, L=LINES/PAGE, W=PAGE
WIDTH m=1
PAGE HEADING? (Y/N) y
ENTER PAGE HEADING: Check Register
DOUBLE SPACE REPORT? (Y/N) n
ARE TOTALS REQUIRED? (Y/N) n
COL     WIDTH,CONTENTS
001     4,CHECK:NO
ENTER HEADING: >Chck No.
002     20,TO:WHOM
ENTER HEADING: <To Whom paid
003     20,REASON
ENTER HEADING: <Purpose
004     12,AMOUNT
ENTER HEADING: >Amount
005     8,DATE
ENTER HEADING: <Date
006
```

The REGREPT.CMD command file uses the REGISTER.FRM format to print the report. The pseudocode for REGREPT is displayed in Figure 17.3.

The REGREPT command file begins by clearing the screen and displaying the message "Updating register file . . ." since the update from

> Clear the screen
> Use the trans file
> Send all written, nonregistered check transactions
>   from the trans file to a temp file
> Flag all registered checks in the trans file as registered
>
> Update register from temp file
>
> Sum checks and deposits
>
> Ask about date range and printer
>
> Set printer on if requested
>
> Print the report using REGISTER.FRM
> Print the balance
>
> Set the printer off
> Release memory variables
> Return to menu

Figure 17.3: Pseudocode for REGREPT.CMD command file.

the trans file may take a little time:

```
* * * * * * * * * * * * * * * * * * * * * * * * * * * REGREPT.CMD
* * * * * * * * * Update check register file and print it.
ERASE
? "Updating register file . . ."
```

Now, before printing the check register, all records on the trans file that involve checks that have been written, but have not been sent to the check register yet, need to be added to the REGISTER.DBF data file. We can begin this procedure by copying all the written, nonregistered check transactions from the trans file to a temp (temporary) file. Then, the copied records should be flagged as having been registered. These lines handle those jobs:

```
* * * * Send all written, nonregistered check transactions
* * * * from the trans file to a temp file.
USE TRANS
COPY TO TEMP FOR WRITTEN .AND. .NOT.;
    REGISTERED .AND. TYPE = 1
REPL ALL REGISTERED WITH T FOR WRITTEN .AND. .NOT.;
    REGISTERED .AND. TYPE = 1
```

Now the program can use the register file and append the records from the temp file into it. Only those field names which are identical on both data files (CHECK:NO, TO:WHOM, REASON, AMOUNT, DATE) will be appended. So we simply need to use the register file and APPEND FROM TEMP, as shown below:

```
********************* Update register from temp file.
USE REGISTER
APPEND FROM TEMP
```

Next, the command file needs to sum the amounts for the checks and deposits in the register data file. The sum of the checks is stored in a memory variable called EXPENSE, and the deposit total is stored in INCOME:

```
************ Sum checks and deposits.
? "Calculating balance . . . ."
SUM AMOUNT FOR .NOT. DEPOSIT TO EXPENSE
SUM AMOUNT FOR DEPOSIT TO INCOME
```

Now the program can ask the user about the range of dates to print checks for, and whether or not to send the report to the printer:

```
********************* Ask about date range and printer.
ERASE
STORE " " TO START,FINISH
STORE " " TO YN,COND
3,2 SAY "Enter starting date " GET START PICT "99/99/99"
4,2 SAY "Enter ending date " GET FINISH PICT "99/99/99"
6,2 SAY "Send to printer (Y/N) " GET YN PICT "!"
READ
```

If the user opts to print the report, the command file will set the printer on:

```
****************** Set printer on if requested.
IF YN = "Y"
   SET PRINT ON
ENDIF (yn – y)
SET EJECT OFF
```

Now the program prints the report using the REGISTER.FRM report format, displaying only those records whose dates are greater than or equal to the requested starting date, and less than or equal to the ending date:

```
************ Print the report using REGISTER.FRM.
ERASE
REPO FORM REGISTER FOR DATE > = START .AND.;
   DATE < = FINISH
```

Managing the Check Register 279

Then it prints a couple of blank lines and the account balance, and sets the printer off:

```
?
?
? "    Balance        ",INCOME – EXPENSE
SET PRINT OFF
```

If the report is not being sent to the printer, the program should pause to allow the user time to read the data on the screen:

```
* * * * * * * * * If report not sent to printer, pause.
IF YN # "Y"
   ?
   ?
   ? "Press any key to continue . . ."
   WAIT
ENDIF (yn – y)
```

Finally, the program releases the memory variables, and returns to the menu program:

```
* * * * * * * * * * * * * * Release memory variables
* * * * * * * * * * * * * * and return to reports menu.
RELEASE INCOME,EXPENSE,YN,START,FINISH
RETURN
```

The REGREPT.CMD command file is displayed in Figure 17.4.

```
********************************* REGREPT.CMD
********* Update check register file and print it.
ERASE
? "Updating register file..."

**** Send all written, nonregistered check transactions
**** from the trans file to a temporary file.
USE TRANS
COPY TO TEMP FOR WRITTEN .AND. .NOT.;
 REGISTERED .AND. TYPE=1
REPL ALL REGISTERED WITH T FOR WRITTEN .AND. .NOT.;
 REGISTERED .AND. TYPE=1

********************** Update register from temp file.
USE REGISTER
APPE FROM TEMP

************ Sum checks and deposits.
? "Calculating balance...."
SUM AMOUNT FOR .NOT. DEPOSIT TO EXPENSE
SUM AMOUNT FOR DEPOSIT TO INCOME
```

Figure 17.4: The REGREPT.CMD command file.

```
*********************** Ask about date range and printer.
ERASE
STORE "          " TO START,FINISH
STORE " " TO YN,COND

@ 3,2 SAY "Enter starting date " GET START PICT "99/99/99"
@ 4,2 SAY "Enter ending date " GET FINISH PICT "99/99/99"
@ 6,2 SAY "Send to printer (Y/N) " GET YN PICT "!"
READ

******************** Set printer on if requested.
IF YN="Y"
   SET PRINT ON
ENDIF (yn-y)
SET EJECT OFF

************ Print the report using REGISTER.FRM.
ERASE
REPO FORM REGISTER FOR DATE >= START .AND.;
   DATE <=FINISH
?
?
? "     Balance           ",INCOME-EXPENSE

SET PRINT OFF

********** If report not going to printer, pause.
IF YN # "Y"
   ?
   ?
   ? "Press any key to continue..."
   WAIT
ENDIF (yn # y)

************* Release memory variables
************* and return to menu.
RELEASE INCOME,EXPENSE,YN,START,FINISH
RETURN
```

Figure 17.4: The REGREPT.CMD command file (continued).

Summary

In this chapter, we've developed the command file to manage the check register:

1. REGISTER.CMD, which allows the user to add deposits to the check register and to check the current balance.
2. REGREPT.CMD, which updates the check register file from the file of income and expense transactions. Then, it allows the user to display the check register and current balance. The user may

specify that only checks that fall within a given range of dates be displayed in the report.

In the next chapter, we'll develop programs to display additional bookkeeping reports including the income statement and chart of accounts with account balances. We'll also develop a command file to print checks.

CHAPTER 18
THE BOOKKEEPING SYSTEM REPORTS

In this chapter, we'll develop programs 1) to write checks, 2) to print the current transactions report (income statement), and 3) to print the chart of accounts with monthly, quarterly, and yearly balances. These command files, including the REGREPT.CMD command file we developed in the last chapter, are called from the BREPORTS.CMD command file. BREPORTS is called from the BOOKS.CMD main menu program. The relationship among the command files is shown in Figure 18.1.

```
                          From BOOKS.CMD
                                │
                                ▼
                    ┌───────────────────────────┐
                    │ BREPORTS.CMD              │
                    │ Reports Menu              │
                    │ 1. Income Statement       │
                    │ 2. Chart of Accounts      │
                    │ 3. Checks                 │
                    │ 4. Check Register         │
                    └───────────────────────────┘
```

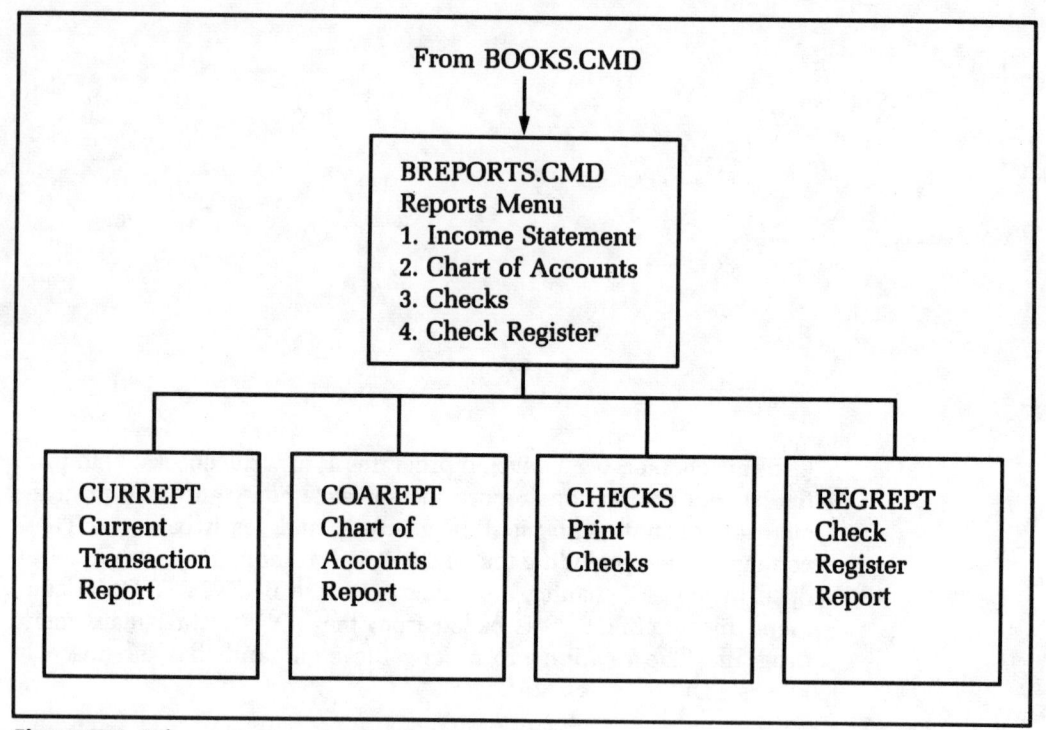

```
┌──────────────┐  ┌──────────────┐  ┌──────────────┐  ┌──────────────┐
│ CURREPT      │  │ COAREPT      │  │ CHECKS       │  │ REGREPT      │
│ Current      │  │ Chart of     │  │ Print        │  │ Check        │
│ Transaction  │  │ Accounts     │  │ Checks       │  │ Register     │
│ Report       │  │ Report       │  │              │  │ Report       │
└──────────────┘  └──────────────┘  └──────────────┘  └──────────────┘
```

Figure 18.1: Software structure for report command files.

Bookkeeping System Reports Menu

When the user selects option 4 (Print Reports) from the main menu, the BREPORTS.CMD command file presents the following menu of report options:

Bookkeeping Report Options
1. Income Statement
2. Chart of Accounts
3. Write Checks
4. Check Register
5. Return to Main Menu

BREPORTS is a simple menu program, and is displayed in Figure 18.2.

```
*********************************** BREPORTS.CMD
********************** Ask user which report
******************** to use, and branch accordingly.
STORE 0 TO REPCHOICE
DO WHILE REPCHOICE <> 5
   ERASE
   TEXT
                  Bookkeeping Report Options

                     1. Income Statement
                     2. Chart of Accounts
                     3. Write checks
                     4. Check Register

                     5. Return to Main Menu

   ENDTEXT
   @ 12,10 SAY "Enter choice (1-5) from above ";
      GET REPCHOICE PICTURE "9"
   READ

   DO CASE
      CASE REPCHOICE=1
         DO CURREPT

      CASE REPCHOICE=2
         DO COAREPT

      CASE REPCHOICE=3
         DO CHECKS

      CASE REPCHOICE=4
         DO REGREPT

   ENDCASE
ENDDO (while repchoice <> 5)
RETURN
```

Figure 18.2: The BREPORTS.CMD command file.

Income Statement

The income statement report allows the user to print transactions for either the current month or any range of dates. Furthermore, the user can opt to have the transactions displayed in either account-number order or date order. When the user opts to print this report, the screen first asks:

Transactions for this month only? :_:

If the user answers Y, only transactions for the current month are displayed. If the user answers N, the screen asks for a range of dates for which to print transactions, as shown below:

```
Enter starting date :_ /   /   :
Enter ending date  :   /   /   :
```

Once the user specifies a date range, the screen displays a menu of sorting options:

Sort Orders
1. By Account Number
2. By Date

Enter choice (1-2) :   :

The user can then specify a sort order. If the user requests account-number order, the report is printed in that order with the account-number field in the left column. If the user opts for date order, the records are displayed in chronological order with the date in the left column, as in Figure 18.3.

Two report format files are used for printing the report. ACCTS.FRM prints the report with account numbers in the left column, and was created by typing in the commands:

```
USE TRANS
REPORT FORM ACCTS
```

and filling in the report form as follows:

```
ENTER OPTIONS, M=LEFT MARGIN, L=LINES/PAGE, W=PAGE
WIDTH m=1
PAGE HEADING? (Y/N) n
DOUBLE SPACE REPORT? (Y/N) n
ARE TOTALS REQUIRED? (Y/N) n
COL     WIDTH,CONTENTS
001     6,ACCT
ENTER HEADING: Acct.
002     8,DATE
ENTER HEADING: Date
003     20,REASON
ENTER HEADING: Description
004     10,AMOUNT
ENTER HEADING: >Amount
005     1,MARKER
ENTER HEADING:
006
```

DATES.FRM is very similar, except that the date, rather than the account number, is placed in the left column. To create the report,

```
              Income Statement for Joe Smith
          For transactions from 01/01/84 to 02/28/84
```

INCOME:

Date	Acct.	Description	Amount
01/15/84	100.00	Regular Income	5555.55
01/15/84	120.00	Interest Income	500.00
02/01/84	100.00	Regular Income	1500.00
Total Income			7555.55

EXPENSES:

Date	Acct.	Description	Amount
01/15/84	300.00	Payment on rental	999.99
01/15/84	300.10	House Interest	400.00*
01/15/84	300.20	House Principal	500.00*
01/15/84	400.00	Car Payment	223.13
01/15/84	500.00	Insurance	123.45
01/15/84	500.00	Insurance	222.22
02/15/84	600.00	Lunch at Bob's	17.50
02/15/84	600.00	Lunch with Bob	32.12
02/28/84	300.00	House Payment	600.00
Total Expenses			2218.41
Total Income			7555.55
Total Expenses			2218.41
Balance			5537.14

NOTE: Subaccounts marked with a * are not included in totals.

Figure 18.3: Sample income statement report.

enter the command REPORT FORM DATES from the dot prompt, and fill out the report questionnaire as below:

```
ENTER OPTIONS, M = LEFT MARGIN, L = LINES/PAGE, W = PAGE
WIDTH m = 1
PAGE HEADING? (Y/N) n
DOUBLE SPACE REPORT? (Y/N) n
ARE TOTALS REQUIRED? (Y/N) n
COL    WIDTH,CONTENTS
001    8,DATE
```

```
ENTER HEADING: Date
002      6,ACCT
ENTER HEADING: Acct.
003      20,REASON
ENTER HEADING: Description
004      10,AMOUNT
ENTER HEADING: >Amount
005      1,MARKER
ENTER HEADING:
006
```

The CURREPT command file uses one of these report formats to print the income statement from the TRANS.DBF data file, depending on whether the user requested account-number or date order. The pseudocode for CURREPT is presented in Figure 18.4.

We'll begin writing the CURREPT.CMD command file by getting the company name from the general information file, and storing it to a memory variable called COMPANY:

```
********************************* CURREPT.CMD
********** Print report of current transactions.

********** First get company name from geninfo file.
USE GENINFO
STORE COMPANY TO COMPANY
```

Then, we will write lines so that the program will ask the user if it should print transactions for the current month only:

```
********** Get information on dates, and store
********** to search macro (COND)
ERASE
STORE " " TO YN
5,2 SAY "Transactions for this month only? ";
   GET YN
   READ
```

If the user answers Y to the question above, the program stores the words "DATE = " and the month (first two characters in the T:DATE memory variable) to a variable called COND, and makes the memory variable RANGE false:

```
********** Set up search condition
********** according to user's request.
IF !(YN) = "Y"
    STORE "DATE = '" + $(T:DATE,1,2) + "'" TO COND
    STORE F TO RANGE
```

If the user wants to print the report for a specified range of dates, the program asks for the starting (START) and ending (FINISH) dates of

The Bookkeeping System Reports

> Get company name from general information file for title
>
> Ask if report should print transactions fo this month only
> If not, ask for range of dates to print transactions for
> Set up a macro for perfoming the search
>
> Display sort options and get sort order
> Set up sort order and appropriate report format
>
> Ask about printer, and set on if necessary
>
> Mark subaccounts for display on report
>
> Calculate income totals, leaving out subaccounts
> Calculate expense totals, leaving out subaccounts
>
> Print title and appropriate subtitle
> Print income transactions and totals
> Print expense transactions and totals
> Display balance at bottom of sheet
> Display message about subaccounts
>
> Move to next page in printer
> Turn the printer off
>
> If report not going to printer, pause on screen
>
> Release memory variables
> Return to BREPORTS program

Figure 18.4: Pseudocode for the CURREPT command file.

the range. Then it stores the words "DATE >= START .AND. DATE <= FINISH" to the COND memory variable, and makes the RANGE variable true, since the program will be printing for a range of dates. The following lines handle these tasks:

```
ELSE
   STORE "        " TO START,FINISH
   @ 7,2 SAY "Enter starting date ";
      GET START PICT "99/99/99"
   @ 9,2 SAY "Enter ending date ";
      GET FINISH PICT "99/99/99"
   READ
   STORE "DATE >=START .AND. DATE <=FINISH" TO COND
   STORE T TO RANGE
ENDIF (yn = y)
```

The COND variable will be used as a macro to calculate totals and determine which transactions are printed, and the RANGE variable will be used to select the proper subheading for the report.

Next, the command file asks the user for a sort order for displaying the transactions:

```
********************* Next, get sort order.
ERASE
STORE 0 TO SCHOICE
3,10 SAY "Sort Orders"
5,8 SAY "1. By Account Number"
6,8 SAY "2. By Date"
8,8 SAY "Enter choice (1-2) " GET SCHOICE PICT "9"
READ
```

If the user selects option 2, the program uses the trans database with the DATES index file, and stores the report format name "DATES" to a variable called ROPTION. If the user wants transactions in account number order, the program uses trans with the ACCT index, and stores "ACCTS" to the ROPTION variable. ROPTION will later be used as a macro to select the report name:

```
************* Set up sort order and report type.
IF SCHOICE = 2
   USE TRANS INDEX DATES
   STORE "DATES" TO ROPTION
ELSE
   USE TRANS INDEX ACCT
   STORE "ACCTS" TO ROPTION
ENDIF (schoice = 2)
```

Next the program asks the user about the printer, and sets it on if requested:

```
********************* Ask about printer . . .
ERASE
STORE " " TO YN
@ 5,2 SAY "Send Report to printer? " GET YN
READ

***************** and set on if necessary.
IF !(YN)="Y"
   SET PRINT ON
ENDIF (yn=y)
```

In order to mark subaccounts in the report, the program must place an asterisk in the MARKER field of all subaccounts in the trans file. To assure accuracy, it will first remove the existing asterisks, then fill in asterisks in the subaccounts (those which have nonzero decimal places):

```
************ Mark subaccounts for report.
REPLACE NOUPDATE ALL MARKER WITH " "
REPLACE NOUPDATE ALL MARKER WITH "*";
   FOR ACCT < > INT(ACCT)
```

Next, the command file calculates totals for the transactions in the appropriate range of dates, excluding the subaccount amounts. It calculates the income and expense totals separately, as shown below:

```
*********** Calculate totals, leaving out subaccounts.
SUM AMOUNT FOR ACCT<300 .AND. &COND .AND.;
   INT(ACCT) = ACCT TO INCOME
SUM AMOUNT FOR ACCT> = 300 .AND. &COND .AND.;
   INT(ACCT) = ACCT TO EXPENSE
```

Now it can print the report. Before doing so, it displays the title with the company name:

```
********************* Print the report using
******************* predefined report formats.
SET EJECT OFF
ERASE
? "          Income Statement For &COMPANY"
?
```

If the report will be printed for a range of dates (RANGE is true), it prints the dates in the subtitle, otherwise it prints today's date (T:DATE):

```
***************** Print appropriate subheading.
IF RANGE
   ? "For transactions from &START to &FINISH"
ELSE
   ? "For &T:DATE"
ENDIF (range)
```

The program then prints income transactions using the appropriate report form (stored in the ROPTION variable) and search condition (stored in the COND variable). When done, it displays the income total:

```
****************** Print income transactions.
?
? "INCOME:"
REPO FORM &ROPTION FOR ACCT<300 .AND. &COND PLAIN
? "Total Income              " +STR(INCOME,10,2)
?
```

Then it uses an identical procedure for printing expense transactions:

```
* * * * * * * * * * * * * * * * * * * Print expense transactions.
? "EXPENSES:"
REPO FORM &ROPTION FOR ACCT> = 300 .AND. &COND PLAIN
? "Total Expenses                  " +STR(EXPENSE,10,2)
* * * * * * * * * * * * * * * * * * * Display balance at bottom of sheet.
?
```

At the bottom of the report, it displays the balance and a reminder about the subaccounts:

```
? "Total Income                   " +STR(INCOME,10,2)
? "Total Expenses                 " +STR(EXPENSE,10,2)
? "                                ---------"
? "Balance                        " +STR(INCOME – EXPENSE,10,2)
?
? " NOTE: Sub-accounts marked with a *"
?? "are not included in totals."
EJECT
SET PRINT OFF
```

If the report was displayed on the screen only, the program pauses to give the user time to read it. Then it releases the memory variables and returns to the BREPORTS menu:

```
* * * * * * * * * * * * * * If report not going to printer,
* * * * * * * * * * * * * * pause on screen.
IF !(YN) # "Y"
  ?
  ?
  ? "Press any key to continue"
  WAIT
ENDIF (yn = y)

RELEASE COMPANY,YN,COND,START,FINISH,RANGE
RELEASE SCHOICE,ROPTION,INCOME,EXPENSE
RETURN
```

Figure 18.5 displays the CURREPT.CMD command file.

Chart of Accounts Report

Option 2 from the reports menu prints the chart of accounts. When this option is selected, the screen asks:

Send report to printer? (Y/N) :   :

```
*********************************** CURREPT.CMD
********** Print report of current transactions.

********** First get company name from geninfo file
USE GENINFO
STORE COMPANY TO COMPANY

********** Get information on dates, and store
********** to search macro (COND)
ERASE
STORE " " TO YN
@ 5,2 SAY "Transactions for this month only? ";
  GET YN
  READ

********** Set up search condition
********** according to user's request.
IF !(YN)="Y"
   STORE "DATE = '"+$(T:DATE,1,2)+"'" TO COND
   STORE F TO RANGE
ELSE
   STORE "        " TO START,FINISH
   @ 7,2 SAY "Enter starting date ";
      GET START PICT "99/99/99"
   @ 9,2 SAY "Enter ending date ";
      GET FINISH PICT "99/99/99"
   READ
   STORE "DATE >=START .AND. DATE <=FINISH" TO COND
   STORE T TO RANGE
ENDIF (yn=y)

********************* Next, get sort order.
ERASE
STORE 0 TO SCHOICE
@ 3,10 SAY "Sort Orders"
@ 5,8 SAY "1. By Account Number"
@ 6,8 SAY "2. By Date"
@ 8,8 SAY "Enter choice (1-2) ";
  GET SCHOICE PICT "9"
READ

************** Set up sort order and report type.
IF SCHOICE = 2
   USE TRANS INDEX DATES
   STORE "DATES" TO ROPTION
ELSE
   USE TRANS INDEX ACCT
   STORE "ACCTS" TO ROPTION
ENDIF

********************* Ask about printer.
ERASE
STORE " " TO YN
@ 5,2 SAY "Send Report to printer? " GET YN
READ
```

Figure 18.5: The CURREPT.CMD command file.

```
***************** and set on if necessary.
IF !(YN)="Y"
   SET PRINT ON
ENDIF (yn=y)

************** Mark subaccounts for report.
REPLACE NOUPDATE ALL MARKER WITH " "
REPLACE NOUPDATE ALL MARKER WITH "*";
     FOR ACCT <> INT(ACCT)

**** Calculate totals, leaving out subaccounts.
SUM AMOUNT FOR ACCT<300 .AND. &COND .AND.;
    INT(ACCT)=ACCT TO INCOME
SUM AMOUNT FOR ACCT>=300 .AND. &COND .AND.;
    INT(ACCT)=ACCT TO EXPENSE

****************** Print the report using
****************** predefined report formats.
SET EJECT OFF
ERASE
? "              Income Statement For &COMPANY"
?
***************** Print appropriate subheading.
IF RANGE
   ? "For transactions from &START to &FINISH"
ELSE
   ? "For &T:DATE"
ENDIF (range)

****************** Print income transactions.
?
? "INCOME:"
REPO FORM &ROPTION FOR ACCT<300 .AND. &COND PLAIN
? "Total Income                      "+;
   STR(INCOME,10,2)
?
******************* Print expense transactions.
? "EXPENSES:"
REPO FORM &ROPTION FOR ACCT>=300 .AND. &COND PLAIN
? "Total Expenses                    "+;
   STR(EXPENSE,10,2)
******************* Display balance at bottom of sheet.
?
? "Total Income                      "+;
   STR(INCOME,10,2)
? "Total Expenses                    "+;
   STR(EXPENSE,10,2)
? "                                      ---------"
? "Balance                           "+;
   STR(INCOME-EXPENSE,10,2)
?
? " NOTE: Subaccounts marked with a *"
?? "are not included in totals."
EJECT
SET PRINT OFF

*************** If report not going to printer,
```

Figure 18.5: *The CURREPT.CMD command file (continued).*

```
*************** pause on screen.
IF !(YN) # "Y"
   ?
   ?
   ? "Press any key to continue"
   WAIT
ENDIF (yn=y)

RELEASE COMPANY,YN,COND,START,FINISH,RANGE
RELEASE SCHOICE,ROPTION,INCOME,EXPENSE
RETURN
```

Figure 18.5: *The CURREPT.CMD command file (continued).*

then briefly displays the message:

   Calculating totals . . . . .

The command file then prints the chart of accounts with balances, as shown in Figure 18.6.

The body of the report is printed with a report format file called COA.FRM. It was created by typing in the commands:

   USE COA
   REPORT FORM COA

from the dot prompt, and filling out the report form as follows:

   ENTER OPTIONS, M=LEFT MARGIN, L=LINES/PAGE, W=PAGE WIDTH m=1
   PAGE HEADING? (Y/N) n
   DOUBLE SPACE REPORT? (Y/N) n
   ARE TOTALS REQUIRED? (Y/N) n
   COL   WIDTH,CONTENTS
   001   6,ACCT
   ENTER HEADING: Acct. No.
   002   20,TITLE
   ENTER HEADING: <Title
   003   12,AMOUNT
   ENTER HEADING: Month;to-date
   004   12,QTD
   ENTER HEADING: Quarter;to-date
   005   12,YTD
   ENTER HEADING: Year;to-date
   006   1,MARKER
   ENTER HEADING:
   007

The COAREPT.CMD command file uses the COA.FRM report format to print the chart of accounts report from the COA.DBF database. The pseudocode for COAREPT.CMD is displayed in Figure 18.7.

Chart of Accounts for Joe Smith

Last Update: 02/01/84

INCOME:

Acct. No.	Title	Month to-Date	Quarter to-Date	Year to-Date
100.00	Regular Income	22166.10	38776.65	38776.65
110.00	Royalty Income	0.00	0.00	0.00
120.00	Interest Income	500.00	1000.00	1000.00
Total Income		22666.10	39776.65	39776.65

EXPENSES:

Acct. No.	Title	Month to-Date	Quarter to-Date	Year to-Date
300.00	Federal Witholding	1999.99	3999.98	3999.98
310.00	State Witholding	0.00	0.00	0.00
400.00	House Payment	7266.34	14532.68	14532.68
400.10	House Interest	200.00	400.00	400.00*
400.20	House Principal	300.00	600.00	600.00*
500.00	Car payment	345.67	691.34	691.34
510.00	Car Insurance	0.00	0.00	0.00
520.00	Gasoline	0.00	0.00	0.00
530.00	Car Repairs	0.00	0.00	0.00
600.00	Medical Expense	172.62	345.24	345.24
610.00	Pharmacy Expense	12.00	24.00	24.00
620.00	Dental Expense	0.00	0.00	0.00
630.00	Medical Insurance	0.00	0.00	0.00
700.00	Entertainment (Pers)	0.00	0.00	0.00
710.00	Entertainment (Bus.)	17.50	35.00	35.00
Total Expenses		9814.12	19628.24	19628.24
Total Income		22666.10	39776.65	39776.65
Total Expenses		9814.12	19628.24	19628.24
Balance		12851.98	20148.41	20148.41

NOTE: Subaccounts marked with a * are not included in totals.

Figure 18.6: Sample chart of accounts program.

> Get date of last update and company name from
>   the general information file
>
> Use the chart of accounts data and index files
>
> Ask about hardcopy
>
> Calculate MTD, QTD, and YTD income and expense totals,
>   leaving out subaccounts
>
> Mark subaccounts with asterisk for display on report
>
> If printer requested, set print on
> Print report heading
> Print subheading
>
> Print income accounts
> Print income totals
> Print expense accounts
> Print expense totals
> Display balance at bottom of sheet
> Print note about subaccounts
> Set the printer off
>
> If report not going to printer, pause screen
>
> Release memory variables
> Return to reports menu

Figure 18.7: *Pseudocode for the COAREPT.CMD command file.*

The COAREPT.CMD command file begins by pulling the date of the last update and company name from the general information file, as shown in the first lines of the program below:

```
* * * * * * * * * * * * * * * * * * * * * * * * * * * * * * * * * *
COAREPT.CMD
* * * * * * * * * * * * Print chart of accounts and balances.

* * * * * * * * * Get date of last update and company name.
USE GENINFO
STORE LAST:UPDAT TO LAST:DATE
STORE COMPANY TO COMPANY
```

Next, it sets up the COA.DBF and COA.NDX database files:

```
* * * * * * * * Use the chart of accounts file and index.
USE COA INDEX COA
```

Then the program asks about the printer, and stores the user's answer to a variable called YN:

```
* * * * * * * * * * * * * * * * * * * * * * * * * * * * * Ask about hardcopy.
ERASE
STORE " " TO YN
@ 5,2 SAY "Send report to printer? " GET YN PICT "!"
READ
```

The program then calculates income and expense totals for the month-to-date (AMOUNT field), quarter-to-date (QTD field) and year-to-date (YTD field) balances, excluding the subaccounts:

```
* * * Calculate income and expense totals, for MTD,
* * * QTD, and YTD; leaving out subaccounts.
ERASE
? "Calculating totals . . . ."

SUM AMOUNT FOR ACCT<300 .AND. INT(ACCT)=ACCT TO TOT:MTD1
SUM AMOUNT FOR ACCT>=300 .AND. INT(ACCT)=ACCT TO TOT:MTD2
SUM QTD FOR ACCT<300 .AND. INT(ACCT)=ACCT TO TOT:QTD1
SUM QTD FOR ACCT>=300 .AND. INT(ACCT)=ACCT TO TOT:QTD2
SUM YTD FOR ACCT<300 .AND. INT(ACCT)=ACCT TO TOT:YTD1
SUM YTD FOR ACCT>=300 .AND. INT(ACCT)=ACCT TO TOT:YTD2
```

Now we need to place a marker next to all the subaccounts for display on the report:

```
* * * * * * * * * * * * * * * * Mark subaccounts with asterisk.
REPL NOUPDATE ALL MARKER WITH " "
REPL NOUPDATE ALL MARKER WITH "*";
    FOR INT(ACCT) # ACCT
```

If the user requested that the report be sent to the printer, the command file sets the printer on:

```
* * * * * * * * * * * * * * * * * If printer selected, set it on.
ERASE
IF YN="Y"
   SET PRINT ON
ENDIF (yn=y)
SET EJECT OFF
```

Now the command file can print the report title and subtitle:

```
* * * * * * * * * * * * * * * * * * * * * * * * * * * Print report title.
? "              Chart of Accounts for &COMPANY"
?

* * * * * * * * * * * * * * * * * * * * * * * * * * * * * * Print subtitle.
? "Last Update: &LAST:DATE"
```

Then it prints all the income accounts using the COA.FRM report format:

```
*************** Print income accounts and totals.
?
? "INCOME:"
REPO FORM COA FOR ACCT<300 PLAIN
```

Then, it prints the totals of the income accounts (TOT:MTD1, TOT:QTD1, TOT:YTD1). The string function (STR) is used to help make lining up the totals in their columns a little easier:

```
? "Total Income               " +STR(TOT:MTD1,10,2) +;
  "        " +STR(TOT:QTD1,10,2) +"      " +STR(TOT:YTD1,10,2)
?
```

Next it prints the expense accounts and their totals (TOT:MTD2, TOT:QTD2, TOT:YTD2):

```
************* Print expense accounts and totals.
? "EXPENSES:"
REPO FORM COA FOR ACCT> =300 PLAIN
? "Total Expenses             " +STR(TOT:MTD2,10,2) +;
  "        " +STR(TOT:QTD2,10,2) +"      " +STR(TOT:YTD2,10,2)
```

Now the program can display the income and expense totals at the bottom of the report, as well as the balance for each period (which is the income total minus the expense total):

```
************ Display balance at bottom of sheet.
?
? "Total Income               " +STR(TOT:MTD1,10,2) +;
  "        " +STR(TOT:QTD1,10,2) +"      " +STR(TOT:YTD1,10,2)
? "Total Expenses             " +STR(TOT:MTD2,10,2) +;
  "        " +STR(TOT:QTD2,10,2) +"      " +STR(TOT:YTD2,10,2)
?
? "Balance               ",;
   STR(TOT:MTD1-TOT:MTD2,10,2) +"        " +;
   STR(TOT:QTD1-TOT:QTD2,10,2) +"      " +;
   STR(TOT:YTD1-TOT:YTD2,10,2)
```

Then it prints a few blank lines and displays the subaccounts message at the bottom of the report:

```
?
?
?
? "NOTE: Subaccounts marked with a *"
?? "are not included in totals."
```

For convenience, the command file ejects the page in the printer, then sets the printer off:

```
EJECT
SET PRINT OFF
```

If the report was not sent to the printer, the program pauses:

```
*************** If report not going to printer,
*************** pause screen.
IF YN # "Y"
    ?
    ?
    ? "Press any key to continue"
    WAIT
ENDIF (yn # y)
```

Then it releases the memory variables and returns to the BREPORTS.CMD menu:

```
RELEASE COMPANY,LAST:DATE,YN,TOT:MTD1,TOT:MTD2
RELEASE TOT:QTD1,TOT:QTD2,TOT:YTD1,TOT:YTD2
RETURN
```

Figure 18.8 shows the complete COAREPT.CMD command file.

Writing Checks

In order for the computer to write checks, it must convert the numeric check amount (such as $1234.56), to its English equivalent (one thousand two hundred thirty four and 56/100 dollars).

We can simplify this problem by finding a pattern that all numbers follow. For example, if we look at a number below one thousand, we can see this pattern:

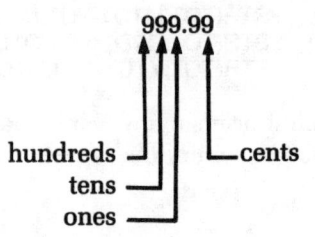

```
            999.99
            ↑↑↑ ↑
            ||| |
hundreds ───┘|| └─cents
     tens ───┘|
     ones ────┘
```

Cents are always to the right of the decimal point, ones are one digit to the left; tens are two digits to the left, and hundreds are 3 digits to the

```
*************************************** COAREPT.CMD
*********** Print chart of accounts and balances.

******* Get date of last update and company name.
USE GENINFO
STORE LAST:UPDAT TO LAST:DATE
STORE COMPANY TO COMPANY

****** Use the chart of accounts file and index.
USE COA INDEX COA

***************************** Ask about hardcopy.
ERASE
STORE " " TO YN
@ 5,2 SAY "Send report to printer? " GET YN PICT "!"
READ

*** Calculate income and expense totals, for MTD,
*** QTD, and YTD; leaving out subaccounts.
ERASE
? "Calculating totals...."

SUM AMOUNT FOR ACCT<300 .AND. INT(ACCT)=ACCT;
    TO TOT:MTD1
SUM AMOUNT FOR ACCT>=300 .AND. INT(ACCT)=ACCT;
    TO TOT:MTD2
SUM QTD FOR ACCT<300 .AND. INT(ACCT)=ACCT;
    TO TOT:QTD1
SUM QTD FOR ACCT>=300 .AND. INT(ACCT)=ACCT;
    TO TOT:QTD2
SUM YTD FOR ACCT<300 .AND. INT(ACCT)=ACCT;
    TO TOT:YTD1
SUM YTD FOR ACCT>=300 .AND. INT(ACCT)=ACCT;
    TO TOT:YTD2

**************** Mark subaccounts with asterisk.
REPL NOUPDATE ALL MARKER WITH " "
REPL NOUPDATE ALL MARKER WITH "*";
     FOR INT(ACCT) # ACCT

***************** If printer selected, set it on.
ERASE
IF YN="Y"
   SET PRINT ON
ENDIF (yn=y)
SET EJECT OFF

***************************** Print report title.
? "             Chart of Accounts for &COMPANY"
?
********************************* Print subtitle.
? "Last Update: &LAST:DATE"
*************** Print income accounts and totals.
?
? "INCOME:"
REPO FORM COA FOR ACCT<300 PLAIN
```

Figure 18.8: The COAREPT.CMD command file.

```
? "Total Income              "+STR(TOT:MTD1,10,2)+;
  "    "+STR(TOT:QTD1,10,2)+"    "+STR(TOT:YTD1,10,2)
?
************** Print expense accounts and totals.
? "EXPENSES:"
REPO FORM COA FOR ACCT>=300 PLAIN
? "Total Expenses            "+STR(TOT:MTD2,10,2)+;
  "    "+STR(TOT:QTD2,10,2)+"    "+STR(TOT:YTD2,10,2)

************* Display balance at bottom of sheet.
?
? "Total Income              "+STR(TOT:MTD1,10,2)+;
  "    "+STR(TOT:QTD1,10,2)+"    "+STR(TOT:YTD1,10,2)

? "Total Expenses            "+STR(TOT:MTD2,10,2)+;
  "    "+STR(TOT:QTD2,10,2)+"    "+STR(TOT:YTD2,10,2)
?
? "Balance                   ",;
   STR(TOT:MTD1-TOT:MTD2,10,2)+"    "+;
   STR(TOT:QTD1-TOT:QTD2,10,2)+"    "+;
   STR(TOT:YTD1-TOT:YTD2,10,2)
?
?
?
? "NOTE: Subaccounts marked with a *"
?? "are not included in totals."
EJECT
SET PRINT OFF
************** If report not going to printer,
************** pause screen.
IF YN # "Y"
   ?
   ?
   ? "Press any key to continue"
   WAIT
ENDIF (yn # y)

RELEASE COMPANY,LAST:DATE,YN,TOT:MTD1,TOT:MTD2
RELEASE TOT:QTD1,TOT:QTD2,TOT:YTD1,TOT:YTD2
RETURN
```

Figure 18.8: *The COAREPT.CMD command file (continued).*

left. A much larger figure uses a similar pattern:

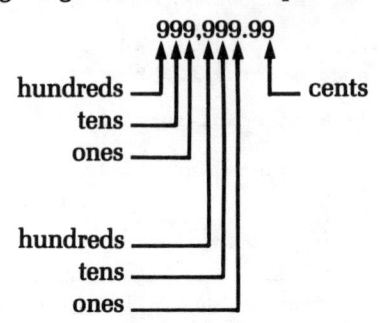

```
                999,999.99
       hundreds ─┘│││  └─ cents
           tens ──┘││
           ones ───┘│
                    │
                    │
       hundreds ────┘│
           tens ─────┘│
           ones ──────┘
```

Our task is to change two three-digit numbers, each in hundreds-tens-ones format, to their English equivalent. We can change the pennies into a fraction (e.g. 99/100).

Let's look at another fact about numbers. The numbers one through nineteen all have unique names (one, two, eleven, nineteen, etc.). After nineteen, only numbers that are evenly divisible by ten have unique names (twenty, thirty, forty, etc.). After ninety, the next highest unique names are hundred and thousand. We can store all of these English words as memory variables.

We can store these words in a way that makes the translation very easy. dBASE memory variable names must begin with a letter, but may contain numbers. Therefore, we can store the numbers using a pattern as follows:

```
STORE "ONE" TO U1
STORE "TWO" TO U2
STORE "THREE" TO U3
STORE "TWENTY" TO U20
```

After storing the numbers in this fashion, to see the English equivalent of one, just ask dBASE to print U1, as shown below:

```
? U1
```

dBASE replies with:

ONE

To see the English equivalent of 23, just ask dBASE to:

```
? U20,U3
```

and dBASE replies with:

TWENTY THREE

Although this is simple, it gets more complicated as we approach a million.

Before we can write the checks program, we need to store all of the English equivalent words for numbers to memory variables. We can do so, then store them all to a *memory file*. We can write a command file to do this for us. The command file name will be MAKEMEMS.CMD, and its job will be to store all the English number words to a memory file called ENGLISH.MEM. That command file is presented in Figure 18.9.

Notice that the MAKEMEMS command file releases all memory variables, stores all the unique English words to memory variables that

```
***************************** MAKEMEMS.CMD
*************** Sets up memory file for
*************** storing English equivalents.
SET DEFA TO B
SET TALK OFF
RELE ALL

STORE " " TO U,ENGLISH
STORE "ONE" TO U1
STORE "TWO" TO U2
STORE "THREE" TO U3
STORE "FOUR" TO U4
STORE "FIVE" TO U5
STORE "SIX" TO U6
STORE "SEVEN" TO U7
STORE "EIGHT" TO U8
STORE "NINE" TO U9
STORE "TEN" TO U10
STORE "ELEVEN" TO U11
STORE "TWELVE" TO U12
STORE "THIRTEEN" TO U13
STORE "FOURTEEN" TO U14
STORE "FIFTEEN" TO U15
STORE "SIXTEEN" TO U16
STORE "SEVENTEEN" TO U17
STORE "EIGHTEEN" TO U18
STORE "NINETEEN" TO U19
STORE "TWENTY" TO U20
STORE "THIRTY" TO U30
STORE "FORTY" TO U40
STORE "FIFTY" TO U50
STORE "SIXTY" TO U60
STORE "SEVENTY" TO U70
STORE "EIGHTY" TO U80
STORE "NINETY" TO U90

SAVE TO ENGLISH
DISP MEMO
RETURN
```

Figure 18.9: MAKEMEMS command file to store English equivalents.

have the corresponding number in the variable name, then saves all the memory variables to a memory file called ENGLISH. Before writing the CHECKS command file, you must write and do the MAKEMEMS command file.

The command file to print the checks is called CHECKS.CMD. Its pseudocode is presented in Figure 18.10.

Now let's develop the CHECKS.CMD command file. We'll begin by writing a few lines that will display some opening messages on the screen:

```
******************************* CHECKS.CMD
**************** Write checks.
```

```
ERASE
SET TALK OFF
? "Preparing checks file"
?
? "Load checks into printer"
```

Now, to make room in memory for the English memory variables, we will add lines that will allow the program to store all existing memory variables to a memory file called THOUGHT, then to read in the English variables from the ENGLISH.MEM memory file:

```
*** Save existing memory variables to THOUGHT.MEM,
*** and bring in English equivalent variables.
SAVE TO THOUGHT
RESTORE FROM ENGLISH
```

Next, our program takes all the unwritten checks from the trans file and stores them to a temporary data file called temp:

```
** Create temporary file of checks to be written.
USE TRANS INDEX ACCT
COPY TO TEMP FOR CHECK:NO>0 .AND. .NOT. WRITTEN
```

Then, it sorts the temp file into check-number order:

```
USE TEMP
INDEX ON CHECK:NO TO CHECKNOS
```

Now the program begins at the top of the temp file, and tells the user the number of the first check to be printed. It then gives him time to finish loading the checks into the printer:

```
GO TOP
?
? "First check to be printed will be ",CHECK:NO
?
?
? "Press any key to begin writing checks"
WAIT
```

When the user is ready to print, the program clears the screen, sets the printer on, and begins a loop through the temp file:

```
ERASE
SET PRINT ON
DO WHILE .NOT. EOF
```

To perform the translation, the program's first task will be to store the numeric amount to a character string of predictable size (nine digits with two decimal places). That way, the program can predict the value of every digit. For example, the numbers:

```
"     1.23"
"   123.00"
" 11234.40"
"999999.99"
```

all have their hundreds, tens, ones, and cents digits in precisely the same position in the string (for example, the "one dollar" digit is always exactly the fourth character from the left). Also, since the program will be making two passes through the string (one for each three-digit set of numbers), we'll need a counter to count the loops, and a starting position for each three-digit set. These lines set up the memory variables and store the numeric check amount to a character variable called STRING:

```
***************** Translate AMOUNT to English.
STORE 1 TO COUNTER,START
STORE STR(AMOUNT,9,2) TO STRING
```

Now we set up a loop to pass twice through the number to be translated:

```
********** Loop through thousands and hundreds.
DO WHILE COUNTER < 3
```

First, starting at START, the program will store three digits to a variable called CHUNK, and then break out the hundreds, tens, and ones digits from the CHUNK:

```
**** Split out hundreds, tens, and ones.
STORE $(STRING,START,3) TO CHUNK
STORE $(CHUNK,1,1) TO HUN
STORE $(CHUNK,2,2) TO TEN
STORE $(CHUNK,3,1) TO ONE
```

Let's try out an example with this program. If the amount of the check to be written is 123456.78, the following memory variables now have these contents, and all are character types:

Memory Variable	Contents
STRING	"123456.78"
CHUNK	"123"
HUN	"1"
TEN	"23"
ONE	"3"

The next job is to store the English equivalent of the hundreds digit, plus the word HUNDRED to a variable called ENGLISH, assuming that CHUNK is greater than 99:

```
*********************** Handle hundreds.
IF VAL(CHUNK) > 99
    STORE ENGLISH + U&HUN + ' HUNDRED ' TO ENGLISH
ENDIF (chunk > 99)
```

Using the number in our example, the memory variable ENGLISH just got U&HUN (U1, which is "ONE") and the word HUNDRED tacked onto it, so the memory variable ENGLISH is now ONE HUNDRED.

Next, the program must translate the second two digits in CHUNK. First it stores the numeric value of the TEN variable to a variable called X. Then it makes sure that X is greater than zero:

```
********************* Handle second two digits.
STORE VAL(TEN) TO X
IF X > 0
```

If so, there are three possibilites to deal with. First, the two digits are either teens (11-19) or evenly divisible by ten (20, 30, etc.). With these numbers, the program simply tacks the English word for the TEN memory variable onto the ENGLISH variable:

```
DO CASE
        ********** Case 1: Handle teens or even tens.
    CASE (INT(X/10.0) = X/10.0) .OR. (X>9 .AND. X<20)
        STORE ENGLISH + U&TEN TO ENGLISH
```

The second possibility is that the two digits are greater than nine, but not divisible by ten (21-29, 31-39, etc.). With these numbers, the program tacks the English equivalent for both the ten and the one portion onto the ENGLISH variable (twenty one, ninety nine, etc.):

```
        ********** Case 2: Handle greater than 10,
        ********** but not evenly divisible.
    CASE X > 9 .AND. (INT(X/10.0) # X/10.0)
        STORE $(TEN,1,1) + '0' TO TEN
        STORE ENGLISH + U&TEN + ' ' + U&ONE TO ENGLISH
```

Our sample number, 123456.78, falls into this category. So first the routine stores the first character of the TEN variable (which is 2, since TEN contains 23) and a zero character (0) to the TEN variable. So now the TEN variable contains 20. Next, line STORE ENGLISH + U&TEN

+ " " + U&TEN TO ENGLISH attaches U&TEN (which becomes U20, and hence the English word TWENTY) to the ENGLISH variable. It also attaches a blank space (+ " " +) and U&ONE (which becomes U3; the word "THREE") to the ENGLISH variable. So at this point, the ENGLISH variable contains ONE HUNDRED TWENTY THREE.

The third possibility is that the last two digits are less than ten (01, 07, 09). In this case, the program adds only the English equivalent of the ONES portion onto the ENGLISH string:

```
********** Case 3: Handle less than 10.
CASE X < 10
   STORE ENGLISH + U&ONE TO ENGLISH
ENDCASE
ENDIF (x > 0)
```

Now, if the program just translated the three-digit chunk in the thousands portion of the number to English, and the amount is over 999.99, it tacks on the word "THOUSAND." These lines handle that:

```
*************** Add "THOUSAND" if necessary.
IF AMOUNT > 999.99 .AND. COUNTER = 1
   STORE ENGLISH +' THOUSAND ' TO ENGLISH
ENDIF (need to add "thousand")
```

Using our sample number again, ENGLISH is now ONE HUNDRED TWENTY THREE THOUSAND.

Now the program needs to perform the same task for the next three-digit chunk of numbers. Those begin at the fourth character in STRING. Therefore, the starting place for the next translation is four, and the loop counter is at two:

```
********** Prepare for pass through hundreds.
STORE 4 TO START
STORE COUNTER +1 TO COUNTER

ENDDO (while counter < 3)
```

Using our sample number through the second loop, the memory variables become:

Memory Variable	Contents
STRING	"123456.78"
CHUNK	"456"

Display opening message on screen telling user to
  load checks into the printer

Save existing memory variables to a memory file

Bring in and bring in English-equivalent memory
  variables from ENGLISH.MEM

Create a temporary file of checks to be written
  from the transaction file

Index the temporary file into check number order

Wait for user to put checks in the printer

Begin loop through the temporary file of checks
  Store three digits of number to a character
      string
  Start loop for two passes through number
      Split out hundreds, tens, and ones
      Translate hundred portion to English

      Handle second two digits
      If second two digits are teens or even tens
          Translate to appropriate English

      If second two digits are greater than 10,
          but not evenly divisible by ten
              Translate the two digits independently

      If the two digits are less than 10
          Translate the single digit

      If in the "thousands" portion of the number,
          and the amount is greater than
          999.99, add the word "thousand"

  Repeat loop for second three-digit portion of number

  Tack on the pennies
  Print the check

  Skip to the next check to be written in the
      temporary file

Continue loop through the temporary file

Figure 18.10: Pseudocode for the CHECKS.CMD command file.

> When all checks have been written . . .
> Flag all checks as written in trans
>
> Get rid of English memory variables, and bring back the originals
>
> Return to the menu program

Figure 18.10: *Pseudocode for the CHECKS.CMD command file (continued).*

```
HUN                    "4"
TEN                    "56"
ONE                    "6"
```

Using the same procedure as before on the second pass through the DO WHILE loop, the ENGLISH memory variable becomes ONE HUNDRED TWENTY THREE THOUSAND FOUR HUNDRED FIFTY SIX. At that point, the program only needs to tack on the pennies, the last two digits in the STRING variable. Of course, we need to add the word "AND" (e.g. ONE HUNDRED TWENTY THREE *AND* 56/100 cents), for checks that are over $1.00 dollar. This small routine handles that task:

```
* * * * * * * * * * * * * * * * * * * * * * * * * * * * * * Tack on cents.
IF INT(AMOUNT) > 0
   STORE ENGLISH + " AND " TO ENGLISH
ENDIF (int(amount)>0))
STORE ENGLISH + $(STRING,8,2)+"/100" TO ENGLISH
```

At this point, the ENGLISH variable for our example is ONE HUNDRED TWENTY THREE THOUSAND FOUR HUNDRED FIFTY SIX AND 78/100, and the translation is complete (assuming the word "Dollars" is preprinted on the check).

Now that the translation is complete, the program can print the date, payee, amount, and English equivalent on the check. You will need to modify this portion of the program to fit your own preprinted check format. You might use photocopies of the checks for determining proper alignment, because perfect alignment usually takes a few tries. These CHECKS program lines print the check:

```
? "                      ",DATE
?
? "        ",TO:WHOM,"        ",AMOUNT
?
```

```
?  "       ",ENGLISH
?
?
?
?
```

Once the check is written, the program should skip to the next record and continue looping through the temp file. But first, it must set ENGLISH back to blank. These lines accomplish the task:

```
SKIP
STORE " " TO ENGLISH
```

ENDDO (while not eof)

The completion of this loop means that all the checks are written. We can set the printer off, and then go back into the trans file and flag all checks as having been printed by making the WRITTEN field true:

```
SET PRINT OFF
*************** Flag checks as written in trans.
USE TRANS
REPLACE ALL WRITTEN WITH T FOR TYPE = 1
USE
```

Now we can have the program release all the English memory variables, and bring back the variables that were originally in memory from the THOUGHT.MEM memory file. Then, the program can return to the reports menu. These lines take care of these jobs:

```
*************** Get rid of English memory
*************** variables, and bring back originals.
RELEASE ALL
RESTORE FROM THOUGHT
RETURN
```

The entire CHECKS.CMD command file is displayed in Figure 18.11. It is a fairly large program, but it is worth studying closely because it solves a difficult problem with a minimum of programming effort. It also runs quite quickly.

Summary

In this chapter, we've completed writing the command files to display bookkeeping data in formatted reports. These programs are:

1. BREPORTS.PRG, which displays a menu of report options to the user.

```
*********************************** CHECKS.CMD
*********************************** Write checks.
ERASE
SET TALK OFF
? "Preparing checks file"
?
? "Load checks into printer"

*** Save existing memory variables to THOUGHT.MEM,
*** and bring in English-equivalent variables.
SAVE TO THOUGHT
RESTORE FROM ENGLISH

** Create temporary file of checks to be written.
USE TRANS INDEX ACCT
COPY TO TEMP FOR CHECK:NO>0 .AND. .NOT. WRITTEN
USE TEMP
INDEX ON CHECK:NO TO CHECKNOS
GO TOP
?
? "First check to be printed will be ",CHECK:NO
?
?
? "Press any key to begin writing checks"
WAIT
ERASE
SET PRINT ON
DO WHILE .NOT. EOF

   **************** Translate AMOUNT to English.
   STORE 1 TO COUNTER,START
   STORE STR(AMOUNT,9,2) TO STRING

   ********* Loop through thousands and hundreds.
   DO WHILE COUNTER < 3

      **** Split out hundreds, tens, and ones.
      STORE $(STRING,START,3) TO CHUNK
      STORE $(CHUNK,1,1) TO HUN
      STORE $(CHUNK,2,2) TO TEN
      STORE $(CHUNK,3,1) TO ONE

      ********************** Handle hundreds.
      IF VAL(CHUNK) > 99
         STORE ENGLISH + U&HUN + ' HUNDRED ' TO ENGLISH
      ENDIF (chunk > 99)

      ******************* Handle second two digits.
      STORE VAL(TEN) TO X
      IF X > 0
        DO CASE
          ********** Case 1: Handle teens or even tens.
          CASE (INT(X/10.0)=X/10.0) .OR. (X>9 .AND. X<20)
               STORE ENGLISH + U&TEN TO ENGLISH

          ********** Case 2: Handle greater than 10,
```

Figure 18.11: The CHECKS.CMD command file.

```
              ********** but not evenly divisible.
              CASE X > 9 .AND. (INT(X/10.0) # X/10.0)
                   STORE $(TEN,1,1) +'0' TO TEN
                   STORE ENGLISH + U&TEN+' '+U&ONE TO ENGLISH

              ********** Case 3: Handle less than 10.
              CASE X < 10
                   STORE ENGLISH + U&ONE TO ENGLISH
           ENDCASE
        ENDIF (x > 0)

        *************** Add "Thousand" if necessary.
        IF AMOUNT > 999.99 .AND. COUNTER = 1
           STORE ENGLISH+' THOUSAND ' TO ENGLISH
        ENDIF (need to add "thousand")

        ********** Prepare for pass through hundreds.
        STORE 4 TO START
        STORE COUNTER+1 TO COUNTER

    ENDDO (while counter < 3.)

    ******************************* Tack on cents.
    IF INT(AMOUNT) > 0
        STORE ENGLISH + " AND " TO ENGLISH
    ENDIF (int(amount)>0))
    STORE ENGLISH + $(STRING,8,2)+"/100" TO ENGLISH

    **************************** Print the check.
    ? "                          ",DATE
    ?
    ? "     ",TO:WHOM,"         ",AMOUNT
    ?
    ? "     ",ENGLISH
    ?
    ?
    ?
    SKIP
    STORE " " TO ENGLISH

ENDDO  (while not eof)

SET PRINT OFF
*************** Flag checks as written in the trans file.
USE TRANS
REPLACE ALL WRITTEN WITH T FOR TYPE = 1
USE
**************** Get rid of English memory
**************** variables, and bring back originals.
RELEASE ALL
RESTORE FROM THOUGHT
RETURN
```

Figure 18.11: *The CHECKS.CMD command file (continued).*

2. CURREPT.CMD, which displays the income statement based upon transactions in the trans file. It also allows the user to print transactions for the current month only or for any range of dates, and to specify a sort order from a menu.
3. COAREPT.CMD, which prints the chart of accounts with month-to-date, quarter-to-date, and year-to-date balances. It also calculates and displays all totals, and demonstrates techniques for performing complex sums and bookkeeping data.
4. CHECKS.CMD, which prints checks and demonstrates techniques for translating numeric amounts to English words.

CHAPTER 19
EDITING THE BOOKKEEPING DATA

All bookkeepers know they must make changes and adjustments throughout the course of a year. In this chapter, we'll develop editing programs which allow the user to make necessary changes and adjustments without harming the audit trail. These changes will be accounted for in all balances and totals when the bookkeeping reports are reprinted.

The user needs to be able to 1) edit and delete data on the chart of accounts, transaction, and check reqister data files, 2) add new accounts to the chart of accounts, 3) perhaps add data to the check register, and 4) change data in the general information file.

To edit the bookkeeping system, the user chooses option 5 from the main menu. This selection calls up the edit menu as follows:

Bookkeeping System Edit Menu

1. Chart of Accounts
2. Transaction File
3. Check Register
4. General Information
5. Return to Main Menu

If the user selects option 1, the screen asks:

(A)dd, (C)hange, or (D)elete?

If the user wishes to change data for an account, he selects C, and the screen asks:

What account number? :   . :

The user types in an account number, and the screen displays data for that account along with brief instructions for editing, as shown below:

```
Cursor Control :   ^E up  :  ^X down  :  ^D right  :  ^S left  :  ^G delete
Screen Control :   ^C next account    :  ^R previous account :  ^W save
```

Account Number :100.00: Title :Regular Income :

Month to date   : 2500.00:

Quarter to date   : 5000.00:

Year to date   : 5000.00:

–CAUTION: Changing balances will destroy audit trail!
Use adjustment transactions to maintain audit trail.

At this point, the user can make changes, move to the next or previous record, and/or save the changes. The caution at the bottom of the screen reminds the user of dangers in changing the balance fields. In bookkeeping systems, the preferred approach is to use adjustment transactions, as we'll discuss later.

Bookkeeping Edit Screens

The user handles all of the edits and additions to the data files with custom screens. The screen for editing and adding data to the chart of accounts was first drawn as a SED screen, as shown below:

| Cursor Control : | ^E up : | ^X down : | ^D right : | ^S left : | ^G delete |
| Screen Control : | ^C next account : | | ^R previous account : | ^W save |

Account Number <ACCT   Title <TITLE

Month to date   <AMOUNT

Quarter to date <QTD

Year to date   <YTD

The SED program generator was used to create the command file COA, which is displayed below:

```
* B:COA.
@ 1,1 SAY "Cursor Control: ^E up : ^X down : ^D right : ^S left :"
@ 1,56 SAY " ^G delete"
@ 3,1 SAY "Screen Control: ^C next account : ^R previous account :"
@ 3,57 SAY " ^W Save"
@ 4,1 SAY "─────────────────────────────────────────────────────────"
@ 4,56 SAY "─────────"
@ 6,1 SAY "Account Number"
@ 6,17 GET ACCT
@ 6,25 SAY "Title"
@ 6,32 GET TITLE
@ 8,1 SAY "Month to date"
@ 8,19 GET AMOUNT
@ 10,1 SAY "Quarter to date"
@ 10,19 GET QTD
@ 12,1 SAY "Year to date"
@ 12,19 GET YTD
@ 16,1 SAY "−CAUTION: Changing balances will destroy audit trail!"
@ 17,3 SAY "Use adjustment transactions to maintain audit trail."
```

Remember, if you use SED to create a format file, you'll need to exit SED back to the A> prompt and type in the command:

   RENAME B:COA. B:COA.FMT

This adds the .FMT extension to the filename so dBASE will recognize it as a format file.

You can create the remaining three edit screens in the same fashion. The TRANS.FMT format screen should be drawn on the SED screen as shown below:

```
Cursor Control :   ^E up :  ^X down :    ^D right :  ^S left  :  ^G delete
Screen Control :   ^C next trans.    :   ^R previous trans.  :  ^W save
------------------------------------------------------------------------
Account number <ACCT              Description <REASON

Amount <AMOUNT                    Date <DATE!"99/99/99"

Type (1 = Check, 2 = Other) <TYPE

Check Number <CHECK:NO

Pay check to <TO:WHOM
```

SED will generate the following format file:

```
* B:TRANS.
@ 1,1 SAY "Cursor Control: ^E up :  ^X down :  ^D right :  ^S left :"
@ 1,56 SAY " ^G delete"
@ 3,1 SAY "Screen Control: ^C next trans. :  ^R previous trans. :"
@ 3,56 SAY " ^W save"
@ 4,1 SAY "--------------------------------------------------------------"
@ 4,56 SAY "---------"
@ 6,1 SAY "Account number"
@ 6,17 GET ACCT
@ 6,28 SAY "Description"
@ 6,41 GET REASON
@ 8,1 SAY "Amount"
@ 8,9 GET AMOUNT
@ 8,28 SAY "Date"
@ 8,34 GET DATE PICTURE "99/99/99"
@ 10,1 SAY "Type (1 = Check, 2 = Other)"
@ 10,26 GET TYPE
@ 12,1 SAY "Check Number"
@ 12,15 GET CHECK:NO
@ 14,1 SAY "Pay check to"
@ 14,15 GET TO:WHOM
```

You can create the GENINFO.FMT format file with SED by drawing the screen as shown below:

```
Cursor Control :   ^E up :  ^X down  :   ^D right :  ^S left  :  ^G delete
------------------------------------------------------------------------
Company name : <COMPANY

Last check number used <LAST:CHECK
```

Then, use the SED program generator to create the format file, which is displayed below:

```
* B:GENINFO.
@ 1,1 SAY "Cursor Control: ^E up :  ^X down :  ^D right :  ^S left :"
```

Editing the Bookkeeping Data

```
@ 1,56 SAY " ^G delete"
@ 2,1 SAY "----------------------------------------------------------------"
@ 2,56 SAY "---------"
@ 4,1 SAY "Company name :"
@ 4,17 GET COMPANY
@ 6,1 SAY "Last check number used"
@ 6,25 GET LAST:CHECK
```

You can create the check register edit screen, REGISTER.FMT, by drawing an SED screen as shown below:

```
Cursor Control :   ^E up :  ^X down :   ^D right :   ^S left :   ^G delete
Screen Control :   ^C next check   :   ^R previous check   :   ^W save
-----------------------------------------------------------------------------
Check Number <CHECK:NO      Paid to <TO:WHOM

Amount <AMOUNT              Reason <REASON

Date <DATE!"99/99/99"       Is this a deposit? (Y/N) <DEPOSIT
```

Then SED will generate the following format file:

```
* B:REGISTER.
@ 1,1 SAY "Cursor Control: ^E up :  ^X down :  ^D right :  ^S left :"
@ 1,56 SAY " ^G delete"
@ 3,1 SAY "Screen Control:  ^C next check :  ^R previous check :"
@ 3,56 SAY " ^W Save"
@ 4,1 SAY "----------------------------------------------------------------"
@ 4,56 SAY "---------"
@ 6,1 SAY "Check Number"
@ 6,15 GET CHECK:NO
@ 6,28 SAY "Paid to"
@ 6,37 GET TO:WHOM
@ 8,1 SAY "Amount"
@ 8,9 GET AMOUNT
@ 8,28 SAY "Reason"
@ 8,37 GET REASON
@ 10,1 SAY "Date"
@ 10,7 GET DATE PICTURE "99/99/99"
@ 10,28 SAY "Is this a deposit? (Y/N)"
@ 10,54 GET DEPOSIT
```

Of course, you can use ZIP to generate the editing screens if you prefer. With ZIP, however, you can't use the ! symbol to create a PICTURE statement. You'll need to add PICTURE statements to the format file after creating the screens.

Add, Change, or Delete Bookkeeping Data

We can save ourselves programming effort by developing one command file to handle edits to all four files. To do so, we will create quite a few macros. We will develop the command file to edit the bookkeeping data files, BEDIT.CMD, along the lines of the pseudocode displayed in Figure 19.1.

OK, let's start developing the BEDIT program. First, we must set up macros that will link data files and format screens directly to menu choices. For example, if the user opts to edit the chart of accounts, the program needs to USE COA INDEX COA and set the format to the COA.FMT file (SET FORMAT TO COA) for editing. If he opts to edit the transaction file (menu option 2), the program needs to USE TRANS INDEX ACCT,DATES, and also needs to SET FORMAT TO TRANS (the TRANS.FMT format file) to do the edit. The first lines in the program set up macros accordingly that will determine which databases and format files to use based upon the user's choice:

```
******************************* BEDIT.CMD
******** Edit program for the bookkeeping system.

******** Set up macros for linking database and
******** format file names to menu choice.

STORE "COA INDEX COA" TO FILE1
STORE "COA" TO FORMAT1
STORE "TRANS INDEX ACCT, DATES" TO FILE2
STORE "TRANS" TO FORMAT2
STORE "REGISTER" TO FILE3,FORMAT3
STORE "GENINFO" TO FILE4,FORMAT4
```

The user is also given the choice to (A)dd, (C)hange, or (D)elete data. If the user selects A, the command file should append. If the user selects C, the command file should edit. The next lines set up the command macros and store them in the memory variables COMMANDA and COMMANDB.

```
*************************** Store commands.
STORE "APPEND" TO COMMANDA
STORE "EDIT #" TO COMMANDC
```

Now that the macros are set up, the program needs to display the menu of edit options, and wait for a reply. Here are the lines that will

Set up macros for linking database and
   format file names to menu choice

Store commands for appending and deleting to macros

Set up loop for menu
   Clear the screen
   Display the menu
   Wait for a response

   Make sure valid selection was entered . . .
      If not, display error message and repeat

   If user not exiting . . .
      Use appropriate database

      If editing coa, ask for command
      If not adding a new account . . .
         Ask for account to edit or delete
         Find that account

      If editing transaction file, ask for command
         Ask for account number and date of record to edit
         Count how many records have that account
            number and date
         If more than one record meets criterion,
            display and ask for record number
         If only one record has that account number
            and date, just locate that record

      If editing check register, ask for command
         Ask for check number to edit

      If record that user requested is found . . .
         If user requested append or edit, use edit screen
            Append or edit, depending on user's choice

         If user requested delete . . .
            Delete that record
            Pack the database

         If no record found, warn user.

Continue loop through menu (while not exit)

Figure 19.1: Pseudocode for the BEDIT.CMD command file.

accomplish the task:

```
******* Set up loop for menu.
STORE " " TO ECHOICE
DO WHILE ECHOICE # "5"
   ERASE
   TEXT

      Bookkeeping System Edit Menu

      1. Chart of Accounts
      2. Transaction File
      3. Check Register
      4. General Information
      5. Return to Main Menu

   ENDTEXT
   @ 11,12 SAY "Enter choice (1-5) " GET ECHOICE
   READ
```

Since the program will use the user's menu choice (ECHOICE) as a macro later in the program, only valid menu selections can be accepted here. The following routine makes sure that the user's entry was a number between one and five. If it was not, an error message is displayed and the menu reappears on the screen. The following lines handle an invalid selection:

```
****** Make sure valid selection was entered.
IF ECHOICE < "1" .OR. ECHOICE > "5"
   * If not, display error message and repeat.
   @ 13,12 SAY "Invalid selection!"
   ? CHR(7)
   ******* Count to 20 just to take up time.
   STORE 1 TO COUNT
   DO WHILE COUNT < 21
      STORE COUNT+1 TO COUNT
   ENDDO (count < 21)
   LOOP
ENDIF (invalid selection made)
```

The DO WHILE loop in the routine above takes 20 seconds. During this time, the error message "Invalid selection" stays on the screen. Then the screen is erased and the menu is redisplayed.

If the user does not choose to exit, the program can proceed. The next lines allow the user to continue:

```
************** If not exiting, get
************** information for finding record.
IF ECHOICE # "5"
   ERASE
```

First, the program needs to use the proper file. If the user wants to edit the transaction file, the program needs to USE TRANS INDEX ACCT,DATES. Recall that the macro FILE2 contains this information. Therefore, the program needs to USE &FILE2. The 2 is actually the user's menu choice, which is stored in the variable ECHOICE. So the program needs to USE &FILE&ECHOICE, which dBASE interprets first as USE &FILE2, then USE TRANS INDEX ACCT,DATES. The next line sets up the appropriate file:

    USE &FILE&ECHOICE

Now, depending upon which file the user is editing, the program needs to find out what action to perform—A(dd), C(hange), or D(elete)—and what record to edit. The action to perform is stored in the variable SUBCOMM as A, C, or D. SUBCOMM, is initialized as a blank:

    STORE " " TO SUBCOMM

Now, we need a CASE clause to handle the various files to edit. If the user selected option 1 (Chart of Accounts), he can either add, change, or delete an account. The first CASE statement asks the user what he wants to do:

```
DO CASE
    ******* If COA, ask for command, then
    ******* look up by account number.
    CASE ECHOICE = "1"
        ERASE
        @ 3,5 SAY "(A)dd, (C)hange or (D)elete? ";
        GET SUBCOMM PICT "!"
        READ
```

If he is not adding a new account, the command file needs to ask which account to edit or delete, then find that account on the database:

```
IF SUBCOMM # "A"
    STORE "      " TO FINDER
    @ 5,5 SAY "What account number ";
        GET FINDER PICT "999.99"
    READ
    FIND &FINDER
ENDIF (command # a)
```

If the user is editing the transaction file (menu option 2), things are a bit trickier. First of all, we should not allow him to add records through this program, because it does not have all the safety features that the ADDTRANS command file does. Therefore, the program displays options to change or delete only:

```
******* If editing a transaction, look up by account and date.
CASE ECHOICE = "2"
   @ 3,5 SAY "(C)hange or (D)elete? ";
      GET SUBCOMM PICT "!"
```

Next, the program needs to pinpoint the record to edit. The account number and date are good search fields, so the program asks for those:

```
STORE "       " TO FINDER
STORE "       " TO FIND2
@ 5,5 SAY "What account number ";
   GET FINDER PICT "999.99"
@ 7,5 SAY "What date? ";
   GET FIND2 PICT "99/99/99"
READ
```

Now the program needs to find the approriate record. First, it counts how many records in the trans file have the requested account number and date:

```
********* Locate exact record number.
COUNT FOR ACCT = &FINDER .AND. DATE = FIND2 TO HOWMANY
```

If several records have the requested number and date, the program displays them on the screen and gets the record number from the user:

```
IF HOWMANY > 1
   ERASE
   LIST FOR ACCT = &FINDER .AND. DATE = FIND2 ACCT,;
      DATE,REASON,AMOUNT
   ?
   INPUT "Which one? " TO RECNO
   GOTO RECNO
```

If only one record has the requested account number and date, the command file can locate that record directly:

```
ELSE
   LOCATE FOR ACCT = &FINDER .AND. DATE = FIND2
ENDIF (howmany > 1)
```

If the user opted to edit the check register, he can add, change, or delete it. These lines will make this possible:

```
******** If register, look up by check number.
CASE ECHOICE = "3"
```

```
@ 3,5 SAY "(A)dd, (C)hange or (D)elete? ";
    GET SUBCOMM PICT "!"
READ
```

If the user is not adding a check, then the program can locate the record to edit by asking for the check number, and finding that check on the data file:

```
IF SUBCOMM # "A"
    STORE "      " TO FINDER
    @ 5,5 SAY "What check number ";
        GET FINDER PICT "9999"
    READ
    LOCATE FOR CHECK:NO = &FINDER
ENDIF (command # a)

ENDCASE
```

If the user is editing the general information file, he can only change data because there is only one record in that file. Therefore, no searching routine is necessary.

If the program successfully found a record to edit, it can proceed:

```
****** If record found, edit or delete.
IF # > 0 .AND. .NOT. EOF

    DO CASE
```

If the user is appending or changing data (SUBCOMM = "A" or SUBCOMM = "C") the program needs to set the format to the appropriate screen and perform the appropriate command. For example, if the user is adding an account to the chart of accounts, then he would select menu option 1. At that point, ECHOICE = 1. He would also select A, for (A)dd, and so SUBCOMM would equal A. Therefore, the command SET FORMAT TO &FORMAT&ECHOICE, will become SET FORMAT TO &FORMAT1, then SET FORMAT TO COA after substituting the macros. And we can give the command &COMMAND&SUBCOMM, which becomes &COMMANDA, and then APPEND after macro substitution. This case statement handles edits and appends for all data files by using ECHOICE and SUBCOMM as macros to fill in FORMAT and COMMAND macros:

```
* If append or edit, use edit screen.
CASE SUBCOMM = "A" .OR. SUBCOMM = "C"
    SET FORMAT TO &FORMAT&ECHOICE
    &COMMAND&SUBCOMM
    SET FORMAT TO SCREEN
```

If the user wishes to delete, the program deletes the record and packs the database in the second case statement below:

```
* If delete, delete and pack.
CASE SUBCOMM = "D"
   ? "Deleting Record " + STR(#,4)
   DELETE
   PACK
ENDCASE
```

If the record that the user requested was not found at all, the program warns him:

```
ELSE
   *** If no record found, warn user.
   @ 10,10 SAY "Not found!"
   ? CHR(7)
```

Now, we just need to close the IF statements above, as well as the DO WHILE loop for displaying the menu:

```
      ENDIF (#>0 and not eof)
   ENDIF (choice # 5)
ENDDO (while echoice # 5)
```

When the user opts to exit, the program releases the memory variables and returns to the main menu:

```
******* Release memory variables and
******* return to main menu.
RELEASE ALL LIKE FILE?
RELEASE ALL LIKE FORMAT?
RELEASE ALL LIKE COMMAND?
RELEASE ECHOICE,FINDER,FIND2,COUNT
RELEASE SUBCOMM,DELMARKER,HOWMANY
RETURN
```

Figure 19.2 shows the complete BEDIT.CMD command file.

Adjustment Transactions

Since the program updates chart of accounts balances directly from the transaction file, those amounts always reflect an ongoing summary of the individual transactions. This provides a complete audit trail for all the balances. If the user goes directly into the chart of accounts and changes a balance, it will destroy the audit trail.

```
*************************************** BEDIT.CMD
******** Edit program for the bookkeeping system.

******** Set up macros for linking database and
******** format file names to menu choice.

STORE "COA INDEX COA" TO FILE1
STORE "COA" TO FORMAT1
STORE "TRANS INDEX ACCT, DATES" TO FILE2
STORE "TRANS" TO FORMAT2
STORE "REGISTER" TO FILE3,FORMAT3
STORE "GENINFO" TO FILE4,FORMAT4
*************************** Store commands.
STORE "APPEND" TO COMMANDA
STORE "EDIT #" TO COMMANDC

******* Set up loop for menu.
STORE " " TO ECHOICE
DO WHILE ECHOICE # "5"
    ERASE
    TEXT
            Bookkeeping System Edit Menu

            1. Chart of Accounts
            2. Transaction File
            3. Check Register
            4. General Information
            5. Return to Main Menu

    ENDTEXT
    @ 11,12 SAY "Enter choice (1-5) " GET ECHOICE
    READ

    ****** Make sure valid selection was entered.
    IF ECHOICE < "1" .OR. ECHOICE > "5"
        * If not, display error message and repeat.
        @ 13,12 SAY "Invalid selection!"
        ? CHR(7)
        ******* Count to 20 just to take up time.
        STORE 1 TO COUNT
        DO WHILE COUNT < 21
            STORE COUNT+1 TO COUNT
        ENDDO (count < 21)
        LOOP
    ENDIF (invalid selection made)

    ************** If not exiting, get
    ************** information for finding record.
    IF ECHOICE # "5"
        ERASE
        USE &FILE&ECHOICE
        STORE " " TO SUBCOMM
        DO CASE
```

Figure 19.2: *The BEDIT.CMD command file.*

330   Advanced Techniques in dBASE II

```
******* If coa, ask for command then
******* look up by account number.
CASE ECHOICE = "1"
     ERASE
     @ 3,5 SAY "(A)dd, (C)hange or (D)elete? ";
       GET SUBCOMM PICT "!"
       READ
     IF SUBCOMM # "A"
        STORE "      " TO FINDER
        @ 5,5 SAY "What account number ";
           GET FINDER PICT "999.99"
        READ
        FIND &FINDER
     ENDIF (command # a)

******* If trans, look up by account and date.
CASE ECHOICE = "2"
     @ 3,5 SAY "(C)hange or (D)elete? ";
       GET SUBCOMM PICT "!"
     STORE "      " TO FINDER
     STORE "        " TO FIND2
     @ 5,5 SAY "What account number ";
       GET FINDER PICT "999.99"
     @ 7,5 SAY "What date? ";
       GET FIND2 PICT "99/99/99"
     READ
     ********* Locate exact record number.
     COUNT FOR ACCT = &FINDER .AND.;
           DATE = FIND2 TO HOWMANY
     IF HOWMANY > 1
        ERASE
        LIST FOR ACCT= &FINDER .AND.;
           DATE = FIND2 ACCT,DATE,REASON,AMOUNT
        ?
        INPUT "Which one? " TO RECNO
        GOTO RECNO
     ELSE
        LOCATE FOR ACCT = &FINDER .AND.;
           DATE = FIND2
     ENDIF (howmany > 1)

******** If register, look up by check number.
CASE ECHOICE = "3"
     @ 3,5 SAY "(A)dd, (C)hange or (D)elete? ";
       GET SUBCOMM PICT "!"
     READ
     IF SUBCOMM # "A"
        STORE "    " TO FINDER
        @ 5,5 SAY "What check number ";
           GET FINDER PICT "9999"
        READ
        LOCATE FOR CHECK:NO = &FINDER
           ENDIF (command # a)
     ENDCASE

     ****** If record found, edit or delete.
     IF # > 0 .AND. .NOT. EOF
```

Figure 19.2: The BEDIT.CMD command file (continued).

```
            DO CASE
               * If append or edit, use edit screen.
               CASE SUBCOMM="A" .OR. SUBCOMM = "C"
                    SET FORMAT TO &FORMAT&ECHOICE
                    &COMMAND&SUBCOMM
                    SET FORMAT TO SCREEN

               * If delete, delete and pack.
               CASE SUBCOMM = "D"
                    ? "Deleting Record "+STR(#,4)
                    DELETE
                    PACK
               ENDCASE

            ELSE
               *** If no record found, warn user.
               @ 10,10 SAY "Not found!"
               ? CHR(7)

            ENDIF (#>0 and not eof)

      ENDIF (choice # 5)

ENDDO (while echoice # 5)

******* Release memory variables and
******* return to main menu.
RELEASE ALL LIKE FILE?
RELEASE ALL LIKE FORMAT?
RELEASE ALL LIKE COMMAND?
RELEASE ECHOICE,FINDER,FIND2,COUNT
RELEASE SUBCOMM,DELMARKER,HOWMANY
RETURN
```

Figure 19.2: The BEDIT.CMD command file (continued).

To make corrections while still maintaining the audit trail, the user can add adjustment transactions to the transaction file. We need not do any additional programming to provide this capability, as it is already built into the system.

Let's suppose that the user adds $500 to account 100 (regular income), then later realizes that the amount should have been posted to account 110 (royalty income). Now, the balance of account number 100 is too large by $500, and account 110 too small by that amount. The user can select main menu option 1 (add new transactions), and add two adjustment transactions as follows:

```
Account number :100.00:    Regular Income
Description    :Adjustment for error    :
Amount : -500.00:
Date   :12/12/84:
```

The second transaction would be:

    Account number :110.00:   Royalty Income
    Description   :Royalty Income   :
    Amount :   500.00:
    Date   :12/12/84:

Next time the user updates the chart of accounts, $500 will be subtracted from account 100 (because of the negative number), and $500 will be added to account 110, so the balances will be correct once again. There will also be a permanent record of the adjustment on the database.

Similarly, if the user accidentally posted $10,000 to account 100, and actually only meant to post $1,000, he could enter a single adjustment transaction to correct the error. In this case, he would subtract $9000 from account 100, by adding the transaction below:

    Account number :100.00:   Regular Income
    Description   :Adjustment for error   :
    Amount : –9000.00:
    Date   :12/12/84:

As in the previous example, the chart of accounts balances will be correct after the next update, and the trans file will have a permanent record of the correction.

Expanding the Bookkeeping System

Our sample bookkeeping system is fairly simple compared to many of the full-blown accounting systems that many businesses use, but the basic design is expandable. For example, to provide for a double-entry system, the trans file needs to have two account numbers for each transaction, a debit account and a credit account. During the update phase, both accounts would need to be updated on the chart of accounts file.

Many bookkeeping systems allow the user to specify totalled accounts. These are accounts that automatically reflect the totals of several subaccounts. For example, the selling expenses account below reflects the totals of the accounts beneath it:

Selling Expenses	$30,700
Sales salaries expense	18,500
Rent expense, selling space	8,100

Advertising expense	700
Store supplies expense	400
Depreciation expense, store equipment	3,000

If you wish to develop a system that allows this sort of automatically totalled account, you'll first need to develop some means of identifying totalled accounts. You could do so by reserving all account numbers that are evenly divisible by 100, and have a zero in the decimal portion for this purpose. Then you'll need to specify a rule for identifying the accounts that are to be totalled into this account. Here is a simple rule: the subaccount should have the same number as the totalled account, but a decimal value greater than zero. The accounts below adhere to this identifying scheme:

100.00 Selling Expenses	$30,700
100.10 Sales salaries expense	18,500
100.20 Rent expense, selling space	8,100
100.30 Advertising expense	700
100.40 Store supplies expense	400
100.50 Depreciation expense, store equipment	3,000

Then you would need to build a routine that could locate all the totalled accounts in the chart of accounts, and calculate the totals. The routine below would do this with the account numbering system we've just described:

```
USE TRANS INDEX ACCTS
STORE 0 TO TOT:ACCT
DO WHILE .NOT. EOF
   STORE 100.00 + TOT:ACCT TO TOT:ACCT
   STORE STR(TOT:ACCT,6,2) TO FINDER
   FIND &FINDER
   IF # > 0
      REPLACE AMOUNT WITH 0
      SUM AMOUNT WHILE INT(ACCT) = TOT:ACCT TO SUB:TOT
      FIND &FINDER
      REPLACE AMOUNT WITH SUB:TOT
   ENDIF (#>0)
ENDDO (not eof)
```

The routine fills in totalled account balances by finding each account that is evenly divisible by 100. First it zeroes out any previous amount in the totalled account. Then, it sums the amounts for those records whose integer portion account number is equal to the totaling account number. The sum of the subaccounts is stored in a variable called

SUB:TOT. Then, the routine replaces the amount in the totaling account with the SUB:TOT amount.

Summary

In this chapter, we've completed our sample bookkeeping system. Many of the techniques we used are identical to those used in the inventory system, particularly those which involve updating the master file, COA.DBF, from the bookkeeping transaction file, TRANS.DBF. We used similar techniques, like error trapping, to ensure that only valid account numbers be entered into the system.

The major difference betweeen the inventory and bookkeeping systems lies in the problems that arise when you start dealing with income versus expense accounts, and subaccounts versus regular accounts. However, these problems can be solved if all the programs in the system can readily identify the various accounts without confusion. If you set up an account numbering scheme that is easy to detect with dBASE commands and functions, you can write programs that can handle many types of accounts without lengthy DO CASE and IF clauses.

In this chapter, we've also looked at advanced uses of macros. In the check-writing program, we used macros to help solve the problem of translating numeric dollar amounts to English words. In the editing section, we set up a single command file to handle edits to four different database files. We also developed a general-purpose editing program that substitutes in database and format file names as well as commands, based upon user menu choices.

CHAPTER 20
A LIBRARY CROSS-REFERENCING SYSTEM

In this chapter, we'll design and begin developing a software system to manage a library. Here are some new programming techniques we'll discuss:

1. Allowing the user to perform complex searches through a simple menu.
2. Formatting with ragged right margin.
3. Printing reports in two columns.
4. Building a subjects file as a cross-referencing aid.
5. Converting dates to English (01/10/85 to January 10, 1985).

Library System Goals

The library system is useful for any user who needs quick access to published information. The user can search for references by author, title, publication or publisher, date, and up to six *keywords* (topics). The references can be printed out in standard bibliographic form and placed directly into the user's written document.

The user will edit data and add data to the file through custom screens that include instructions for managing the cursor. He can also accomplish complex searches by filling in the blanks on a simple custom screen. The user can define the fields to search on, the values to search for, the logic of the search (AND vs. OR), and whether or not the keywords and abstract should be included on the printout. Furthermore, the user can send the resulting bibliography to the screen, printer, or separate text file for inclusion in a word-processing document.

The reports in the library system will be printed to look hand-typed, i.e., the data will be printed with a ragged right edge, as it would look if typed with a typewriter. When the user wishes to sort or search, he will enter dates in MM/DD/YY format, but in the report, dates will be printed in their English equivalent.

Library System Database Structure

The library system will consist of two data files. The first, LIBRARY.DBF, will hold the reference data for journal articles and books. Here is the structure:

STRUCTURE FOR FILE: B:LIBRARY .DBF

FLD	NAME	TYPE	WIDTH	DEC	CONTENTS
001	AUTHOR	C	030		Author name(s)
002	TITLE	C	040		Book or article title
003	PUB	C	030		Publication or publisher
004	VOLUME	C	020		Volume (for journal)
005	PLACE	C	020		Place of publication (book)
006	PAGES	C	008		Pages (article)
007	DATE	C	008		Date (MM/DD/YY)
008	KEY1	C	025		Topic
009	KEY2	C	025		Topic
010	KEY3	C	025		Topic
011	KEY4	C	025		Topic
012	KEY5	C	025		Topic
013	KEY6	C	025		Topic
014	ABSTRACT	C	244		Summary of content

For sorting and searching purposes, the primary sort order will be by author name. However, the user can also list articles in chronological order. The names of the index files will be AUTHORS and DATES, which can be created with these commands:

```
USE LIBRARY
INDEX ON !(AUTHOR) TO AUTHORS
INDEX ON $(DATE,7,2) + $(DATE,1,6) TO DATES
```

Notice that we've indexed on the uppercase-equivalent of the author name(s), and we've moved the year to the front of the date for proper sorting.

The system will also generate an alphabetized summary of all subjects stored on the database, along with a number indicating how many references refer to that topic. These data will be structured as follows:

```
STRUCTURE FOR FILE: B:TOPICS .DBF

FLD  NAME      TYPE  WIDTH  DEC  CONTENTS
001  SUBJECT   C     025         Keyword (or topic)
002  QTY       N     004         Number of associated references
```

You should create the two data files and two index files prior to developing and testing any programs.

Library System Software Design

The library system will consist of five command files:

1. LIBRARY.CMD, the main menu,
2. LIBEDIT.CMD, for editing,
3. LIBDEL.CMD, for deleting,
4. LIBSEARC.CMD, for searching and printing reports,
5. SUBJECTS.CMD, for creating the subjects list.

Also, there will be three format (.FMT) files:

1. LIBADD.FMT, for adding new references,
2. LIBEDIT.FMT, for editing,
3. LIBSEARC.FMT for menu-driven searches.

The relationships among the command files is shown in Figure 20.1.

Library System Main Menu

The main menu for the library system will display the following options to the user:

Library Referencing System Main Menu
1. Add references
2. Change references
3. Delete references
4. Search references
5. Print subjects list
6. Exit

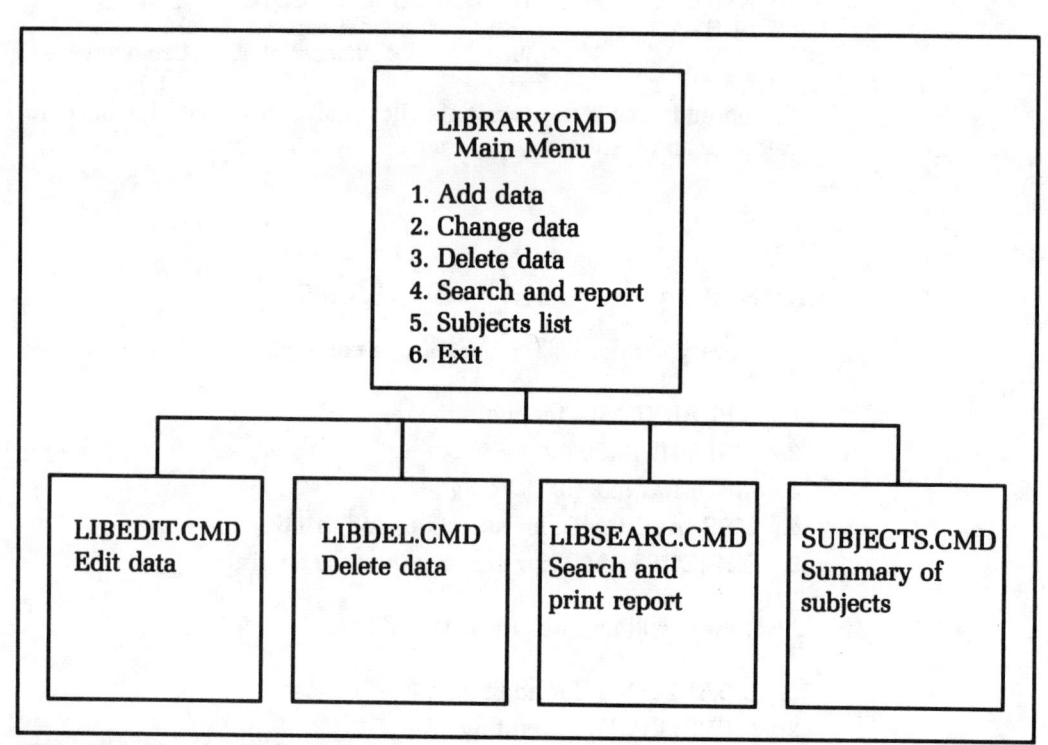

```
                    ┌──────────────────────┐
                    │     LIBRARY.CMD      │
                    │      Main Menu       │
                    │                      │
                    │   1. Add data        │
                    │   2. Change data     │
                    │   3. Delete data     │
                    │   4. Search and report│
                    │   5. Subjects list   │
                    │   6. Exit            │
                    └──────────┬───────────┘
          ┌──────────┬─────────┴─────────┬──────────┐
  ┌───────┴─────┐ ┌──┴────────┐ ┌────────┴────┐ ┌───┴──────────┐
  │ LIBEDIT.CMD │ │LIBDEL.CMD │ │LIBSEARC.CMD │ │ SUBJECTS.CMD │
  │ Edit data   │ │Delete data│ │Search and   │ │ Summary of   │
  │             │ │           │ │print report │ │ subjects     │
  └─────────────┘ └───────────┘ └─────────────┘ └──────────────┘
```

Figure 20.1: Library system software structure.

The main menu segment of the LIBRARY system is similar to the ones in the other systems we've developed. The difference is that when the user opts to add new data, the LIBRARY program does not branch to another command file. Instead, it sets the format to the LIBADD.FMT format file, appends, and then sets the format back to the screen (see CASE CHOICE = "1" clause in Figure 20.2). The LIBRARY.CMD command file is shown in Figure 20.2.

```
*************************************** LIBRARY.CMD
*************** Main menu for the library system.
SET TALK OFF
SET DEFA TO B
STORE " " TO CHOICE
DO WHILE CHOICE # "6"
   ERASE
   TEXT
           Library Referencing System Main Menu

                1. Add references
                2. Change references
                3. Delete references
                4. Search references
                5. Print subjects list

                6. Exit
   ENDTEXT
   @ 11,10 SAY "Enter choice (1-6) " GET CHOICE
   READ

   ****** Do appropriate task.
   DO CASE

      CASE CHOICE  = "1"
           USE LIBRARY INDEX AUTHORS, DATES
           SET FORMAT TO LIBADD
           APPEND
           SET FORMAT TO SCREEN

      CASE CHOICE = "2"
           DO LIBEDIT

      CASE CHOICE = "3"
           DO LIBDEL

      CASE CHOICE = "4"
           DO LIBSEARC

      CASE CHOICE = "5"
           DO SUBJECTS

   ENDCASE

ENDDO (while choice # 6)
QUIT
```

Figure 20.2: *The LIBRARY.CMD command file.*

Adding References

You'll also need to create the LIBADD.FMT file to allow the user to add new data. You can use the ZIP or SED program to generate the code. Figure 20.3 shows how to draw the screen using SED. Once the screen is drawn, use the SED G (generate) option to create the LIBADD format file, which is shown in Figure 20.4. Then, from the A>, use the RENAME B:LIBADD B:LIBADD.FMT to add the .FMT extension to the SED-generated file.

The user can store references to either books or journal articles on this screen. Generally, book references include author, title, publisher, location of publisher, and publication date. Figure 20.5 shows a data-entry screen with a book reference filled in. Note that the publisher is stored in the publication field.

The user generally includes the author, title, publication, volume and number, pages, and date in journal entries. Figure 20.6 shows the library system data-entry screen with a magazine reference filled in.

Editing References

The LIBEDIT.CMD command file and the LIBEDIT.FMT format file handle changes to the library system data. You can create the format file by drawing a SED screen, as in Figure 20.7.

```
        Cursor Control:  ^E up  :  ^X down  :  ^D right  :  ^S left
                      :  ^G delete character  :  ^V insert mode
       ─────────────────────────────────────────────────────────────
       Author <AUTHOR
       Title <TITLE
       Publication <PUB                        Volume <VOLUME
       Date <DATE!"99/99/99" Pages <PAGES     Location <PLACE
       Subjects:
       ─────────
       1.<KEY1              2.<KEY2
       3.<KEY3              4.<KEY4
       5.<KEY5              6.<KEY6
       Abstract:
       ─────────
       <ABSTRACT
```

Figure 20.3: *SED screen for the LIBADD.FMT file.*

Once the screen is drawn, use the SED G option and the RENAME command to create the LIBEDIT.FMT format file shown in Figure 20.8.

The LIBEDIT.CMD command file works by first asking the user for the author of the reference to edit, as shown below:

Edit which? (lead author name) :_

If the user presses RETURN, the program stops and the main menu is redisplayed. If the user enters an author name for which there is no reference, the program presents this message:

Not found!

```
* B:LIBADD
@ 1,1 SAY "Cursor Control: ^E up : ^X down : ^D right : ^S left"
@ 2,15 SAY ": ^G delete character : ^V insert mode"
@ 3,1 SAY "-----------------------------------------------------"
@ 4,1 SAY "Author"
@ 4,9 GET AUTHOR
@ 6,1 SAY "Title"
@ 6,9 GET TITLE
@ 8,1 SAY "Publication"
@ 8,14 GET PUB
@ 8,47 SAY "Volume"
@ 8,55 GET VOLUME
@ 10,1 SAY "Date"
@ 10,7 GET DATE PICTURE "99/99/99"
@ 10,24 SAY "Pages"
@ 10,31 GET PAGES
@ 10,45 SAY "Location"
@ 10,55 GET PLACE
@ 12,1 SAY "Subjects:"
@ 13,1 SAY "---------"
@ 14,1 SAY "1."
@ 14,4 GET KEY1
@ 14,34 SAY "2."
@ 14,37 GET KEY2
@ 15,1 SAY "3."
@ 15,4 GET KEY3
@ 15,34 SAY "4."
@ 15,37 GET KEY4
@ 16,1 SAY "5."
@ 16,4 GET KEY5
@ 16,34 SAY "6."
@ 16,37 GET KEY6
@ 18,1 SAY "Abstract:"
@ 19,1 SAY "---------"
@ 20,2 GET ABSTRACT
```

Figure 20.4: *The LIBADD format file.*

```
Cursor Control:  ^E up  :  ^X down  :  ^D right  :  ^S left
                 :  ^G delete character  :  ^V insert mode
```

Author :**Simpson, Alan**   :
Title :**Understanding dBASE II**   :
Publication :**SYBEX, Inc.**   :   Volume :   :
Date :**03/00/84**: Pages :   :   Location :**Berkeley, CA**   :
Subjects:

1. :**dBASE II**   :   2. :**Database management** :
3. :**Mailing System**: 4. :**Multiple databases**   :
5. :**Programming**   :   6. :   :
Abstract:

   :An introduction to dBASE II for the novice computerist or   :
:dBASE II beginner. Provides numerous examples for creating,   :
: editing, modifying, sorting, and searching a database.   :

Figure 20.5: A book reference filled in.

```
Cursor Control:  ^E up  :  ^X down  :  ^D right  :  ^S left  :  ^V insert
                 :  ^G delete character  :  ^V insert mode
```

Author :**Smith, P. and Jones, J.**   :
Title :**Access Manager 86: A Review** :
Publication :**Microsystems**   :   Volume :**Vol. 1, No. 4** :
Date :**03/00/84**: Pages   :**12-17** :   Location :   :
Subjects:

1. :**Custom screens**:   2. :**Indexing**   :
3. :**CB-86**   :   4. :**Sorting**   :
5.:   :   6. :   :
Abstract:

   :A review of the Access Manager retrieval system for the 80   :
:86 processor. Includes sample programs using the CB-86 comp   :
:ilable programming language.   :

Figure 20.6: A journal article reference.

and the user can try again. If the user enters a valid name, the first reference for that author is displayed on the edit screen, and the user can make changes. In addition, the user can use ^C to view and edit the next reference in the database, or ^R to view and edit the previous reference. Since the data file is indexed on the author name, the next and previous references will appear in alphabetical order by author.

The pseudocode for the LIBEDIT.CMD command file is shown in Figure 20.9.

The LIBEDIT.CMD command file begins by using the LIBRARY data file with the author and dates index, as shown below:

```
*********************************  LIBEDIT.CMD
**************************** Edit the library file.
USE LIBRARY INDEX AUTHORS,DATES
```

It then sets up loop so that the user can either edit several references or exit by pressing RETURN instead of typing in an author name:

```
*****************  Set up loop for editing.
STORE "X" TO SEARCH
DO WHILE SEARCH # " "
    STORE "                    " TO SEARCH
    ERASE
    @ 5,5 SAY "Edit which? (lead author name) ";
      GET SEARCH
    READ
```

Cursor Control: ^E up : ^X down : ^D right : ^S left : ^V insert
  ^G delete : ^C next : ^R previous : ^W SAVE : ^Q abandon

Author <AUTHOR
Title <TITLE
Publication <PUB   Volume <VOLUME
Date <DATE!"99/99/99" Pages <PAGES   Location <PLACE
Subjects:

1.<KEY1   2.<KEY2
3.<KEY3   4.<KEY4
5.<KEY5   6.<KEY6
Abstract:

<ABSTRACT

Figure 20.7: *SED screen as drawn for the LIBEDIT.FMT file.*

The command file then converts the author name to uppercase, since the index is in uppercase. Then, the program trims off the trailing blanks left by the READ command. This allows the user to enter only the last name of the lead author when looking up a reference. For example, if the user enters Smith, the FIND command could still locate an article with the author name:

Smith, A. and Jones, P.

The lines below do the uppercase conversion, trim the trailing blanks,

```
* B:LIBEDIT.FMT
@ 1,1 SAY "Cursor Control: ^E up : ^X down : ^D right : ^S left :"
@ 1,56 SAY "^V insert"
@ 2,3 SAY "^G delete : ^R next : ^R previous  : ^W SAVE : ^Q aband"
@ 2,58 SAY "on"
@ 3,1 SAY "------------------------------------------------------------"
@ 3,56 SAY "---------"
@ 4,1 SAY "Author"
@ 4,9 GET AUTHOR
@ 6,1 SAY "Title"
@ 6,9 GET TITLE
@ 8,1 SAY "Publication"
@ 8,14 GET PUB
@ 8,47 SAY "Volume"
@ 8,55 GET VOLUME
@ 10,1 SAY "Date"
@ 10,7 GET DATE PICTURE "99/99/99"
@ 10,24 SAY "Pages"
@ 10,31 GET PAGES
@ 10,45 SAY "Location"
@ 10,55 GET PLACE
@ 12,1 SAY "Subjects:"
@ 13,1 SAY "---------"
@ 14,1 SAY "1."
@ 14,4 GET KEY1
@ 14,34 SAY "2."
@ 14,37 GET KEY2
@ 15,1 SAY "3."
@ 15,4 GET KEY3
@ 15,34 SAY "4."
@ 15,37 GET KEY4
@ 16,1 SAY "5."
@ 16,4 GET KEY5
@ 16,34 SAY "6."
@ 16,37 GET KEY6
@ 18,1 SAY "Abstract:"
@ 19,1 SAY "---------"
@ 20,2 GET ABSTRACT
```

Figure 20.8: *The LIBEDIT.FMT format file.*

and search for the requested reference:

```
******** Find first article by that author.
STORE !(TRIM(SEARCH)) TO SEARCH
FIND &SEARCH
```

Now, we must create a DO CASE clause so that the user can proceed. If the user did not enter a name to edit, the command file can simply clear the screen and skip over the remaining CASE statements. Here are the lines that would accomplish this:

```
DO CASE
    ** If exit requested, just clear the screen.
    CASE SEARCH = " "
        ERASE
```

If the program finds an appropriate reference, it can set the screen to the LIBEDIT.FMT format, allow editing, then set the screen back to normal, as shown in the lines below:

```
    ** If reference found, enter edit mode.
    CASE # > 0
        SET FORMAT TO LIBEDIT
        EDIT #
        SET FORMAT TO SCREEN
```

Open the library file and indexes

Set up loop for editing
  Ask for author of reference

  Find first article by that author

    If exit requested, just clear the screen
      and return to main menu

    If reference found, enter edit mode with
      custom LIBEDIT.FMT screen

    If reference not found, warn user and try again

Continue loop for editing (until exit requested)

Release memory variables
Return to main menu

Figure 20.9: Pseudocode for the LIBEDIT.CMD command file.

If it finds no reference, the command file can display a warning message. These lines allow for that condition:

```
*** If not found, warn user and try again.
CASE # = 0
   @ 10,5 SAY "Not found! . . . ."
   ?
   WAIT
ENDCASE
```

Then, we only need to add commands to close the DO WHILE loop, release the memory variable, and return to the main menu:

```
ENDDO (while search # " ")
RELEASE SEARCH
RETURN
```

The complete LIBEDIT.CMD command file is shown in Figure 20.10.

Deleting References

To delete names from the library system database, you will use a procedure identical to the one used earlier in the DELNAMES command file for deleting names from the mailing system. Refer to Chapter 7 for a detailed discussion of the procedure. Here, we'll simply display the command file in its entirety in Figure 20.11. Its name is LIBDEL.CMD. Create and save it as you would any other command file.

```
************************************* LIBEDIT.CMD
************************** Edit the library file.

USE LIBRARY INDEX AUTHORS,DATES

***************** Set up loop for editing.
STORE "X" TO SEARCH
DO WHILE SEARCH # " "
   STORE "                          " TO SEARCH
   ERASE
   @ 5,5 SAY "Edit which? (lead author name) ";
      GET SEARCH
   READ

   ******** Find first article by that author.
   STORE !(TRIM(SEARCH)) TO SEARCH
   FIND &SEARCH
```

Figure 20.10: The LIBEDIT.CMD command file.

```
       DO CASE

          ** If exit requested, just clear the screen.
          CASE SEARCH = " "
             ERASE

          ** If reference found, enter edit mode.
          CASE # > 0
             SET FORMAT TO LIBEDIT
             EDIT #
             SET FORMAT TO SCREEN

          *** If not found, warn user and try again.
          CASE # = 0
             @ 10,5 SAY "Not found!...."
             ?
             WAIT

       ENDCASE

ENDDO (while search # " ")
RELEASE SEARCH
RETURN
```

Figure 20.10: *The LIBEDIT.CMD command file (continued).*


```
       ******************************** LIBDEL.CMD
       ***************************** Delete references.
USE LIBRARY INDEX AUTHORS,DATES

********* First, get author of record to delete.
STORE "X" TO SEARCH
DO WHILE SEARCH # " "
   ERASE
   ACCEPT " Delete which? (lead author name) ";
     TO SEARCH
   ERASE

   ******** Translate to uppercase, then count how
   ******** many idiviuduals have that last name.
   STORE !(SEARCH) TO SEARCH
   FIND &SEARCH
   COUNT WHILE !(AUTHOR) = SEARCH TO HOWMANY

   ****** Respond accordingly, depending on how
   ****** many records have the author's last name.
```

Figure 20.11: *The LIBDEL.CMD command file.*

```
DO CASE
    **** If no name entered, just clear screen.
    CASE SEARCH=" "
        ERASE

    ** If nobody has that last name, warn user.
    CASE HOWMANY = 0
        ? "There is no &SEARCH on the database"
        ?
        ? "Press any key to try again...."
        WAIT

    *** If one person has that last name, delete.
    CASE HOWMANY=1
        FIND &SEARCH
        ? "Deleting ",TRIM(AUTHOR),TRIM(TITLE)
        DELETE

    ***** If several people have that last name,
    ***** display them and get further information
    CASE HOWMANY > 1
        FIND &SEARCH
        LIST WHILE !(AUTHOR)=SEARCH;
        TRIM(AUTHOR),TRIM(TITLE)
        ?
        ACCEPT "Which one? (by number) " TO RECNO
        IF VAL(RECNO)>0
            GOTO &RECNO
            DELETE
        ENDIF (value of recno > 0)
ENDCASE

ENDDO   (while search # " ")

****************** Before packing the database
****************** and returning to the main menu
****************** get permission to pack.
COUNT FOR * TO NO:DELS
STORE "N" TO PACKEM
DO WHILE !(PACKEM) # "Y" .AND. NO:DELS > 0
    ERASE
    DISPLAY ALL FOR * TRIM(AUTHOR),TRIM(TITLE)
    ?
    ACCEPT "Delete all these references? (Y/N) ";
        TO PACKEM

    ****************** If not OK to pack everyone,
    ****************** find out who to recall.
    IF !(PACKEM) # "Y"
        ?
        ACCEPT "Recall which one (left-column number) ";
            TO SAVE
        IF VAL(SAVE)>0
            RECALL RECORD &SAVE
            STORE NO:DELS-1 TO NO:DELS
```

Figure 20.11: The LIBDEL.CMD command file (continued).

```
        ENDIF (val(save>0))
   ENDIF (packem # "Y")

ENDDO (while packem # Y)

*********** When OK to pack, do so if there are names to delete.
ERASE
IF NO:DELS > 0
   ? "Deleting requested references....."
   PACK
ENDIF (number of names to delete > 0).

***** Release memory variables and return to main menu.
RELEASE ALL EXCEPT CHOICE
?
? "Returning to main menu..."
RETURN
```

Figure 20.11: *The LIBDEL.CMD command file (continued).*

Summary

In this chapter, we've designed a system for storing and retrieving references to books and periodicals. References can include up to seven keywords (topics) which allow the user to look up information by subject. The user can also store an abstract (summary) up to 254 characters in length with each reference. References are stored in a database named LIBRARY.DBF.

A second database named TOPICS.DBF will be used by the system to create an alphabetized listing of all keywords used in the database, and the number of records associated with each topic.

In this chapter, we've developed the following command and format files for the referencing system:

1. LIBRARY.CMD, which is the library system main menu.
2. LIBADD.FMT, which is a custom screen for entering references into the database.
3. LIBEDIT.CMD, which allows the user to edit references on the database.
4. LIBEDIT.FMT, which is a custom screen for editing references.
5. LIBDEL.CMD, which is a command file that allows the user to delete references from the database.

CHAPTER 21
LIBRARY SYSTEM REPORTS

The library system produces two reports. The first is a bibliography that can be printed with or without keywords and abstracts. Unlike previous reports in the system, the bibliography prints each line of the report in a continuous form, rather than in columnar blocks. Figure 21.1 shows a sample report with the keywords and abstract for each reference included.

A bibliography printed without the keywords and abstracts is shown in Figure 21.2. Both reports are printed via the "Search for References" option from the main menu. The user can specify any search criteria, and may request that data be presented in either alphabetical order (by author) or chronological order. In each of the two figures, the dates appear in English format (i.e., January 10, 1984), even though they are stored in the standard MM/DD/YY format.

The system is also capable of printing an alphabetized listing of all the subjects available on the system. The number of articles on the database that refer to each topic is also included on the report. Figure 21.3 shows a sample subjects list.

Searching for References

The searching program for the library system is unique. It allows the user to perform complex searches easily when otherwise they would

---

Bibliography

Levine, Joel H., Hard Disks for Portables, Portable Computer, Vol. 2, No. 3, 38–41, March 10, 1984.
KEYWORDS: Hard Disks, Winchesters, Portable Computers.
ABSTRACT: Discusses the proper care and feeding of hard disks for portable computers. Includes portable computer stress, temperature, and humidity.

Trost, S., and King, R., Doing Business with Multiplan, SYBEX Inc., Berkeley, CA, 1984.
KEYWORDS: Multiplan, budgeting, sales.
ABSTRACT: This book is an introduction to using Multiplan in business.

Simpson, Alan, Data File Programming On Your IBM PC, SYBEX Inc., Berkeley, CA, May 1984.
KEYWORDS: BASIC, IBM PC, Data File Programming, Sorting, Searching, Data Files.
ABSTRACT: This book discusses advanced BASIC programming techniques. Discusses sequential and random access data files, as well as sorting and searching in BASIC.

Figure 21.1: *Sample bibliography with keywords and abstracts.*

be very difficult. The user can type search parameters into the screen as shown in Figure 21.4.

Bibliography

Glass, Jim, Word Processor File Conversion, PC Tech Journal, Vol. 1, No. 2, 168–179, September 1983.

Levine, Joel H., Hard Disks for Portables, Portable Computer, Vol. 2, No. 3, 38–41, March 10, 1984.

Trost, S. and King, R. Doing Business with Multiplan. SYBEX Inc., Berkeley, CA, 1984.

Simpson, Alan, Understanding dBASE II, SYBEX, Inc., Berkeley, CA, February 1984.

Simpson, Alan, Data File Programming On Your IBM PC, SYBEX Inc., Berkeley, CA, May 1984.

Zaks, Rodnay, The CP/M Handbook, SYBEX Inc., Berkeley, CA, 1982.

Figure 21.2: *Sample bibliography without keywords or abstracts.*

Subjects List

Subject	No.	Subject	No.
Assembly Language	11	BASIC	22
Copying	9	CP/M	42
Data File Programming	13	Data Files	19
Database management	43	dBASE II	21
File Conversion	1	File Management	2
Formatting disks	3	Graphics	37
Hard Disks	12	IBM PC	22
Input/Output	7	Kaypro	19
Mailing lists	33	PIP	7
Portable Computers	24	SBASIC	8
Searching	44	Sorting	51
Winchesters	11	Word Processing	12
WordStar	21		

Figure 21.3: *Sample subjects list.*

Advanced Techniques in dBASE II

Suppose the user wants to see everything written by P. Smith on the topic of dBASE II. He would simply have to fill out the screen as shown in Figure 21.5.

Notice that the author field and one subject field are filled in. Furthermore, under searching criteria the ALL criteria field is marked Y,

```
Cursor Control: ^E up : ^X down : ^D right : ^S left : ^V insert
-Fill in search criteria, or leave all blank for all references-
```

Author :	:
Title :	:
Publication :	:
Date : / / :	
Subjects:	
1. :	: 2. : :
3. :	: 4. : :
5. :	: 6. : :

Searching Logic:	ALL criteria : :	ANY criterion : :
Format:	Show keywords? : :	Abstract? : :
Output:	To printer? : :	To text file? : :

Figure 21.4: *A blank search screen.*

```
Cursor Control: ^E up : ^X down : ^D right : ^S left : ^V insert
-Fill in search criteria, or leave all blank for all references-
```

Author :**Smith, P**	:
Title :	:
Publication :	:
Date : / / :	
Subjects:	
1. :**dBASE II**	: 2. : :
3. :	: 4. : :
5. :	: 6. : :

Searching Logic:	ALL criteria :**Y**:	ANY criterion : :
Format:	Show keywords? :**Y**:	Abstract? :**Y**:
Output:	To printer? :**Y**:	To text file? : :

Figure 21.5: *A search for articles on dBASE II by P. Smith.*

meaning that the references displayed must be by P. Smith *and* deal with the topic of dBASE II. The format options "Show keywords?" and "Abstract?" are also marked Y, meaning that these will be displayed for each reference on the report. Also, the "To printer?" box is marked Y, so the report will go to the printer.

Now let's suppose the user wishes to see articles dealing with database management, dBASE II, database design, and programming techniques. He does not want the abstracts or keywords displayed, and he wants the resulting report to be sent to a separate disk file as well as to the printer. In this case, he would fill out the screen as shown in Figure 21.6.

The search for references in Figure 21.6 shows the ANY criterion box marked Y. This ensures that a reference dealing with *any one* of these topics will be displayed on the report. If the user marked the ALL criteria box Y instead, then references covering *all four* topics would be displayed. In other words, the ALL criteria box, when marked Y, performs an AND search. The ANY criterion box when marked Y performs a broader OR search.

The LIBSEARC.CMD command file performs the search, and also produces the bibliographic reports shown earlier in Figure 21.1. It is quite a complex program for two reasons. First, it needs to build search conditions out of the user's request from the search screen. Second, it must ensure that a long string never breaks in the middle of a word in the right-hand margin.

Cursor Control: ^E up : ^X down : ^D right : ^S left : ^V insert
-Fill in search criteria, or leave all blank for all references-

Author :   :
Title :   :
Publication :   :
Date : / / :
Subjects:
1. :**Database management**   : 2. : **dBASE II**   :
3. :**Database design**   : 4. : **Programming techniques**   :
5. :   : 6. :   :

Searching Logic: ALL criteria : :   ANY criterion :**Y**:
Format: Show keywords? :**Y**:   Abstract? :**Y**:
Output: To printer? :**Y**:   To text file? :**Y**:

Figure 21.6: *A search for references to four topics.*

358   Advanced Techniques in dBASE II

You can create the search screen with the ZIP or SED program. Its name is LIBSEARC.FMT. Figure 21.7 shows how to draw it on the SED screen.

The SED program then created the LIBSEARC.FMT format file, as shown in Figure 21.8.

As usual, you will need to use the DOS command RENAME b:LIBSEARC b:LIBSEARC.FMT after exiting SED to give the generated file the proper filename extension.

The pseuducode for the LIBSEARC.CMD command file is shown in Figure 21.9.

We'll begin developing the LIBSEARC.CMD command file now. First, we need to set up the variables to be used in the program:

```
******************************* LIBSEARC.CMD
*************************** Search for references.

********************** Set up memory variables.
STORE "                     " TO M:AUTHOR,M:PUB
STORE "                     " TO M:TITLE
STORE "        " TO M:DATE
STORE "            " TO M:KEY1,M:KEY2,M:KEY3
STORE "            " TO M:KEY4,M:KEY5,M:KEY6
STORE " " TO ANY,ALL,SHOW:KEYS,SHOW:ABS,PRINTER,TO:TEXT
STORE "         " TO TEXT:FILE
```

Cursor Control: ^E up : ^X down : ^D right : ^S left : ^V insert
-Fill in search criteria, or leave all blank for all references-

Author <M:AUTHOR
Title <M:TITLE
Publication <M:PUB
Date <M:DATE!"99/99/99"
Subjects:
1.<M:KEY1   2.<M:KEY2
3.<M:KEY3   4.<M:KEY4
5.<M:KEY5   6.<M:KEY6

Searching Logic: ALL criteria <ALL   ANY criterion <ANY
Format: Show keywords? <SHOW:KEYS   Abstract? <SHOW:ABS
Output: To printer? <PRINTER   To text file? <TO:TEXT

Figure 21.7: The library screen as drawn with SED.

Variables beginning with M: are memory-variable equivalents of field names. For example, M:AUTHOR is the name of the author to search for, M:KEY1 is a keyword to search for, and so forth. The variables ANY, ALL, SHOW:KEYS, SHOW:ABS, PRINTER, TO:TEXT are all used as flags (Y or N) to determine whether the search should include ALL criteria or ANY criteria selected by the user, whether the report should display keywords (SHOW:KEYS) or the abstract (SHOW:ABS), and whether or not the report should be sent to the printer (PRINTER)

```
* B:LIBSEARC.FMT
@ 1,1 SAY "Cursor Control:  ^E up : ^X down : ^D right : ^S left :"
@ 1,56 SAY "^V insert"
@ 2,1 SAY "-Fill in search criteria, or leave all blank for all re"
@ 2,56 SAY "ferences-"
@ 3,1 SAY "-------------------------------------------------------"
@ 3,56 SAY "---------"
@ 4,1 SAY "Author"
@ 4,9 GET M:AUTHOR
@ 6,1 SAY "Title"
@ 6,9 GET M:TITLE
@ 8,1 SAY "Publication"
@ 8,14 GET M:PUB
@ 10,1 SAY "Date"
@ 10,7 GET M:DATE PICTURE "99/99/99"
@ 12,1 SAY "Subjects:"
@ 13,1 SAY "1."
@ 13,4 GET M:KEY1
@ 13,36 SAY "2."
@ 13,39 GET M:KEY2
@ 14,1 SAY "3."
@ 14,4 GET M:KEY3
@ 14,36 SAY "4."
@ 14,39 GET M:KEY4
@ 15,1 SAY "5."
@ 15,4 GET M:KEY5
@ 15,36 SAY "6."
@ 15,39 GET M:KEY6
@ 16,1 SAY "-------------------------------------------------------"
@ 16,56 SAY "---------"
@ 17,1 SAY "Searching Logic:   ALL criteria"
@ 17,33 GET ALL
@ 17,44 SAY "ANY criterion"
@ 17,59 GET ANY
@ 19,1 SAY "Format:          Show keywords?"
@ 19,33 GET SHOW:KEYS
@ 19,48 SAY "Abstract?"
@ 19,59 GET SHOW:ABS
@ 21,1 SAY "Output:          To printer?"
@ 21,32 GET PRINTER
@ 21,44 SAY "To text file?"
@ 21,59 GET TO:TEXT
```

Figure 21.8: *The LIBSEARC.FMT format file.*

Set up memory variables

Set up month names for translating dates to English

Get search criteria from user using LIBSEARC.FMT format file

If report going to a separate text file, ask user for file name

Ask user for sort order

Use appropriate index file based upon user's sort request

Set up a macro for AND or OR search

Build a search string for author, title, publication, and date

Add keywords to search condition

Remove last .AND. or .OR. from search macro if necessary

If no search criteria selected, make it always true

If printer selected, set on

If text file selected, set one up

Print title and start line counter

Begin the search at top of the database file

Put keywords together for search and print

Check for match up

If record matches search criteria

   Set up bibliography line
   Translate date to English
   Print the line properly formatted

   If user wants keywords displayed
     First, remove trailing comma, and add leading title
       and ending period
     Display keywords properly formatted

   If user wants abstract displayed
     Add leading title to abstract
     Display in proper format

   Print a blank line between each reference
Increment line counter

Figure 21.9: *Pseudocode for the LIBSEARC.CMD command file.*

> Count lines printed, and eject or pause if necessary
> Skip to the next record in the database
>
> Continue loop (unless end of file encountered)
>
> Close and terminate alternate file if necessary
>
> Pause on screen if not being sent to printer
>
> Release all memory variables except choice
>
> Return to main menu

Figure 21.9: Pseudocode for the LIBSEARC.CMD command file (continued).

or a text file (TO:TEXT). If the user wishes to store the data resulting from the search to a text file, the name of that file is stored in the memory variable TEXT:FILE.

Next, the command file needs to set up month names for changing the numeric dates to English. Note that the last two characters of each variable name match the month they represent, that is, January is stored in MO01, and December is stored in MO12. This simplifies the translation later:

```
*************************** Set up month names.
STORE " " TO MO00
STORE "January " TO MO01
STORE "February " TO MO02
STORE "March " TO MO03
STORE "April " TO MO04
STORE "May " TO MO05
STORE "June " TO MO06
STORE "July " TO MO07
STORE "August " TO MO08
STORE "September " TO MO09
STORE "October " TO MO10
STORE "November " TO MO11
STORE "December " TO MO12
```

Next, we will add lines to the program to display the screen for specifying search and report parameters. This is handled by the LIBSEARC.FMT format file, and the following lines:

```
********************* Get search criteria from user.
SET FORMAT TO LIBSEARC
READ
SET FORMAT TO SCREEN
```

If the user requested that a text file be created, the program needs to ask for a filename, as shown below:

```
********************** If going to a separate file,
********************** ask for filename.
IF !(TO:TEXT) = "Y"
   ERASE
   @ 5,5 SAY "Enter name of text file to send to ";
      GET TEXT:FILE
      READ
ENDIF (to:text = y)
```

Now the program can ask the user for the order in which to display the data:

```
********************** Next, ask for sort order.
ERASE
STORE " " TO ORDER
TEXT

     Sort Options

  1. Alphabetically by Author
  2. By Date
  3. Original Order

ENDTEXT
@ 8,10 SAY "Enter sort order " GET ORDER
READ
```

The program then assigns the appropriate index file, or uses the data file without an index:

```
******* Use appropriate index file.
DO CASE
   CASE ORDER = "1"
      USE LIBRARY INDEX AUTHORS

   CASE ORDER = "2"
      USE LIBRARY INDEX DATES

   OTHERWISE
      USE LIBRARY
ENDCASE
```

If the user specifies that a match to ANY search parameter was sufficient for displaying a reference, then the result would be an OR search. Otherwise, it would be an AND search. The lines below set up the search by storing the appropriate relational operator to a variable called LOGIC.

```
********** Set up macro for AND or OR search.
IF !(ANY) = "Y"
    STORE ".OR." TO LOGIC
ELSE
    STORE ".AND." TO LOGIC
ENDIF (any # " ")
```

The next major step in the program is to develop a character string that can be used as a macro in performing the search. For instance, if the user wishes to locate an article by Smith, P. with the title "Welcome Home," then the search string should be:

M:AUTHOR $!(AUTHOR) .AND. M:TITLE $!(TITLE)

so that when used with an IF clause, as shown below:

IF M:AUTHOR $!(AUTHOR) .AND. M:TITLE $!(TITLE)

it will display only those references with SMITH, P embedded in the uppercase-equivalent of the author field, and WELCOME HOME embedded in the uppercase-equivalent of the title field.

Since the user has so many options in defining search parameters, it takes several steps for the program to build the search string. The variable named COND stores the search parameter string. It is first set to a blank:

```
* Build search string for author, title, publication, and date.
STORE " " TO COND
```

If the user wishes to search by author, the program translates the name in the M:AUTHOR memory variable to uppercase, and trims off the trailing blanks. Then it tacks the phrase M:AUTHOR $!(AUTHOR) to the COND string, as well as an .AND. or an .OR., depending on the logic of the search:

```
** Search by author.
IF M:AUTHOR # " "
    STORE !(TRIM(M:AUTHOR)) TO M:AUTHOR
    STORE "M:AUTHOR $!(AUTHOR)" + LOGIC TO COND
ENDIF (m:author # " ")
```

If the user is searching by title, a similar series of events takes place for the M:TITLE field, and the phrase M:TITLE $!(TITLE) is added to the COND variable, as well as another .AND. or .OR.:

```
** Search by title.
IF M:TITLE # " "
    STORE !(TRIM(M:TITLE)) TO M:TITLE
```

```
      STORE COND+"M:TITLE $!(TITLE)"+LOGIC TO COND
ENDIF (m:title # " ")
```

The same procedure is used for the PUB and DATE fields, except that there is no need to translate to uppercase or trim the blanks off the date:

```
** Search by publication
IF M:PUB # " "
   STORE !(TRIM(M:PUB)) TO M:PUB
   STORE COND+"M:PUB $!(PUB)"+LOGIC TO COND
ENDIF (m:pub # " ")
** Search by date.
IF M:DATE # " "
   STORE COND+"M:DATE = DATE"+LOGIC TO COND
ENDIF (m:date # " ")
```

At this point, the COND string contains the necessary dBASE syntax for searching on any of the fields except keywords. Since there are six keywords, all with a number in the variable names (M:KEY1, M:KEY2, M:KEY3 . . .), we can handle all six keywords with a loop. We start the loop at one, and continue looping until the counter reaches six:

```
******* Add keywords to search condition.
STORE 1 TO COUNTER
DO WHILE COUNTER < 6
```

Then we store the string equivalent of the counter to a variable called SUB, so we can tack it on to the variable name as a macro. That is, the first time through the loop, we look at M:KEY&SUB, (M:KEY1). The second pass through the loop looks at M:KEY&SUB, which is M:KEY2, and so forth through all six:

```
   STORE STR(COUNTER,1) TO SUB
```

For each of the six M:KEY memory variables, if it is not a blank, then its search criterion is tacked onto the COND string with the format M:KEY1 $!(KEYWORDS). To speed the search, all six keywords from the data file will be placed in one long string called KEYWORDS which has this format:

   Data Files, dBASE II, Database Design, Program Design,

To assure maximum accuracy, the M:KEY being searched for will be padded with a leading blank and a trailing comma, like so:

   " Database,"

That way, when the substring function ($) scans the KEYWORDS string for a given keyword, it will not match to a portion of any single keyword in the list.

The routine below checks to make sure that the M:KEY keyword is not a blank, and if not, it adds the appropriate phrase to the COND string, and tacks on the logical .AND. or .OR. operator:

```
IF M:KEY&SUB # " "
   STORE " " + !(TRIM(M:KEY&SUB)) + "," TO M:KEY&SUB
   STORE COND + "M:KEY&SUB $!(KEYWORDS)" + LOGIC;
      TO COND
ENDIF (key&sub # " ")
```

The COUNTER variable is then incremented by one, and the loop through the six M:KEY variables continues:

```
   STORE COUNTER + 1 TO COUNTER
ENDDO (counter < 6)
```

At this point, if the user had asked to search for all references by Smith dealing with the topic dBASE II, the COND string would look like this:

   M:AUTHOR $!(AUTHOR) .AND. M:KEY1 $!(KEYWORDS) .AND.

M:AUTHOR and M:KEY1 have already been trimmed and translated to uppercase for maximum search reliability. Of course, the COND string might end up being much longer and more complex than this, depending upon how many search criteria the user selects from the screen.

There is one small bug in the COND variable above: the last .AND. should be trimmed off. This can be accomplished by storing all but the last five letters of COND back into COND. However, if the use is performing an OR search, then the last four characters, .OR., must be trimmed off. The next routine takes care of the trimming:

```
******** Remove last ".and." or ".or.".
IF !(ANY) = "Y"
   STORE $(COND,1,LEN(COND) - 4) TO COND
ELSE
   STORE $(COND,1,LEN(COND) - 5) TO COND
ENDIF (and # " ")
```

The user also has the option to leave all of the search criteria fields on the screen blank, thereby listing all references on the database. If the user selects this, the COND string will still be only a blank. We'll need to put an always-true search criterion into the program, such as

1 = 1, to handle this situation. The next routine takes care of this:

```
********* If no search criteria selected,
********* make it always true.
IF LEN(COND) = 1
   STORE "1 = 1" TO COND
ENDIF (cond = " ")
```

Now the search condition string (COND) is complete. The program can turn on the printer if the user selected it:

```
********* If printer selected, set on.
IF !(PRINTER) = "Y"
   SET PRINT ON
ENDIF
```

If the user wants the references to be stored on a separate text file, the program must create and open an alternate file with the user-supplied name:

```
********* If text file selected, set on.
IF !(TO:TEXT) = "Y"
   SET ALTERNATE TO &TEXT:FILE
   SET ALTERNATE ON
ENDIF (to:text = y)
```

Now the program can clear the screen, print the report title, go to the first record in the database, start a variable for counting printed lines (LF), and start a loop to the end of the file:

```
********* Print title and start line counter.
ERASE
? "                    Bibliography"
?
STORE 2 TO LF
********* Now begin the search, and format
********* references to bibliography format.
GO TOP
DO WHILE .NOT. EOF
```

For each record in the database, all of the keywords (KEY1 – KEY6) must first be placed into a single memory variable called KEYWORDS. The program will automatically place commas between each one for a neatly printed appearance, and for improved accuracy, as discussed above. Again, we'll use a loop, from one to six, to deal with each KEY field:

```
********** Put keywords together for search
********** and print.
```

```
STORE 1 TO COUNTER
STORE " " TO KEYWORDS
DO WHILE COUNTER < = 6
   STORE STR(COUNTER,1) TO SUB
   IF KEY&SUB # " "
      STORE KEYWORDS + TRIM(KEY&SUB) + ", " TO KEYWORDS
   ENDIF (key&sub # " ")
   STORE COUNTER + 1 TO COUNTER
ENDDO (counter<6)
```

Since the entire COND string is already put together, the program can see if the current record from the data file matches all the search criteria by simply substituting the COND variable into an IF clause as a macro:

```
********* Check for match up.
IF &COND
```

And now the fun begins. First of all, if the data from the current record are to be printed, the AUTHOR, TITLE, and PUB fields need to be placed into a long string with commas and a space in between. These will be stored in a memory variable called LONG:

```
********* Set up format string.
STORE TRIM(AUTHOR) + ", " + TRIM(TITLE) + ", " + ;
   TRIM(PUB) + ", " TO LONG
```

If a volume number (VOLUME), location (PLACE), or page numbers (PAGES) are included in this reference, they too should be placed in the LONG memory variable:

```
IF VOLUME # " "
   STORE LONG + TRIM(VOLUME) + ", " TO LONG
ENDIF
IF PLACE # " "
   STORE LONG + TRIM(PLACE) + ", " TO LONG
ENDIF
IF PAGES # " "
   STORE LONG + TRIM(PAGES) + ", " TO LONG
ENDIF
```

Of course, the date must be added. But since dates in the 10/10/84 format are not used in bibliographies, we'll translate the date to English. We'll accomplish this by storing the first two characters from the date (MM) to a variable called MONTH; the fourth and fifth characters (DD) to a variable called DAY, and the seventh and eight characters (YY) to YEAR. First, the program breaks the date variable into three separate variables, MONTH, DAY, and YEAR in the lines below:

```
********* Translate date to English.
STORE $(DATE,1,2) TO MONTH
STORE $(DATE,4,2) TO DAY
STORE $(DATE,7,2) TO YEAR
```

We've already assigned the months of the year to variable names such as MO01 (January), MO06 (June), so a simple macro will quickly change the numeric month to English (e.g. MO&MONTH). We'll store this to a variable called ENG:DATE (English date):

```
STORE MO&MONTH TO ENG:DATE
```

At this point, ENG:DATE contains the month in English (e.g., March).

If the date has a day in it (that is, it is not 03/00/84), then we'll put in the day number, followed by a comma and a space:

```
IF VAL(DAY)>0
    STORE ENG:DATE + DAY + ", " TO ENG:DATE
ENDIF
```

If the DATE did indeed contain a date, ENG:DATE might look like "March 31,". Otherwise, it is still just the month name (March). Then for the year, we'll just tack on the number 19 plus the last two digits from the date (YEAR):

```
STORE ENG:DATE +"19"+YEAR TO ENG:DATE
```

Now the ENG:DATE will contain the date in English, such as March 31, 1985 or March 1985.

Once translated to English, we can tack ENG:DATE onto the LONG memory variable:

```
STORE LONG + ENG:DATE +"." TO LONG
```

So far so good. Now, let's use column number 76 as the right margin of our report. If the LONG variable is less than or equal to 76, it can be printed right away, and the line counter (LF) can be incremented by one:

```
********* Print the line.
STORE 76 TO MARGIN
IF LEN(LONG)< = MARGIN
    ? LONG
    STORE LF+1 TO LF
ELSE
```

If LONG is greater than 76 characters, it should be split at the blank space nearest the right margin (this procedure is called *word-wrapping*). To accomplish this, we will set up a loop that counts backwards from 76, and keeps counting until it finds a blank space in the LONG string:

```
DO WHILE $(LONG,MARGIN,1) # " "
    STORE MARGIN - 1 TO MARGIN
ENDDO (rightmost character not blank)
```

That loop will stop spinning when it encounters the blank space nearest the right margin. At that point, the variable MARGIN will equal the position at which to break the line. Therefore, we can print the first part of LONG up to MARGIN on one line, and the second part of LONG from MARGIN (plus one) on the second line, and increment the line counter by two:

```
? $(LONG,1,MARGIN)
? $(LONG,MARGIN + 1)
STORE LF + 2 TO LF
ENDIF (long < = margin)
```

Now, if the user asks that keywords be printed, we can do the same type of formatting with the KEYWORDS string. But first, it needs a little work. The KEYWORDS variable still has a comma at the end (used for the search above), which we can delete and replace with a period. And we'll add the small heading KEYWORDS: to the front of the line to improve the appearance of the report:

```
* * * * * * * If keywords selected, display.
IF !(SHOW:KEYS) = "Y"
    * * * First, remove trailing comma, and
    * * * add leading title and ending period.
    STORE LEN(TRIM(KEYWORDS)) TO LENGTH
    STORE $(KEYWORDS,1,LENGTH - 1) TO KEYWORDS
    STORE "KEYWORDS:" + KEYWORDS TO KEYWORDS
    IF LEN(KEYWORDS) > 10
        STORE KEYWORDS + "." TO KEYWORDS
    ENDIF
```

Then, we can go through the same routine we used with the LONG string above to word-wrap the right margin:

```
STORE 76 TO MARGIN
IF LEN(KEYWORDS) < = MARGIN
    ? KEYWORDS
    STORE LF + 1 TO LF
ELSE
```

```
              DO WHILE $(KEYWORDS,MARGIN,1) # " "
                  STORE MARGIN – 1 TO MARGIN
              ENDDO (rightmost character not " ")
              ? $(KEYWORDS,1,MARGIN)
              ? "           " + $(KEYWORDS,MARGIN + 1)
              STORE LF + 2 TO LF
          ENDIF (len(keywords) < = margin)
      ENDIF (!(show:keys = y)
```

Now if the user asks that the abstract be displayed, the program will add the small heading ABSTRACT:, and store all of that to the memory variable LONG:

```
      * * * * * * If abstract selected, print it.
      IF !(SHOW:ABS) = "Y"
          STORE "ABSTRACT: " + TRIM(ABSTRACT) TO LONG
```

Formatting the abstract is a bit tougher. Since its maximum length is up to 254 characters (including the heading ABSTRACT:), it may take up three or four lines on the report. Here is the logic. First of all, we set up a loop that continues breaking down the LONG abstract into smaller pieces that do not exceed 76 characters:

```
      DO WHILE LEN(LONG) > 76
```

Within the loop, the margin is set to 76, and another loop finds the nearest blank space to the left of the 76th character:

```
      STORE 76 TO MARGIN
          DO WHILE $(LONG,MARGIN,1) # " "
              STORE MARGIN – 1 TO MARGIN
          ENDDO
```

Once the nearest blank is found, the characters within the margin limit are printed on the report, and the line counter is incremented:

```
      ? $(LONG,1,MARGIN)
      STORE LF + 1 TO LF
```

Then, the remaining portion of the LONG abstract is put into LONG, and if that portion is still longer than 76, the program again passes through the outer loop and breaks off another section of the LONG abstract. This process continues until only a portion of the original abstract that is less than 76 characters remains in LONG:

```
          STORE $(LONG,MARGIN + 1) TO LONG
      ENDDO (len(long>76))
```

When a portion that will fit on the line is left, it is printed on the screen and the line counter is incremented:

```
? LONG
STORE LF + 1 TO LF
ENDIF (show:abs = y)
```

At that point, one whole entry is printed. (Believe it or not, it only takes about three seconds for the computer to put together the entire COND string, and about two or three seconds do all the formatting we've just discussed.)

To keep things from getting too cluttered on the page, we'll ensure that a blank line is left between each printed reference, and again increment the line counter:

```
******** Print a blank line between each entry.
?
STORE LF + 1 TO LF
```

If the user wishes to print the report, and 55 or so lines have been printed on the page, the program should advance to the next page, print the title, and reset the line counter:

```
******** Count lines printed, and eject or
******** pause if necessary.
IF !(PRINTER) = "Y" .AND. LF > = 55
    EJECT
    ? "                    Bibliography"
    ?
    STORE 2 TO LF
ENDIF
```

If the user wishes that the report print only on the screen, the program should pause after every 20 or so lines, and reset the line counter:

```
IF !(PRINTER) # "Y" .AND. !(TO:TEXT) # "Y" .AND. LF > = 20
    ?
    ? "Press any key to continue . . ."
    WAIT
    STORE 2 TO LF
    ERASE
ENDIF (not printer)
```

Of course, if the record did not match the search criterion, none of the routines for formatting and printing the reference will be used. Either way, the program should now skip to the next reference in the database, and continue looping until the end of the file:

```
    ENDIF (record meets search criteria)
    SKIP
ENDDO (while .not. eof)
SET PRINT OFF
```

When the DO WHILE .NOT. EOF loop is done, the program is done. If an alternate file was opened, it should now be closed:

```
****************** Close and terminate alternate
****************** file if necessary.
IF !(TO:TEXT) = "Y"
   SET ALTERNATE OFF
   SET ALTERNATE TO
ENDIF (to:text = y)
```

If the references were displayed on the screen only, the program should pause before clearing the screen and returning to the main menu:

```
*** Pause on screen if not being sent to printer.
IF !(PRINTER) # "Y"
   ?
   ? "Press any key to return to menu ..."
   WAIT
ENDIF
```

Now the program can release all the memory variables (except CHOICE from the main menu), and return to LIBRARY.CMD:

```
*** Release all memory variables except choice.
RELE ALL EXCEPT CHOICE
RETURN
```

The entire LIBSEARC.CMD command file is displayed in Figure 21.10. It is a large and complex program, but it displays the power of dBASE II macros, as well as the power and flexibility of the dBASE II language, and is therefore worth studying for the more ambitious dBASE II programmer.

```
************************************ LIBSEARC.CMD
************************* Search for references.
SET TALK OFF

************************* Set up memory variables.
STORE "                          " TO M:AUTHOR,M:PUB
STORE "                              " TO M:TITLE
STORE "            " TO M:DATE
STORE "                   " TO M:KEY1,M:KEY2,M:KEY3
STORE "                   " TO M:KEY4,M:KEY5,M:KEY6
STORE " " TO ANY,ALL,SHOW:KEYS,SHOW:ABS,PRINTER,TO:TEXT
STORE "               " TO TEXT:FILE

************************* Set up month names.
STORE " " TO M00
STORE "January " TO M001
STORE "February " TO M002
```

Figure 21.10: *The LIBSEARC.CMD command file.*

```
STORE "March    " TO MO03
STORE "April    " TO MO04
STORE "May      " TO MO05
STORE "June     " TO MO06
STORE "July     " TO MO07
STORE "August   " TO MO08
STORE "September" TO MO09
STORE "October  " TO MO10
STORE "November " TO MO11
STORE "December " TO MO12

***************** Get search criteria from user.
SET FORMAT TO LIBSEARC
READ
SET FORMAT TO SCREEN

********************* If going to a separate file,
********************* ask for file name.
IF !(TO:TEXT)="Y"
   ERASE
   @ 5,5 SAY "Enter name of text file to send to ";
      GET TEXT:FILE
      READ
ENDIF (to:text=y)

********************* Next, ask for sort order.
ERASE
STORE " " TO ORDER
TEXT
                Sort Options

           1. Alphabetically by Author
           2. By Date
           3. Original Order
ENDTEXT
@ 8,10 SAY "Enter sort order " GET ORDER

READ

******* Use appropriate index file.
DO CASE
   CASE ORDER = "1"
        USE LIBRARY INDEX AUTHORS

   CASE ORDER = "2"
        USE LIBRARY INDEX DATES

   OTHERWISE
        USE LIBRARY

ENDCASE

********** Set up macro for AND or OR search.
IF !(ANY) = "Y"
   STORE ".OR." TO LOGIC
ELSE
```

Figure 21.10: *The LIBSEARC.CMD command file (continued).*

```
         STORE ".AND." TO LOGIC
ENDIF (any # " ")

** Build search string for author, title, publication, and date.
STORE " " TO COND

****** Search by author.
IF M:AUTHOR # " "
   STORE !(TRIM(M:AUTHOR)) TO M:AUTHOR
   STORE "M:AUTHOR $!(AUTHOR)"+LOGIC TO COND
ENDIF (m:author # " ")

****** Search by title.
IF M:TITLE # " "
   STORE !(TRIM(M:TITLE)) TO M:TITLE
   STORE COND+"M:TITLE $!(TITLE)"+LOGIC TO COND
ENDIF (m:title # " ")

****** Search by publication.
IF M:PUB # " "
   STORE !(TRIM(M:PUB)) TO M:PUB
   STORE COND+"M:PUB $!(PUB)"+LOGIC TO COND
ENDIF (m:pub # " ")

****** Search by date.
IF M:DATE # " "
   STORE COND+"M:DATE = DATE"+LOGIC TO COND
ENDIF (m:date # " ")

******* Add keywords to search condition.
STORE 1 TO COUNTER
DO WHILE COUNTER < 6
   STORE STR(COUNTER,1) TO SUB
   IF M:KEY&SUB # " "
      STORE " "+!(TRIM(M:KEY&SUB))+"," TO M:KEY&SUB
      STORE COND+"M:KEY&SUB $!(KEYWORDS)"+LOGIC;
          TO COND
   ENDIF (key&sub # " ")
   STORE COUNTER+1 TO COUNTER
ENDDO (counter < 6)

******** Remove last ".AND." or ".OR.".
IF !(ANY) = "Y"
   STORE $(COND,1,LEN(COND)-4) TO COND
ELSE
   STORE $(COND,1,LEN(COND)-5) TO COND
ENDIF (and # " ")

********* If no search criteria selected,
********* make it always true.
IF LEN(COND) = 1
   STORE "1=1" TO COND
ENDIF (cond = " ")

********* If printer selected, set on.
```

Figure 21.10: The LIBSEARC.CMD command file (continued).

```
IF !(PRINTER)="Y"
   SET PRINT ON
ENDIF

********* If text file selected, set on.
IF !(TO:TEXT)="Y"
   SET ALTERNATE TO &TEXT:FILE
   SET ALTERNATE ON
ENDIF (to:text=y)

********* Print title and start line counter.
ERASE
? "                        Bibliography"
?
STORE 2 TO LF
********* Now begin the search, and format
********* references to bibliography format.
GO TOP
DO WHILE .NOT. EOF
   ********** Put keywords together for search
   ********** and print.
   STORE 1 TO COUNTER
   STORE " " TO KEYWORDS
   DO WHILE COUNTER <= 6
      STORE STR(COUNTER,1) TO SUB
      IF KEY&SUB # " "
         STORE KEYWORDS+TRIM(KEY&SUB)+", " TO KEYWORDS
      ENDIF (key&sub # " ")
      STORE COUNTER+1 TO COUNTER
   ENDDO
   ********* Check for match up.
   IF &COND
********* Set up format string.
STORE TRIM(AUTHOR)+", "+TRIM(TITLE)+", "+;
      TRIM(PUB)+", " TO LONG
IF VOLUME # " "
   STORE LONG+TRIM(VOLUME)+", " TO LONG
ENDIF
IF PLACE  # " "
   STORE LONG + TRIM(PLACE) + ", " TO LONG
ENDIF
IF PAGES , " "
   STORE LONG + TRIM(PAGES)+", " TO LONG
ENDIF

********* Translate date to English.
STORE $(DATE,1,2) TO MONTH
STORE $(DATE,4,2) TO DAY
STORE $(DATE,7,2) TO YEAR
STORE MO&MONTH TO ENG:DATE
IF VAL(DAY)<10
   STORE $(DAY,2,1) TO DAY
ENDIF (val(day))
IF VAL(DAY)>0
   STORE ENG:DATE + DAY + ", " TO ENG:DATE
```

Figure 21.10: The LIBSEARC.CMD command file (continued).

```
ENDIF
STORE ENG:DATE+"19"+YEAR TO ENG:DATE
STORE LONG + ENG:DATE+"." TO LONG

********* Print the line.
STORE 76 TO MARGIN
IF LEN(LONG)<=MARGIN
   ? LONG
   STORE LF+1 TO LF
ELSE
   DO WHILE $(LONG,MARGIN,1) # " "
      STORE MARGIN-1 TO MARGIN
   ENDDO (rightmost character not blank)
   ? $(LONG,1,MARGIN)
   ? $(LONG,MARGIN+1)
   STORE LF+2 TO LF
ENDIF (long <= margin)

******* If keywords selected, display.
IF !(SHOW:KEYS) = "Y"
   *** First, remove trailing comma, and
   *** add leading title and ending period.
   STORE LEN(TRIM(KEYWORDS)) TO LENGTH
   STORE $(KEYWORDS,1,LENGTH-1) TO KEYWORDS
   STORE "KEYWORDS:"+KEYWORDS TO KEYWORDS
   IF LEN(KEYWORDS)>10
      STORE KEYWORDS+"." TO KEYWORDS
   ENDIF
   STORE 76 TO MARGIN
   IF LEN(KEYWORDS)<=MARGIN
         ? KEYWORDS
         STORE LF+1 TO LF
      ELSE
         DO WHILE $(KEYWORDS,MARGIN,1) # " "
            STORE MARGIN-1 TO MARGIN
         ENDDO (rightmost character not " ")
         ? $(KEYWORDS,1,MARGIN)
         ? "         "+$(KEYWORDS,MARGIN+1)
         STORE LF+2 TO LF
      ENDIF (len(keywords)<=margin)
ENDIF (!(show:keys=y)

****** If abstract selected, print it.
IF !(SHOW:ABS) = "Y"
   STORE "ABSTRACT: "+TRIM(ABSTRACT) TO LONG
   DO WHILE LEN(LONG) > 76
      STORE 76 TO MARGIN
      DO WHILE $(LONG,MARGIN,1) # " "
         STORE MARGIN-1 TO MARGIN
      ENDDO
      ? $(LONG,1,MARGIN)
```

Figure 21.10: The LIBSEARC.CMD command file (continued).

```
            STORE LF+1 TO LF
            STORE $(LONG,MARGIN+1) TO LONG
        ENDDO (len(long>76))
        ? LONG
        STORE LF+2 TO LF
    ENDIF (show:abs=y)

    ******* Print a blank line between each.
    ?
    STORE LF+1 TO LF

    ******* Count lines printed, and eject or
    ******* pause if necessary.
    IF !(PRINTER)="Y" .AND. LF >= 55
        EJECT
        ? "                         Bibliography"
        ?
        STORE 2 TO LF
    ENDIF

    IF !(PRINTER) # "Y" .AND. !(TO:TEXT) # "Y" .AND. LF >= 20
        ?
        ? "Press any key to continue..."
        WAIT
        STORE 2 TO LF
        ERASE
    ENDIF (not printer)

    ENDIF (record meets search criteria)
    SKIP
ENDDO (while .not. eof)

SET PRINT OFF

****************** Close and terminate alternate
****************** file if necessary.
IF !(TO:TEXT) = "Y"
    SET ALTERNATE OFF
    SET ALTERNATE TO
ENDIF (to:text = y)

*** Pause on screen if not being sent to printer.
IF !(PRINTER) # "Y"
    ?
    ? "Press any key to return to menu..."
    WAIT
ENDIF

*** Release all memory variables except choice.
RELE ALL EXCEPT CHOICE
RETURN
```

Figure 21.10: The LIBSEARC.CMD command file (continued).

Underlining

You may wish to add underlining to the library system or to any custom application of your own. For example, you can print your bibliography with the titles underlined, as shown below:

Bibliography

Glass, Jim, <u>Word Processor File Conversion</u>, PC Tech Journal, Vol. 1, No. 2, 168–179, September 1983.

Levine, Joel H., <u>Hard Disks for Portables</u>, Portable Computer, Vol. 2, No. 3, 38–41, March 10, 1984.

Trost, S., and King, R., <u>Doing Business with Multiplan</u>, SYBEX Inc., Berkeley, CA, 1984.

There are two methods for underlining printed data. The first method requires that you place special printer codes before and after the data to be underlined prior to printing. You can find these codes in the printer manual, or by writing to the printer manufacturer.

Here is an example. The Juki printer uses the character sequence Esc-E to start underlining, and Esc-R to stop underlining. The symbol Esc stands for the escape key, and is expressed in dBASE as CHR(27) (ASCII character number 27). Hence, near the top of the LIBSEARC.CMD command file where the memory variables are set up, you can include the variables to start and stop underlining, as below:

```
STORE CHR(27)+"E" TO BEG:UNDER
STORE CHR(27)+"R" TO END:UNDER
```

As soon as the program encounters the BEG:UNDER variable, it will start underlining on the printer. When it encounters the END:UNDER variable, it will stop underlining.

The LIBSEARC command file stores the author name, title, and publisher for a reference to a variable called LONG in these lines of the program:

```
********* Set up format string.
STORE TRIM(AUTHOR)+", "+TRIM(TITLE)+", "+;
    TRIM(PUB)+", " TO LONG
```

To underline the title, surround the TITLE field with the underlining codes. Since we only want to add the codes if the report is being sent to the printer, we'll need to replace the existing lines with this routine:

```
************* Set up format string.
STORE TRIM(AUTHOR)+", " TO LONG

IF !(PRINTER)="Y"
   STORE LONG+BEG:UNDER+TRIM(TITLE)+END:UNDER+;
   ", " TO LONG
ELSE
   STORE LONG+TRIM(TITLE)+", " TO LONG
ENDIF (printer=Y)

STORE LONG+TRIM(PUB)+", " TO LONG
```

Now, the BEG:UNDER and END:UNDER only surround the TITLE field if the report is being sent to the printer.

After modifying the program the next time you run the LIBSEARC program and ask that data be sent to the printer, the titles will be underlined.

The second method uses the WordStar or other word-processing program to underline. In this approach, the program sends the references to a text file with a random special character surrounding the TITLE field. Then, prior to printing the bibliography, the user can globally find-and-replace all the special characters with the code for underlining.

To use the word-processing approach, you must modify the LIBSEARC program so that it surrounds the TITLE field with a seldom-used character (such as @) when it sends the references to the text file. The LIBSEARC command file uses the variable TO:TEXT to determine whether or not a separate text file is being created. Therefore, we only need to modify LIBSEARC by changing these lines:

```
********* Set up format string.
STORE TRIM(AUTHOR)+", "+TRIM(TITLE)+", "+;
   TRIM(PUB)+", " TO LONG
```

to a routine that places @'s around the TITLE field when the data are being sent to a separate text file:

```
********* Set up format string.
STORE TRIM(AUTHOR)+", " TO LONG

IF !(TO:TEXT)="Y"
   STORE LONG + "@"+TRIM(TITLE)+"@"+", " TO LONG
   ELSE
   STORE LONG + TRIM(TITLE)+", " TO LONG
ENDIF (to:text=y)

STORE LONG+TRIM(PUB)+", " TO LONG
```

After the LIBSEARC program has been modified, the program will put @'s around the titles in the references. For example, suppose the user opts to write a text file from this program, and names the file B:BIBLIO.TXT. The program will then create a text file called BIBLIO.TXT on the disk in drive B. To print BIBLIO.TXT, The user quits dBASE and runs his word processor. If the user is using WordStar, he puts the WordStar disk in drive A and types in the command WS B:BIBLIO.TXT. The references will appear on the screen with @'s around the titles as shown below:

Bibliography

Glass, Jim, @Word Processor File Conversion@, PC Tech Journal, Vol. 1, No. 2, 168–179, September 1983.

Levine, Joel H., @Hard Disks for Portables@, Portable Computer, Vol. 2, No. 3, 38–41, March 10, 1984.

Trost, S., and King, R., @Doing Business with Multiplan@, SYBEX Inc., Berkeley, CA, 1984.

Now, before printing, the user must change all the @'s to the word-processing underline code. In the WordStar example, he types in the command ^QA to do a find-and-replace. WordStar will ask:

FIND? _

The user types in @ and presses RETURN. WordStar will then ask:

REPLACE WITH? _

Next, the user holds down Ctrl and types PS and presses RETURN again. (The WordStar code to start/stop underlining is Ctrl-PS). Next WordStar will ask:

OPTIONS? (? FOR INFO) _

The user must type in GN (for "globally" without asking for permission) and press RETURN. WordStar then changes all the @'s to the Ctrl-PS underlining command as shown below:

Bibliography

Glass, Jim, ^SWord Processor File Conversion^S, PC Tech Journal, Vol. 1, No. 2, 168–179, September 1983.

Levine, Joel H., ^SHard Disks for Portables^S, Portable Computer, Vol. 2, No. 3, 38–41, March 10, 1984.

Trost, S., and King, R., ^SDoing Business with Multiplan^S, SYBEX Inc., Berkeley, CA, 1984.

After performing the find-and-replace procedure, the user can save the BIBLIO.TXT command file by typing in ^KD (holding down Ctrl and typing KD). Then, from the WordStar main menu, select option P (print a document). When WordStar asks:

NAME OF FILE TO PRINT? _

the user types in the filename (e.g. B:BIBLIO.TXT), and the references will be printed with the titles underlined.

The next command file, which creates a file of all the subjects in the library system, and displays them on a two-column report, is not nearly as complex.

Library Subjects Report

As discussed earlier in this chapter, the subjects report displays a list of all the subjects on file, and the number of references on the database that deal with that subject. It is created by reading all six keywords from each record in the LIBRARY file, and placing them on a separate data file called TOPICS.DBF. Prior to doing so, it eliminates all existing subjects from that file, just in case some have been added, changed, or deleted since the last time the report was printed.

The command file to produce the subjects report is called SUBJECTS.CMD, and its pseudocode is displayed in Figure 21.11.

The first step in the SUBJECTS program is to ask the user if he wants the report sent to the printer:

```
**************************** SUBJECTS.CMD
********************* Create a file of keywords.
******** Ask about printer.
ERASE
STORE " " TO YN
@ 5,5 SAY "Send to printer? (Y/N) " GET YN PICT "!"
READ
```

The program then clears all existing records from the TOPICS data file. Since this takes a few seconds, we'll give the user a message on the screen to assure him that the computer is at work:

```
ERASE
? " Preparing subjects file . . ."
```

Ask about printer for the report

Display message about creating files during pause

Eliminate all existing records from the topics data file
Index the empty topics database

Open both the library and temp files

Find out how many records are on the library file to
   keep user posted of progress

Loop through the library file

   Display message about progress
   Loop through the six keywords on library record
      Try to find keyword on topics file
         If found, increment quantity
         If not found, put keyword on file, then
            increment quantity
   Continue loop through six keywords
Skip to next record in library file
Continue loop through library file (until EOF)

Close secondary, and make subjects primary

Set printer on, if requested

Start loop through topics file

   Print topic and quantity in first column
   Skip to the next record
   If not at the end of file, print topic and
      quantity in the next column

   If printer selected, handle printer pagination

   If screen selected, handle screen pauses

Skip to next record in topic file
Continue loop through the topics file

If report not sent to printer, pause before returning to menu

Set printer off, release memory variables,
and return to main menu

Figure 21.11: Pseudocode for the SUBJECTS.CMD command file.

There are two ways to clear out all the records from a data file. The first is to use the commands DELETE ALL and PACK. With a large, indexed file, this can be a painfully slow process. The other method is to copy the structure of a file to a temporary file, then copy the structure back to the original file. This takes only a couple of seconds. Then you can index the empty file, which also only takes a couple of seconds. The routine below uses the COPY STRUCTURE procedure to clear out the TOPICS database:

```
******** First, eliminate all existing records
******** from the TOPICS.DBF data file.
USE TOPICS
COPY STRUCTURE TO TEMP
USE TEMP
COPY STRUCTURE TO TOPICS
USE TOPICS
INDEX ON !(SUBJECT) TO TOPICS
```

Next, we'll perform a type of update on the TOPICS file from the LIBRARY file, so both will have to be open simultaneously:

```
******** Open both the library and temp files.
SELE PRIM
USE LIBRARY
SELE SECO
USE TOPICS INDEX TOPICS
```

The updating process takes a few minutes. We'll keep the user informed of the program's progress by showing how many records need to be accessed to complete the job, and the current record number being processed, as shown below:

```
There are 174 references . . .
Now processing record number: 1
```

As the program proceeds, the counter at the end of the "Now processing record number: " prompt will count from 1 up to the number of references (174 in this example). This way, the user can see how much time is required, and can go get a cup of coffee (now *that's* what I call user-friendly). In order to display this message, we first need to determine how many records are on the LIBRARY file. The program does so by using the LIBRARY file, jumping to the bottom record, and storing its record number to a memory variable called MAX:RECS:

```
******** Find out how many records on the library
******** file to keep user posted of progress.
SELE PRIM
```

```
        GO BOTT
        STORE # TO MAX:RECS
```

The command file then starts at the top of the library file, and starts a loop that proceeds to the end of the file:

```
        ******* Loop through the library file, and
        ******* store keywords to the temp file.
        GO TOP
        ERASE
        DO WHILE .NOT. EOF
```

Within that loop, it displays the progress report on the screen:

```
        @ 5,5 SAY "There are " +STR(MAX:RECS,4)+ " references . . ."
        @ 7,5 SAY "Now processing record number: " +STR(#,4)
```

Next, a small loop to analyze each of the six keywords on each record in the library database is started:

```
        **** Loop through the six keywords.
        STORE 1 TO COUNTER
        DO WHILE COUNTER < = 6
            STORE STR(COUNTER,1) TO SUB
```

For each keyword (that is not a blank) in the record, the program stores the uppercase-equivalent to the variable FINDER. Then it selects the secondary file (TOPICS INDEX TOPICS) and attempts to find that keyword there:

```
        IF KEY&SUB # " "
            STORE !(KEY&SUB) TO FINDER
            SELE SECO
            FIND &FINDER
```

If the keyword already exists on the topics file, the program increments the quantity counter (QTY) by one:

```
        ***** If found, increment counter . . .
        IF # > 0
            REPLACE QTY WITH QTY + 1
```

If the keyword does not already exist on the topics file, the program adds it to the file and sets the QTY counter to one:

```
            ***** Otherwise, put on file.
            ELSE
                APPEND BLANK
                REPLACE SUBJECT WITH KEY&SUB
```

```
        REPLACE QTY WITH 1
      ENDIF (#>0)
    ENDIF (key&sub # " ")
```

The program then increments COUNTER by one to continue the loop through the six keywords:

```
      STORE COUNTER + 1 TO COUNTER
    ENDDO (while counter <= 6)
```

After the program has analyzed all six keywords for a given record, it skips to the next record in the LIBRARY file and repeats the process:

```
    SELE PRIM
    SKIP
  ENDDO (not eof)
```

When the program has analyzed all the records in the LIBRARY.DBF file, the program can close the secondary file, and make the TOPICS file primary:

```
  ****** Close secondary, and make subjects primary.
  SELE SECO
  USE
  SELE PRIM
  USE TOPICS INDEX TOPICS
```

If the user selected the printer, the program sets it on:

```
  *********** Set printer on, if requested.
  IF YN = "Y"
    SET PRINT ON
  ENDIF (yn=y)
```

The program can print the report now. First it clears the screen, prints a heading and subheading, sets the line counter (LF) to four, and begins a loop through the TOPICS file:

```
  **************************** Now print the report
  **************************** in two columns.
  ERASE
  ? "                        Subjects List"
  ?
  ? "     Subject              No."
  ?? "            Subject              No."
  STORE 4 TO LF
  DO WHILE .NOT. EOF
```

Then it prints the SUBJECT and QTY fields, followed by a few blank spaces, from the TOPICS file, and skips to the next record in the database:

```
? SUBJECT,QTY," "
SKIP
```

If the end of the file is not encountered, the program prints the next SUBJECT and QTY fields in the second column of the same line by using a double question mark (??):

```
IF .NOT. EOF
   ?? SUBJECT,QTY
ENDIF (not eof)
```

The program then dutifully increments the line counter (LF) by one, and handles printer pagination and screen pauses as necessary:

```
STORE LF+1 TO LF
***** Format for printer.
IF YN="Y" .AND. LF >= 55
    EJECT
    ? "     Subject              No."
    ?? "         Subject         No."
    STORE 2 TO LF
ENDIF (yn-y and lf >=55)

***** Format for screen.
IF YN # "Y" .AND. LF >= 20
    ?
    ? "Press any key to continue . . ."
    WAIT
    STORE 2 TO LF
ENDIF (yn # y and lf >=20)
```

Then the program skips to the next record to print more data until it reaches the end of the file:

```
SKIP
ENDDO (while not eof)
```

If the report was displayed on the screen only, the program pauses before returning to the main menu:

```
******** If report not sent to printer, pause
******** before returning to menu.
IF YN # "Y"
    ?
    ? "Press any key to return to menu."
    WAIT
ENDIF (yn # y)
```

Then it sets the printer off, releases the memory variables, and returns to the main menu:

```
****** Set printer off, release memory variables,
****** and return to main menu.
USE
RELEASE ALL EXCEPT CHOICE
RETURN
```

Figure 21.12 shows the complete SUBJECTS.CMD command file. At this point, the entire library cross-referencing system is complete.

```
*********************************** SUBJECTS.CMD
********************** Create a file of keywords.

******** Ask about printer.
ERASE
STORE " " TO YN
@ 5,5 SAY "Send to printer? (Y/N) " GET YN PICT "!"
READ

ERASE
? " Preparing subjects file..."

******** First, eliminate all existing records
******** from the TOPICS.DBF data file.
USE TOPICS
COPY STRUCTURE TO TEMP
USE TEMP
COPY STRUCTURE TO TOPICS
USE TOPICS
INDEX ON !(SUBJECT) TO TOPICS

******** Open both the library and TOPICS files.
SELE PRIM
USE LIBRARY
SELE SECO
USE TOPICS INDEX TOPICS

******** Find out how many records on the library
******** file to keep user posted of progress.
SELE PRIM
GO BOTT
STORE # TO MAX:RECS

******* Loop through the library file, and
******* store keywords to the topic file.
GO TOP
ERASE
DO WHILE .NOT. EOF
    @ 5,5 SAY "There are "+STR(MAX:RECS,4)+" references..."
    @ 7,5 SAY "Now processing record number: "+STR(#,4)
    **** Loop through the six keywords.
```

Figure 21.12: *The SUBJECTS.CMD command file.*

```
         STORE 1 TO COUNTER
         DO WHILE COUNTER <= 6
            STORE STR(COUNTER,1) TO SUB
            IF KEY&SUB # " "
               STORE !(KEY&SUB) TO FINDER
               SELE SECO
               FIND &FINDER
               ***** If found, increment counter.
               IF # > 0
                  REPLACE QTY WITH QTY + 1
               ***** Otherwise, put on file.
               ELSE
                     APPEND BLANK
                     REPLACE SUBJECT WITH KEY&SUB
                     REPLACE QTY WITH 1
                  ENDIF (#>0)
               ENDIF (key&sub # " ")
               STORE COUNTER + 1 TO COUNTER
            ENDDO (while counter <= 6)
            SELE PRIM
            SKIP
         ENDDO (not eof)

         ****** Close secondary, and make subjects primary.
         SELE SECO
         USE
         SELE PRIM
         USE TOPICS INDEX TOPICS

         *********** Set printer on, if requested.
         IF YN = "Y"
            SET PRINT ON
         ENDIF (yn=y)

         *************************** Now print the report
         *************************** in two columns.
         ERASE
         ? "               Subjects List"
         ?
         ? "     Subject              No."
         ?? "          Subject              No."
         STORE 4 TO LF
         DO WHILE .NOT. EOF
            ? SUBJECT,QTY,"       "
            SKIP
            IF .NOT. EOF
               ?? SUBJECT,QTY
            ENDIF (not eof)
            STORE LF+1 TO LF
            ***** Format for printer.
            IF YN="Y" .AND. LF >= 55
               EJECT
               ? "     Subject              No."
               ?? "          Subject              No."
               STORE 2 TO LF
            ENDIF (yn=y and lf >=55)
            ***** Format for screen.
```

Figure 21.12: The SUBJECTS.CMD command file (continued).

```
IF YN # "Y" .AND. LF >= 20
   ?
   ? "Press any key to continue..."
   WAIT
   STORE 2 TO LF
ENDIF (yn # y and lf >=20)

SKIP
ENDDO (while not eof)

******** If report not sent to printer, pause
******** before returning to menu.
IF YN # "Y"
   ?
   ? "Press any key to return to menu."
   WAIT
ENDIF (yn # y)


****** Set printer off, release memory variables,
****** and return to main menu.
USE
SET PRINT OFF
RELEASE ALL EXCEPT CHOICE
RETURN
```

Figure 21.12: The SUBJECTS.CMD command file (continued).

Summary

In this final chapter, we've developed programs to display reports in the library reference system and finished developing the library system. We've discussed some very advanced database-management programming techniques here in just two command files:

1. LIBSEARCH.CMD, which allows a user to perform complex searches on the LIBRARY reference database by filling in prompts on a simple screen. Advanced techniques that we've used in this program include:

    - keyword searches,
    - complex menu-driven searches,
    - word-wrapping long character strings,
    - translating dates to English,
    - underlining, and
    - creating text files from reports.

2. SUBJECTS.CMD, which makes a list of all unique keywords in the LIBRARY.DBF database. Some advanced techniques used in this program are:

- transferring multiple fields from each record in a database to a single field in a separate database,
- building a database and counting the number of occurrences of unique items in a database, and
- printing data from a single field in two alphabetized columns.

Though some of the techniques are fairly advanced, the power and convenience that they provide the user make them well worth learning. Assigning multiple keywords to each record in a database is useful in many referencing situations; and searching via a menu is more convenient than writing complex queries at the dot prompt.

INDEX

!, 31, 50, 255
$, 184, 363

ACCEPT, 14
Account numbers, 228, 235
ACCT.NDX, 230
ACCTS.FRM, 286
ADDNUMBS.CMD, 143
ADDTRANS.CMD, 257
Adjustment transactions, 328
ALLMAST.FRM, 144
APPEND, 21, 41, 48
APPEND BLANK, 142, 172
APPEND.CMD, 51
AUTHORS.NDX, 339
Automatic numbering, 170

B:, 5
BAK file, 3
Balance calculation, 256
Balances, current, 292
BEDIT.CMD, 329
Bibliography report, 354
BINSTALL.CMD, 242
Blocks, moving, 6
Bookkeeping database, 228
    edit screens, 317–318
    installation, 236
    reports, 283
    software, 232
    system, 228
    system menu, 245
    transactions, 249
BOOKS.CMD, 245
BREPORTS.CMD, 285
BROWSE, 17

Calculating balances, 256
Calculation, on-screen, 172
CASE, 36
Chart of Accounts, 231, 244
    balance, 296
    report, 292
    update, 256
Checks, printing, 300
Check register, 269, 270, 275
Checking-account balance, 270, 273
CHECKS.CMD, 312

CHR, 378
CHR(7), 142, 153
Closing a file, 173
CMD file, 2
COA.DBF, 231
COA.FMT, 319
COA.FRM, 295
COA.NDX, 231
COAREPT.CMD, 301
Command file, 1
Complex editing, 208
COPY, 17
COPY STRUCTURE, 383
COUNT, 16, 94, 102
CP/M, 2
CREATE, 31
Currency format, 173
Current balances, 292
Current stock report, 144
CURREPT.CMD, 293
Cursor control
    MODI COMM, 2
    SED, 4
    WordStar, 5
Custom edits, 92
Custom reports, 69
Custom screens, 41

Database design, 30
Database structure, 30
Date ranges, 180, 184, 195, 198, 278
Dates, searching, 181, 288
Dates, sorting, 184, 339
DATE( ), 130, 245
Dates-to-English, 361, 368
DATES.FRM, 287
DATES.NDX, 230, 339
DBF file, 128
DELETE, 91
Deleting records, 98
Deleting references, 348
Delimited file, 85
DELNAMES.CMD, 103
Deposits, 270
DIRECTOR.CMD, 75
DO, 2
DO CASE, 9, 36
DO WHILE, 8, 23

Index

DOS, 2
Drive specification, 5
DUPES.CMD, 119
Duplicates, 114

EDIT, 18, 21, 91
Editing
   bookkeeping data, 317
   command files, 3
   complex, 208
   inventory new stock, 215
   library references, 342
   mailing list data, 92
   sales transactions, 208
EDIT.CMD, 97
EJECT, 180
Embedded search, 363
ENDCASE, 9, 36
ENDDO, 8
ENDTEXT, 36
ENGLISH.MEM, 303
EOF, 73
ERASE, 2
Estimating performance, 19
Expense accounts, 236, 291

FILE, 64, 156
File existence, 64, 156
Files, formatting, 42, 47
FIND, 14, 15, 22, 31, 142, 197
FIND (number), 253
FIND and WHILE, 13-15, 94, 96
FIND with two fields, 110
FMT file, 42, 47, 139, 319
FOR, calculated, 150, 153
Form letters, 87
Formatting files, 42, 47
Formatting long strings, 368, 370

General information file, 229
GENINFO.DBF, 229
GENINFO.FMT, 320
GET, 36

Hierarchical design, 33

IF, calculated, 152
IMENU.CMD, 132
Income accounts, 236, 291
Income statement, 285
Indentations, 7
INDEX, 14, 19, 20, 31

Index files, multiple, 20, 34
Index on multiple fields, 31
INPUT, 179
INT, 255
Inventories, 123
   database design, 126, 128
   main menu, 129
   new stock, 188
   reorder report, 145
   sales, 164
   sales reports, 173
   software design, 128
   system, 125
ISCREEN1.FMT, 139, 140, 156

Key field, 125
Keywords, 355, 357, 364

Labels, for mailing, 23, 77-78, 81
LABELS.CMD, 83
Letters, form, 87
LIBADD.FMT, 342
LIBDEL.CMD, 349
LIBEDIT.CMD, 348
LIBEDIT.FMT, 346
Library reference system, 338, 342
   database, 338
   reports, 353
   software, 340
LIBRARY.CMD, 341
LIBRARY.DBF, 338
LIBSEARC.CMD, 372
LIBSEARC.FMT, 359
LIST WHILE, 15
LOCATE, 179
Logical field, 127
Logical flow, 33
Logical search, 362
Long strings, 368, 370
LOOKUP.CMD, 112

Macros, 22, 62, 149, 180, 290, 363, 367
Macro commands, 322
Mail directory, 70
MAIL.CMD, 37
MAIL.DBF, 13, 30
Mailing label alignment, 78, 81
Mailing labels, 23, 77
Mailing list system, 28

MailMerge, 29, 84
MAKEMEMS.CMD, 304
Master files, 123, 136, 203
    editing, 156
    lookup, 167
    reports, 143
    update, 204
MASTER.DBF, 126, 135
MASTER.NDX, 126
Maximizing performance, 12–25
MEDIT.CMD, 160
MEM file, 303
Memory file, 303
Menu, 34
Menu-driven search, 61, 356
Menu-driven sort, 60
MMENU.CMD, 138
MMERGE.CMD, 86
MODIFY COMMAND, 1
Month search, 288
Month-to-date balance, 262
Moving blocks, 6
MREPORTS.CMD, 151
MS-DOS, 2
MSCREEN1.FMT, 46
Multiple file edit, 208
Multiple index files, 20, 34
Multiple keyword search, 364
Multiple keywords, 357
Multiple topic search, 357

NAMES.NDX, 20, 31, 108
NDX file, 128
New stock editing, 215
NEWEDIT.CMD, 222
NEWREPS.CMD, 199
NEWSTOCK.CMD, 194
NEWSTOCK.DBF, 127, 187
NEWSTOCK.FRM, 195
NEWSTOCK.NDX, 128, 187
NMENU.CMD, 190
NOUPDATE, 22, 153, 206
Numbering, 170
Numbers-to-English, 300

OFF, 180
On order report, 146
On-screen calculation, 172
ONORDER.FRM, 147
Order forms, 148
Orders, placing, 147

ORDERS.CMD, 157
OTHERWISE, 60

P., 207
PACK, 91
Page breaks, 73, 371
Pagination, 72
PC-DOS, 2
Performance trade-offs, 21
PICTURE, 36, 49–50
Point-of-sale, 165
POS.CMD, 174
PRG file, 2
PRIMARY, 168, 173
Printed reports, 149, 180
Printer pause, 78
Printing checks, 300
Processing time, 15
Program installation, 236
Program performance, 23
Programmer comments, 7
Programming, structured, 7
Pseudocode, 33

Quarter-to-date balance, 263
Quick lookup, 107

Ragged-right margin, 368, 370
READ, 36
Recalling records, 99
RECORD OUT OF RANGE, 22
Records, deleting, 98
Reference searches, 354
References, deleting, 348
REGISTER.CMD, 274
REGISTER.DBF, 231, 270
REGISTER.FMT, 321
REGISTER.FRM, 276
REGREPT.CMD, 279
RELEASE, 64
RENAME, 47, 319
Reorder report, 145
REORDER.FRM, 145
REPLACE, 21, 153, 204
REPORT, 16, 69, 144, 145, 147, 195
REPORT column, 147
Reports, two-column, 355, 385
REPORTS.CMD, 65
RESTORE, 305
Rolodex, 107

Index

S., 263
SALEDIT.CMD, 216
Sales transaction editing, 208
Sales transactions report, 176
SALES.DBF, 127, 164
SALES.FRM, 177
SALES.NDX, 127
SALREPS.CMD, 182
SAVE, 305
Saving command files, 2
Saving memory variables, 305
SAY, calculated, 172
SCREEN, 48
Screen editor, 3
Screen pause, 74, 371
Search
    embedded, 363
    logical, 362
    menu-driven, 61, 356
    multiple topic, 357
Searching
    by reference, 354
    by subject, 355
SECONDARY, 168, 173
SED, 3–4, 45, 138, 319
SELECT, 168, 173, 207, 208, 253, 383
SET ALTERNATE, 366, 372
SET CONSOLE, 81
SET DEFAULT, 2
SET FORMAT, 48, 51, 95
SET INDEX, 21, 60
SET PRINT, 72
SMENU.CMD, 166, 166
Software design, 28, 32
Software structure, 32
SORT, 19
Sort, menu-driven, 60
Sorting by date, 184
Sorting by zip codes, 43, 321
Stock report, current, 144
STR, 152, 299, 364
Strings, formatting long, 368, 370
Structured programming, 7

Subaccounts, 228, 236, 291, 332
SUBJECTS.CMD, 387
Subtotals, 291, 298
Suggested response, 250
SUM, 16

Templates, 49
TEXT, 36
Text editor, 1
Text files, 361
TOPICS.DBF, 339
Totaled accounts, 332
TRANS.DBF, 229
TRANS.FMT, 320
Transaction files, 124
Transferring data, 167, 250
Truncated REPORT column, 147
Two-column reports, 355, 385
TYPE, 79

Underlining, 378
Uniqueness, 137
UPDATE, 204, 206
Update from edit, 208
UPDATE subtraction, 204
UPDATE.CMD, 264
UPDATER.PRG, 209
Updating, 204, 263
Updating balances, 256
Uppercase, 31
USE, 173
USING, 173

VAL, 96
Validation, 167, 170, 189, 250, 253

WHILE, 13–15, 94–97, 197
Word-wrap, 368, 370
WordStar, 5, 49, 87, 379

Year-to-date balance, 263
YY/MM/DD date format, 184

Zip codes, 43, 321
ZIPS.NDX, 20, 31

Selections from The SYBEX Library

Humor

COMPUTER CRAZY
by Daniel Le Noury
100 pp., illustr., Ref. 0-173
No matter how you feel about computers, these cartoons will have you laughing about them.

MOTHER GOOSE YOUR COMPUTER: A GROWNUP'S GARDEN OF SILICON SATIRE
by Paul Panish and Anna Belle Panish, illustrated by Terry Small
96 pp., illustr., Ref. 0-198
This richly illustrated hardcover book uses parodies of familiar Mother Goose rhymes to satirize the world of high technology.

Special Interest

ESPIONAGE IN THE SILICON VALLEY
by John D. Halamka
200 pp., illustr., Ref. 0-225
Discover the behind-the-scenes stories of famous high-tech spy cases you've seen in the headlines.

Software Specific

Spreadsheets

VISICALC® FOR SCIENCE AND ENGINEERING
by Stanley R. Trost and Charles Pomernacki
203 pp., illustr., Ref. 0-096
More than 50 programs for solving technical problems in science and engineering. Applications range from math and statistics to electrical and electronic engineering.

DOING BUSINESS WITH MULTIPLAN™
by Richard Allen King and Stanley R. Trost
250 pp., illustr., Ref. 0-148
This book will show you how using Multiplan can be nearly as easy as learning to use a pocket calculator. It presents a collection of templates for business applications.

MASTERING VISICALC®
by Douglas Hergert
217 pp., 140 illustr., Ref. 0-090
Explains how to use the VisiCalc "electronic spreadsheet" functions and provides examples of each. Makes using this powerful program simple.

DOING BUSINESS WITH VISICALC®
by Stanley R. Trost
260 pp., illustr., Ref. 0-086
Presents accounting and management planning applications—from financial statements to master budgets; from pricing models to investment strategies.

DOING BUSINESS WITH SUPERCALC™
by Stanley R. Trost
248 pp., illustr., Ref. 0-095
Presents accounting and management planning applications—from financial statements to master budgets; from pricing models to investment strategies.

MULTIPLAN™ ON THE COMMODORE 64™
by Richard Allen King
260 pp., illustr., Ref. 0-231
This clear, straighforward guide will give you a firm grasp on Multiplan's functions, as well as provide a collection of useful template programs.

Word Processing

INTRODUCTION TO WORDSTAR®
by Arthur Naiman
202 pp., 30 illustr., Ref. 0-134
Makes it easy to learn WordStar, a powerful word processing program for personal computers.

PRACTICAL WORDSTAR® USES
by Julie Anne Arca
303 pp., illustr., Ref. 0-107
Pick your most time-consuming office tasks and this book will show you how to streamline them with WordStar.

THE COMPLETE GUIDE TO MULTIMATE™
by Carol Holcomb Dreger
250 pp., illustr., Ref. 0-229
A concise introduction to the many practical applications of this powerful word processing program.

THE THINKTANK™ BOOK
by Jonathan Kamin
200 pp., illustr., Ref. 0-224
Learn how the ThinkTank program can help you organize your thoughts, plans, and activities.

Data Base Management Systems

UNDERSTANDING dBASE III™
by Alan Simpson
250 pp., illustr., Ref. 0-267
For experienced dBASE II programmers, data base and program design are covered in detail; with many examples and illustrations.

UNDERSTANDING dBASE II™
by Alan Simpson
260 pp., illustr., Ref. 0-147
Learn programming techniques for mailing label systems, bookkeeping, and data management, as well as ways to interface dBASE II with other software systems.

Integrated Software

MASTERING SYMPHONY™
by Douglas Cobb
763 pp., illustr., Ref. 0-244
This bestselling book provides all the information you will need to put Symphony to work for you right away. Packed with practical models for the business user.

SYMPHONY™ ENCORE: PROGRAM NOTES
by Dick Andersen
325 pp., illustr., Ref. 0-247
Organized as a reference tool, this book gives shortcuts for using Symphony commands and functions, with troubleshooting advice.

JAZZ ON THE MACINTOSH™
by Joseph Caggiano
400 pp., illustr., Ref. 0-265
The complete tutorial on the ins and outs of the season's hottest software, with tips on integrating its functions into efficient business projects.

MASTERING FRAMEWORK™
by Doug Hergert
450 pp., illustr., Ref. 0-248
This tutorial guides the beginning user through all the functions and features of this integrated software package, geared to the business environment.

ADVANCED TECHNIQUES IN FRAMEWORK™
by Alan Simpson
250 pp., illustr., Ref. 0-267
In order to begin customizing your own models with Framework, you'll need a thorough knowledge of Fred programming language, and this book provides this information in a complete, well-organized form.

SYBEX COMPUTER BOOKS

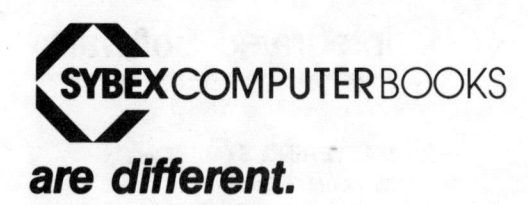

are different.

Here is why . . .

At SYBEX, each book is designed with you in mind. Every manuscript is carefully selected and supervised by our editors, who are themselves computer experts. We publish the best authors, whose technical expertise is matched by an ability to write clearly and to communicate effectively. Programs are thoroughly tested for accuracy by our technical staff. Our computerized production department goes to great lengths to make sure that each book is well-designed.

In the pursuit of timeliness, SYBEX has achieved many publishing firsts. SYBEX was among the first to integrate personal computers used by authors and staff into the publishing process. SYBEX was the first to publish books on the CP/M operating system, microprocessor interfacing techniques, word processing, and many more topics.

Expertise in computers and dedication to the highest quality product have made SYBEX a world leader in computer book publishing. Translated into fourteen languages, SYBEX books have helped millions of people around the world to get the most from their computers. We hope we have helped you, too.

For a complete catalog of our publications please contact:

U.S.A.	FRANCE	GERMANY	UNITED KINGDOM
SYBEX, Inc.	SYBEX	SYBEX-Verlag GmbH	SYBEX, Ltd.
2344 Sixth Street	6–8 Impasse du Curé	Vogelsanger Weg 111	Unit 4–Bourne Industrial Park
Berkeley,	75018 Paris	4000 Düsseldorf 30	Bourne Road, Crayford
California 94710	France	West Germany	Kent DA1 4BZ England
Tel: (415) 848-8233	Tel: 01/203-9595	Tel: (0211) 626441	Tel: (0322) 57717
Telex: 336311	Telex: 211801	Telex: 8588163	Telex: 896939